WEDDING BIBLE

SARAH HAYWOOD

images Susie Barker & Harley Evans

GET ORGANIZED
GET GORGEOUS
BE FABULOUS!

WEDDING BIBLE COMPANY

First published in 2006
by The Wedding Bible Company Ltd

ISBN 0-9547129-0-0

A CIP record of this book is available from the British Library.

Design, typeset and concepts by Yvonne Macken and Harley Evans
Photography by Harley Evans and Susie Barker

Printed and bound in Great Britain by Butler and Tanner Ltd., Frome and London

Cover: Charlotte & Gary
Wedding Gown: Christiana Couture
Accessories: Merola
Hair & Make-up: Carol McNeil, Brothers Hair Sculpting Team
Photography: © Barker Evans

The Wedding Bible Company Limited
The Old Barn
14 The Green
Drayton
Oxfordshire OX14 4HZ
Telephone +44 (0) 1235 532719
www.weddingbible.co.uk

For all the *Wedding Bible* brides

especially Charlotte our cover girl

Contents

detailed contents

introduction

It's official – tying the knot is good for your heath! Scientists say so. Marriage increases health, wealth and your lifespan by up to three years. "The singleton life is seriously bad for your health and can almost be as bad as smoking," says economist, Professor Andrew Oswald of Warwick University. "Being married inspires you to work harder while boosting the immune system." And according to his research, married people earn between ten and twenty percent more than single or cohabiting couples. So congratulations on a longer, healthier and wealthier life ahead. However, Professor Oswald assumes you'll survive the wedding planning!

Are you racing around in every direction, on the phone and on-line talking nothing but weddings? Do you find yourself devouring every bridal magazine you can lay your hands on? Are you faced with seemingly endless choices, lots of 'advice' from family and friends, but feel the wedding countdown clock is ticking? Welcome to the world of the newly engaged! You are about to plan probably the biggest and most expensive party of your life. But it's largely the spontaneous moments that can't be planned for that will define your day when it comes: all you can do is provide the perfect backdrop. The *Wedding Bible* will help you to create it. We will not be telling you how to plan your wedding our way, but offering our advice together with that from dozens of the most respected names in the wedding business. We'll tell you about all things you need to do when planning your big day, and reveal our top tips on everything else you might choose to arrange. Whether you are planning a small informal gathering or a large and lavish affair, if you are a bride on a budget or have serious cash to spend, and whether you have six weeks, six months or a year or more to plan your big day, we will ensure you have all the information you'll need.

Each chapter starts with a brief introduction. The *Wedding Bible* experts are then introduced and their advice presented in 'What the Experts Say'. We regularly work with many of those quoted and have sought their advice precisely because we believe them to be among the best in their fields. We have not paid them and they've not paid us. It's honest, impartial advice. Take what appeals and reject what doesn't – but be informed. You must know what to ask and what to expect from everyone involved in your celebration. Handy checklists, top tips, shopping advice and information for the bride on a budget is easily identifiable in coloured text and charts which appear throughout the book. At the end of those chapters where it is relevant, you will find the *Wedding Bible*'s unique '4-phase timeline'. How to use it is explained on pages 30 and 31. It's designed to help you concentrate on key tasks and major decisions efficiently and effectively. We aim to keep you on-track and organized – which is the key to successful and enjoyable wedding planning. Start at chapter one. The rest of the chapters are self contained and can be read in any order. Some advice is repeated in more than one chapter because, for ease of reference, we have tried to make each one independent. For example, if you are shopping for a wedding gown, all you need to know is in the wedding gown chapter.

Planning any event requires organizational skills, creativity, an eye for detail and the ability to work to a budget. Few individuals possess all these skills or have the time to develop them. But the *Wedding Bible* will guide and steer you in the right direction ensuring that nothing is left to chance. We are your guarantee that come the big day, everything will be in place, leaving you free to really enjoy your celebration – not just another wedding, but a special, personal and unique event that is all your own.

getting started

There is no right or wrong way to plan a wedding. But it could be stressful and time-consuming when it doesn't have to be. We have assembled information that will make your wedding planning journey an enjoyable one. Few people have had to organize an event on the scale of a wedding until it is their turn. Wedding days are complex social events and knowing where to start can be a daunting prospect. Every wedding, no matter how modest, needs organization, planning and attention to detail. As soon as you get engaged there's a temptation to become carried-away and immediately start making decisions about your big day before considering some of the key elements. This can result in your wasting time and making decisions that won't work or that tie you down.

Planning a wedding is not difficult, but is a matter of breaking down the elements of the day and thinking about them in the right order. Traditionally the bride's parents paid for the day and her mother planned it. Nowadays both the financial and organizational burden usually falls on the bridal couple, with some assistance from parents. Early in this chapter we'll ask you to consider the *Wedding Bible* 'Big 5' decisions (how, where and when you'll be married, who you'll invite and how much money you can

spend). Making the big decisions will help you define the style and size of your celebration (formal or informal, large or small) and set a budget. We'll talk you through those decisions, offering advice and assistance where appropriate. We offer hints and tips on setting a budget, compiling your guest list, dealing with the expectations of your families, assembling the right team of helpers around you, and finally we explain how to break down wedding planning into four easy phases with the '4-phase timeline'.

To help you get started we have consulted those working in the heart of the industry as well as recent brides. We've also drawn on our own experience and expertise in planning and hosting weddings. We've interviewed the editor of a best-selling bridal magazine, the organizers of the two largest wedding shows, a bride who worked to a budget and then wrote a book about it, and another who as well as working for two bridal magazines, planned her entire wedding in under eight weeks whilst pregnant! Finally, because we know the path to your wedding day is strewn not only with your own hopes and expectations, but also those of the people you love, we have top tips from a respected psychologist to ensure you survive and thrive as a bride!

what the experts say

ANNOUNCING THE ENGAGEMENT

If not already, you are about to become the focus of much attention. The moment you announce your engagement, the celebration is underway! But before you get caught-up in the excitement, ensure that those who will want to share it with you have been given the opportunity to do so. Who have you told? Has the bride's father been asked for her hand? Will he expect this? Do either of you have children you should be consulting? Avoid a delay between telling the parties, especially if you've got divorced parents or have children. If he'll appreciate it, ask the bride's father, at the very least for his blessing. If either of you have children, how you inform them they are about to acquire a step-parent is important (even when they like them). Get everyone who needs to be, 'on side'. If they haven't already done so, arrange for your parents or immediate families to meet.

In this age of high-speed electronic communication, a wedding announcement is simply a gentle nod to a bygone age when one did things more conventionally. If the traditional route is the one you want to take, then the bride's family announce the engagement in the forthcoming marriages section of a local or national newspaper. If you've been married before, it would be more appropriate for the announcement to be worded as coming from yourselves.

If you'd like an engagement photograph, now is the time to arrange for one to be taken. You might also want to organize a dinner or drinks party to announce your engagement to friends and family. But it is not obligatory. Simply bask in your own afterglow and enjoy feeling fabulous!

SECOND TIME AROUND?

Nearly thirty percent of people marrying in the UK are doing so for a second (or more) time. Usually, such celebrations are less formal affairs – but not necessarily. You may have more money to spare this time around, or one of you may not have been married before. Second marriage celebrations open up whole new possibilities. You may opt to marry on one day, and hold a party later on. Perhaps you'd like to hold a civil ceremony with immediate family present, and a larger religious blessing later in the day or week, followed by a reception. You can break all the rules: do what feels appropriate to your circumstances. The bride could be given-away by her children and the best man could be a woman. Both the bride and groom can make speeches and your children, if you have them, can offer a toast. It's up to you. Simply ensure you make informed decisions you are both comfortable with.

THE 'BIG 5'

Five big decisions need to be made before you can get down to the nitty gritty of planning your wedding day: how and where you will be married, an ideal date for the wedding, who you will invite to the celebration and how much money you choose to spend. The 'Big 5' are your wedding planning starting points and should be considered as soon as possible. It's unlikely you'll be able to agree the answers to all these questions immediately with one another and your families – don't worry, that's a common hazard. Some decisions will be easier to make than others and some will need to be deferred until you have made decisions in other areas. But simply thinking and talking together about the 'Big 5' will focus the mind and steer you in the right direction. You may need to take a flexible approach as some things are likely to change as you progress. But there is little value in getting down to the detail of your day until you have attempted to make these basic but key decisions:

HOW?	Do you want a civil or religious ceremony? Explore your options and the legal criteria (page 56).
WHERE?	Will the ceremony and reception be held at different locations? If so, the reception should ideally be within a thirty minutes' drive of the ceremony. Have a rough geographic area in mind. (See relevant chapters on 'Wedding Day Venues' pages 35–53 and 'Wedding Reception' pages 67–89)
WHEN?	Do you have an approximate date in mind? The more flexible you are, the more options you have. (See 'Naming the Day' page 18.)
WHO?	Who will you invite? This could be dictated by your budget or be determined by how many guests your reception venue can accommodate. But have an approximate figure in mind. (See 'Compiling a Guest List' on page 18.)
BUDGET?	The million-dollar question: how much money can you afford to spend?

THE COST OF LOVING: SETTING A BUDGET

Money can't buy you love. But over the coming months you could be forgiven for thinking that it can. The UK wedding industry is worth several billion pounds a year and all kinds of people and companies want a share of it. Some will play on your anxieties and the vulnerability many couples feel when trying to create their perfect day. It might be subtly suggested to you that simply trying and being your best is not enough and that money, lots of it, is ultimately the route to creating the wonderful wedding day of your dreams. You will be encouraged to spend, spend, spend – and on things you didn't even know existed. You are going to be told to 'invest' in your once-in-a-lifetime big day. It's easy to start believing the hype. Don't! Only plan for the type of wedding you can afford. Before taking out a loan, think carefully about what you can afford to repay and how debt might affect your future plans.

THE WEDDING BIBLE GOLDEN RULE: How much money you spend celebrating your commitment to one another is not a measure of it's strength. Weddings are about people not the pounds and pence. They are joyous occasions where friendships are renewed and we affirm the concept of family. They are about witnessing and sharing one of life's special moments. A wedding is also a rite of passage and a new beginning.

Budgeting is the most important task (and usually the most difficult) you need to undertake when planning a wedding. Whatever you now think you will spend, it is likely to cost you more! But it is impossible to plan anything until you have an idea of how much you can spend. If you start booking venues and signing cheques before you know what you can afford, you could launch yourselves headlong down the road to financial disaster.

The first priority is to decide who is paying for what. Traditionally, the bride's family covered the cost of the wedding day, with the exception of the marriage fees, rings, bridal bouquets, buttonholes and honeymoon, which were paid for by the groom or his family. However, modern couples marry later in life, are financially independent and often finance their own weddings. As soon as you can, establish whether financial assistance is likely to be forthcoming. Sometimes parents contribute cash or offer to pay for a specific part of the celebration (possibly the flowers, wine or food). But if they are contributing significant sums to the wedding fund, they may reasonably want to have a say in how that money is spent. Often bridesmaids, the best man and ushers will be happy to pay for their outfits, or the costs of hiring them. But assume the responsibility unless they offer.

Weddings can be expensive, but they don't have to break the bank. Carole Hamilton, editor of *You & Your Wedding* agrees that you do not need to have lots of money to create a beautiful wedding: "What you have to have is good ideas. I think to a certain extent style is about planning. Through style you can create an amazing, wonderful wedding without spending a fortune." As early as possible work out what you can afford. Do not assume that you and your partner will have the same budget priorities, but you must eventually agree which elements of the day are the most important to you and where you'll allocate the bulk of the funds (that could be food, the wine, the venue, the flowers or your outfits). Have realistic expectations about what you can afford and what you can achieve within your budget. Consult our 'Wedding Budget Checklist' (page 17) and make your own list itemising everything you could spend on your wedding celebration, then cross out what you don't want or need. Concentrate on your 'must haves', prioritize what is left and allocate the money accordingly.

Never guess how much things will cost, do the research. Look through magazines, trawl the internet and ask advice from recently-married friends and colleagues. As well as outfits for the bridal party and rings, you'll probably want flowers, a photographer, a wedding cake, transport, music and wedding stationery. This is all before you have given your guests anything to eat or drink. When you have agreed on guest numbers, work out how much you can spend on each one. A buffet will cost less than a formal meal, a cocktail reception will be cheaper still. A venue will charge more for alcohol than you need to spend if holding your wedding at home, but if you are planning to hire a marquee they can be expensive. A venue where you can hire your own caterers and buy your own alcohol will significantly reduce your overall costs. If you are working to a tight budget and plan to invite a large number of guests then you could opt for an afternoon wedding and serve high-tea or canapés. If you hold an evening reception consider holding the ceremony late in the afternoon so that you can serve pre-dinner drinks followed immediately by a meal. Less waiting around for your guests means they'll consume less! There are more money-saving tips in the later relevant chapters of the *Wedding Bible*. Ensure you know what to ask and what to expect so that you are in charge. If parents are paying for an element of the wedding and you can't agree amongst yourselves, calmly communicate your desires, but be prepared to compromise if it's someone else's money you are spending.

Typically the wedding budget breaks down as follows:
  50% on the Wedding Reception (including food and drink)
  15% on Wedding Outfits
  10% on Flowers
  10% on Photography
  5% on Entertainment
  10% on everything else (stationery, gifts, marriage fees)
The Honeymoon is an additional expense.

Whatever your budget, you are likely to exceed it, so when you have made your own assessment of what your celebration might cost, add an additional 10% contingency. Set-up a wedding account to simplify paying the bills. Create a 'Wedding Expenses' spreadsheet on your PC to keep track of finances. If costs begin to spiral out of control avoid making up the difference by paying on plastic. If you start married life in debt it could be years before you are able to pay it off. Adjust the budget as you go along: if you overspend on one item or area, claw it back by spending less than you'd originally intended elsewhere.

Negotiate with suppliers. Always when you receive a quote ask, "Is this your best price?" You might be surprised how many will knock a percentage off the cost just because you asked. Get every cost quoted in writing and establish whether prices are inclusive of VAT. Always ask what the cancellation or postponement penalties would be, the amount required for a deposit and when the final payment is due. Include that information on your 'Wedding Expenses' spreadsheet. Finally, take out wedding insurance. Don't think about it, or what could go wrong, just do it. It covers most disasters – except postponement if one of you gets cold feet.

BRIDE ON A BUDGET

'Feel a million dollars without actually spending it'. That's the claim real-life bride-on-a-budget, Laura Bloom, makes on the front cover of her book The Wedding Diaries (White Ladder Press). "Please don't despair if you don't have much cash!" Laura says. "Bargains are freely available to anyone prepared to do some legwork. Firstly, borrow rather than buy. Our bridal car was my brother-in-law's gold sports car and my dress was hired. These days you can hire anything from outfits to candelabras and topiary. When looking for cheap decorations, wait until after Christmas when shelves groan with votive candles, or shop around in late summer for discounted garden decorations. Unique stationery can be made by anyone with a PC, and you can make gorgeous confetti by gently microwaving your own rose petals. Finally, enlist the help of talented friends and family – I've seen wonderful home-made bouquets, favours and cakes."

Laura spent less than half the amount the average couple spend on their wedding. Yet she had a beautiful village celebration for ninety people with catered food, champagne and a ceilidh. "Most of our savings came from the extra work we put in and from shopping around." Laura advises you to start by discussing the budget together. "Write a list of all the main items of spending in order of their importance to you. Then allocate a chunk of your budget to each item. I know things will slip (our budget did) but at least you have an agreement on whether food is more important than flowers. Try to keep control of two key figures: guest numbers and price per head. Keep a calculator handy and tap in the figures regularly. Try not to faint when you read the total! The reception venue is a crucial choice as many wedding venues trap couples in fixed-price packages. Remember that each guest will require food and drink. Just this once, read all the small print. If you don't, an additional 17.5% VAT can come as a terrible shock when you receive the final bills. Also, buy from suppliers who will refund unused items. We returned plenty of purchases like bottled water, decorations and table sparklers for welcome cash. Couples are often penniless just after the wedding, so don't be like someone I know who used all their gift list vouchers on their first weekly food shop!" What can you do if you think the budget is running away from you? "I know that I veered from carefully budgeting one minute to thinking: 'I must have it. I'm only getting married once!' the next. Nevertheless, I did quick tallies on how much we were spending and tried to cut back on other items." And very useful words of caution: "My own spending became sillier the closer to the wedding day we got. Panic made me waste money on items like nerve remedies for stress and expensive make-up I didn't even use."

Finally, Laura's top tip: "I discovered that entries to bridal competitions are unexpectedly low. We won our wedding wine, a chef for my Hen Party and an expensive honeymoon. If I had known the odds were so good, I would have entered competitions for at least a year before the wedding!" The only thing Laura regretted was trying to save money on her wedding cake. "With hindsight, I wouldn't have baked my own. Although it was beautiful, it was a white chocolate nightmare! A few hundred pounds would have been a small price to avoid the tears and stress." But in every other way the day was perfect. "It was deeply emotional for us both and our spending allowed us to treat and feast everyone we love in great style. In retrospect, if we hadn't been budgeting we could easily have spent twice the amount – and that really would have been foolish!"

WEDDING BUDGET CHECKLIST

THE CEREMONY

Marriage Licence
Officiant's Fees
Venue Fees
Wedding Ring(s)
Transport
Musicians/Choir/Bell Ringers

THE RECEPTION

Venue/Marquee Hire
Catering (food, drink, crockery & linen hire)
Wedding Cake
Entertainment
Favours
Tips/Service Charge

WARDROBE

Wedding Gown
Bride's Shoes & Accessories
Bridesmaids' Outfits
Groom's Attire
Best Man's & Ushers' Outfits
Hairdressing & Make-up (bridal party)

FLOWERS

PHOTOGRAPHY

VIDEOGRAPHY

MISCELLANEOUS:

Engagement Ring
Announcements
Invitations & Stationery (Orders of Service, menu & place cards)
Postage
Gifts (best man, ushers, bridesmaids, parents)
Wedding Insurance
First Night Accommodation
Honeymoon

LAURA BLOOM'S TOP TIPS FOR THE BRIDE ON A BUDGET

Prioritize the main areas of spending.

Keep control of two key figures: guest numbers and price per head.

Beware of fixed price venue packages.

Read the small print: is VAT included?

Borrow what items you can.

Hire expensive items, don't buy them.

Enlist the help of talented friends.

Shop for decorations after Christmas and in late summer sales.

Microwave rose petals for gorgeous confetti.

Buy from suppliers who will allow you to return unused goods.

Do not spend to alleviate pre-wedding nerves.

Enter bridal competitions – the odds are good.

Focus on what you can afford and go all out to get it.

EXPERT'S TOP TIPS FOR THE BRIDE ON A BUDGET

NAMING THE DAY

If you are not in a hurry, perhaps consider finding a suitable venue to celebrate your wedding before setting the date. You will have more options because the most popular venues are booked-up well in advance. If you have a particular time of year in mind, it is a good idea to consult close family and friends who you'll want to share your day to ensure their availability. Ideally, allow at least six to nine months to plan your wedding so you can comfortably put everything in place. If many of your friends and family have young children avoid summer holiday time. Similarly, avoid other family celebrations such as significant birthdays and wedding anniversaries. If planning a honeymoon abroad at your dream destination, check availability now. But don't book the honeymoon until you are certain the wedding date is fixed. Many couples now send 'Save the Day' cards about six months before the wedding to encourage friends and family to keep the day or weekend free. You could also enclose an accommodation list for out-of-town guests.

COMPILING A GUEST LIST

The starting point for guest numbers is the style of wedding celebration you think you'd like to have. You might be dreaming of a small intimate gathering of immediate family and close friends, or a larger celebration where you'll party into the small hours. If you have set your heart on a particular venue then the number of guests might have to be limited to how many people can be accommodated there. Alternatively, your budget might dictate the number of guests you can afford to invite. But bear in mind that you can adapt your celebration to suit your budget – so a cocktail party will be cheaper than a buffet which will cost less than a sit down meal.

Begin with a wish list and then start pruning. Divide your list into categories: immediate family from both sides, distant relatives, friends you must invite, friends you would like to invite and 'optionals' such as work colleagues. If you are not sure whether someone should be included, try asking yourself if you'd be offended not to be invited to their wedding. If not, there's no requirement for them to be included on your list. Do not feel pressured to include work colleagues, but consider instead who is likely to remain important in the years ahead. Deciding whether to include recent partners of your friends or family can also be a sticky issue. If they are not in a committed relationship you need only include them if you have space at the venue and your budget will stretch. But be clear on your invitations who is invited and speak to people in advance to soften the blow!

It is paramount that you have the people at your wedding with whom you want to share the day. The final guest list is usually an amalgamation of several smaller lists: those of the bride, the groom and their parents.

Managing the list requires diplomacy – it is the one area of wedding planning that rarely passes without incident between a couple and their immediate families. Ultimately, whoever is paying for the celebration should have the final say on guest numbers. However, the modern wedding celebration is often funded by the bride, groom and both sets of parents who might all have strong views on who should and who should not be included on the final list. If your family or families are pressing you to include friends and relatives not on your list, ask yourself not only who is important to you, but who is important to your parents with whom they might want to share the day. Ultimately, it is your celebration, but a part of it also belongs to your families. If possible, try to avoid causing them discomfort or embarrassment by insisting they offend or hurt those closest to them – especially if parents are contributing financially. But it is reasonable to ask them to restrict their numbers to people you actually know. Some couples divide their list into three equal parts: one third for the bride's family, one third for the groom's and one third for the couple's friends. However, this method will only work if you have some idea of guest numbers at the outset and if you have equally small or large families. Always give your parents a number to work to. If they claim not to be able to stick to that number then negotiate.

If you are considering holding an additional evening reception, before drawing-up a guest list carefully consider your options. You might want or need to get married later in the day, therefore will the main celebration be over in time to hold another event later on? If you are compiling an additional list and holding an evening event solely to accommodate a few extra guests, by so doing are you adding an unnecessary extra layer of planning and expense to the day? It might be simpler and cheaper to invite everyone to one inclusive celebration. If there is no 'B' list, then only those people who are really important need be considered.

Not inviting children could dramatically reduce your guest numbers. Some parents will not take kindly to their little ones being excluded, others will jump for joy at the prospect of a day or night out without them! Small children can add a special sparkle to your day, are usually the first on the dance floor, and often provide impromptu entertainment that money can't buy. However, others will scream through your wedding vows, have temper tantrums at the most inopportune moments and will not consider it rude to show their contempt for what they consider to be the boring bits! Ultimately, the decision rests with the hosts. Once you have made a decision stick to it. If that is not to invite children, warn parents in advance so they can make alternative arrangements, be clear on the invitations exactly who is invited (printing 'no children' is not an option!) and do not make any exceptions – except perhaps nursing mothers: their babies will not be an additional expense and their mothers are unlikely

to be able to accept your invitation if they can't bring them. If you decide to include children, if there will be significant numbers of them attending, consider how they will be looked–after and entertained (page 80).

Remember to add your own names and members of the wedding party to the final guest list! People generally love weddings, so expect an eighty–five to ninety percent acceptance rate.

PROFESSIONAL WEDDING PLANNERS

More and more couples are enlisting the services of a professional to plan their wedding. Many are busy working people who don't have the time to put their celebration together and no–one to help them, others simply don't have the inclination. Some might be planning a long distance wedding, or want to marry on a tight schedule. A few couples just find the prospect of planning a wedding so daunting they need someone to hold their hands!

As an event organizer, I believe it is the job of a wedding planner to transform your dreams into reality. It is our task to manage your expectations and within your budget. You have the control and we remove the pressure, responsibility, stress and last minute panics. Nothing is left to chance. We are your guarantee that come the big day everything will be in place, leaving you free to enjoy your celebration. Even the simplest, smallest weddings require hours of detailed planning. A wedding organizer is your event PA: to manage the mountain of paperwork, the endless e–mails and perpetual phone calls. We keep everything on budget and to time.

Often venues have on–site wedding co-ordinators whose services are covered in the hire fee. They are usually good at their job, know their venue inside out and can recommend favoured suppliers. But they are employed by the venue, not you. An independent professional wedding planner will offer a more personal, bespoke, detailed and all–inclusive level of service. We have good contacts, good local knowledge and use tried, tested and trusted venues and suppliers. Many of us are also surprisingly cost–efficient, often securing discounts that more than cover our fees. That's because venues and suppliers usually like working with us. They know they'll be kept informed, that access and delivery times will be accurate and honoured on the day, that they'll be paid on time and that there is a middle–person helping the bride and groom make the crucial decisions saving them time (which in most businesses means money). Additionally, we bring repeat business to suppliers and venues. Wedding planners keep abreast of the latest wedding trends, can advise on costs, negotiate contracts and secure you the best deals ensuring you get value for money. We can do as much or as little as you choose. Sometimes we are hired to assist with a specific aspect or aspects, such as finding a venue or sourcing suppliers. For this service

it's likely you'll be charged a flat fee or an hourly rate. Or we can offer full event management when we take care of everything – right down to organizing your outfits, sending the invitations, booking the honeymoon and having your bags sent to your hotel room on your wedding night. We can work around your schedule, bring suppliers to you, accompany you to dress fittings and menu tastings and make sure everything is perfect and everyone is happy on the day. We pull rabbits out of hats! Expect to pay a percentage of the budget for this service.

It is essential that a wedding consultant or planner comes with a recommendation. If you admired a friend's wedding and hear they secured the services of a wedding planner, immediately take their telephone number! Alternatively, ask for a referral from suppliers such as florists, photographers or caterers who regularly work alongside wedding planners.

Questions to ask a wedding planner would include how many weddings they have worked on before, how many they are working on now, what their budgets were, what range of services they can offer, how they charge and when payments are due. Ask how and when they'll keep in contact with you and how often you can meet. Ask to see photographs of weddings they've organized and references from couples they've worked with recently. It is essential that you like the person or people to whom you entrust your day, so ensure you meet them before hiring them and are confident you can work together. After the initial consultation you should expect to receive a detailed list of what needs to be organized and what it will cost. A contract should then be forthcoming with everything you have agreed put in writing.

GET ORGANIZED!

Planning a wedding is a full–time job and you'll need the right tools to get it done. Buy a fabulous organizer, such as the *Wedding Bible Planner* (see *www.weddingbible.co.uk*) to keep everything together: quotes, swatches, business cards and details of key contacts and suppliers, 'to do' lists and a budget checklist. Run an efficient diary to keep track of appointments. Create a 'Wedding' file on your computer with a budget tracker and a 'Guest Spreadsheet' (page 240). Print and safely store hard copies of important documents and communications. Label two boxes: one 'Ceremony', the other 'Reception' (page 249) and store everything related to these events in them.

Create a 'mood board' or ideas scrap book for cuttings from magazines, adding swatches and photos. This will be useful when you come to make decisions. You may have no clue at this stage what style of event you are hoping to create, what you'll wear or what kind of flowers you will buy. The word 'theme' may cause your heart rate to rise (but it might just mean 'colour scheme' in your case), but by cutting out pictures from magazines a pattern will emerge hinting at your preferred style.

INSPIRATIONS

To assist you to create your day your way, there are many sources of inspiration: bridal magazines, local wedding fairs, national shows and the world wide web. Wedding magazines are a boon for every bride-to-be: packed with pictures and with addictive 'real weddings' pages to inspire you. Magazines advise on the latest and upcoming trends, new products and publications, offer remedies for every problem, and advice on every aspect of your day. They run features on every conceivable topic from how to look fantastic for a fiver and styling your wedding mellow yellow. "We are a huge, glossy, gorgeous treat!" says *You & Your Wedding* editor, Carole Hamilton. "We are a bride's best friend, her stylish shopping guide and we give good advice. We put a huge emphasis on the practical side of how to do things. It is not just about the pretty pictures we present, but how to translate the information and make it real, regardless of budget. Some brides have no clue what kind of wedding they want and have never given it a thought. Others have been planning the day since they were children and know in their head exactly what they want. Magazines help them find it. It's our job to help and inspire both. We are here to hold a bride's hand whether she has just got engaged or is about to be married."

Local and national bridal fairs showcase companies and individuals offering everything you'll need to plan and host your day. It's an opportunity not only to seek inspiration, but to talk to those working full-time on weddings and benefit from their experience and expertise. The National Wedding Show is the largest such event, held each spring and autumn over six days in London and Birmingham (three days at each). "We offer the whole wedding party a unique opportunity to source all their ideas. We have everything from venues, wedding dresses, cakes, flowers, honeymoons, right the way through to unique stationery, favours and jewellery," says Christine Weaver, the show's director. The Designer Wedding Show, which also takes place twice a year, but only in London, is a top-end event where companies exhibit by invitation only. Participants are among the fashion famous and foremost names in the industry: leading couturiers, specialist shoe and accessory designers as well as exclusive caterers, private dining companies and travel specialists who can tailor-make your dream honeymoon. If you do not have a six figure sum to spend on your wedding day, don't let that put you off visiting the show. "Some brides have a yearning to find the perfect designer dress. Others may be planning an overseas wedding and come to speak to specialist travel companies about the perfect location. The Designer Wedding Show has the very best of everything to inspire you," says show Director, Sue Maddix. The highlight of both shows is the professionally styled catwalk presentation which is repeated several times a day. You'll see the latest trends in bridal design and ideas for the groom, bridesmaids and pageboys. Spend the day and take a friend, your fiancé or your mother. Enjoy a glass of champagne and make the most of the opportunity to see in the flesh what the magazines present on paper.

Local bridal fairs are much smaller events, but give you an opportunity to source services, venues and suppliers close to where you live or are getting married. Local brides' guides publications and the web are also valuable tools. There are thousands of wedding websites with more going on-line every month. Many have chat rooms where brides can usefully exchange ideas and information. But beware of those sites that are purely a forum for advertising and are not offering impartial advice.

PLANNING A WEDDING IN A HURRY?
THE SEVEN WEEK WEDDING

It is possible to arrange a wedding in a hurry. The planning principles are the same, but you don't have the luxury of time to deliberate over key decisions. You will need to be organized and make the 'Big 5' decisions quickly.

Zelda Suite-Pedler, Retail Events Editor for magazines *Cosmopolitan Bride* and *You & Your Wedding*, thought she had months to plan her big day, but then discovered she was expecting a baby and planned her entire wedding in just seven weeks. "I just wanted to get on with it, and soon!" she says. Any couple wanting to marry sooner rather than later, for whatever reason, should begin the process by establishing what the most important aspect of the day will be. This is the area that has got to

work without compromise. "For me the service was the most important thing and that was therefore my starting point," says Zelda. "I wanted a Roman Catholic ceremony. The church we were married in therefore dictated the location of the wedding." Having approached her church, Zelda had to wait for confirmation that the dates she had in mind were available. Meanwhile she and her fiancé began working on the guest list. "If you are going to get married very quickly call your families and friends as soon as you know to ensure they'll keep free the date or dates you have in mind. That will also tell you if the people you really want to be there, can be." If key people can't make it, you may want to consider weekdays or a Sunday if that means they can attend.

If you have only a few weeks to arrange a wedding, you might find it easier to restrict the guest list to just close friends and family. "We thought really hard about whom we wanted to invite and decided to restrict the numbers to about sixty – half the number we had thought before the news of the baby. It was a good exercise and meant that everyone who was there at the wedding was very close and important to one or both of us," says Zelda. "From that we knew we had to find a venue that would work for sixty people and was available. We knew we wanted something intimate and relaxed, but at the same time beautiful. We also knew that we and our friends love food and relaxing over a meal, so a restaurant was the obvious choice. It had to be easy to get to from the church, so that narrowed down the area I was looking in. Because we hadn't got long, the choice was then restricted to who could assist us and how nice they were when I spoke to them!" When searching for a reception venue decide what is most important to you: for Zelda it was the food, for you it could be the setting or the proximity to where you live. You may be searching for a venue where you can hold both your ceremony and the reception under one roof. Decide how you would like the day to be and whether you'd prefer a sit-down meal, a buffet or drinks and canapés. If you want dancing, that will also have to be accommodated. Having established guest numbers and the format for the day, you should be able to realistically judge how much it will cost. Then restrict your search among venues that can deliver what you want and are within your budget.

Zelda lined-up a printer and designed the invitations so they could be produced as soon as the details were confirmed. This is a sensible idea that could save you up to ten days. Only print your invitations when you have checked all the details, including the timings, with your venue or venues and the ceremony officiant. You will also need to find outfits, a florist, a photographer and possibly a hairdresser and make-up artist. "I went through magazines and pulled-out pictures I liked. It was then important that when I talked to people I felt confident they could interpret what I wanted. Go on instinct," advises Zelda. Consult the advice in the following chapters about the details of your day and the professionals you will hire. The better informed you are, the easier it will be to make decisions quickly. You should not have to compromise on service or quality because you are in a hurry. "You want to know that people will bend over backwards to make sure you have the best possible day. The restaurant we picked was not my favourite venue, but because they were so nice, and so helpful, I thought I'd much rather be in their hands. I felt totally confident with them and they delivered on the day."

When organizing any wedding, managing the expectations of your family, especially parents, can be tricky. When you are short on time it is imperative you address their concerns at the outset. "The day must reflect who you are and be the day you and your groom want,"

says Zelda. "You must not allow yourself to be bamboozled into ways of doing things if they don't or won't work for you. Even if you do not know what you want, you need to set boundaries so you can work it out yourself. So be clear from the beginning: diplomacy is the key!" Zelda found that by talking to her family and involving them from the outset she was able to reassure them. Keep lines of communication open, but be clear. It will be easier in the long run than allowing others to think the wedding is going to be the way they have envisaged, then having to deal with their disappointment when they discover it is not.

Arranging a wedding at short notice can sometimes work to your advantage. A reception venue that is available a few weeks ahead for example, is unlikely to secure a booking at a late stage. Therefore they'll want your business and might be willing to reduce the price – always ask.

Being organized is important when you've a long time to plan a wedding, and is crucial when you have not. Store everything in one place, keep an open mind and be flexible. Enlist as much help as you can – but only from reliable individuals; good intentions are not enough! "Don't think you have to do everything yourself," agrees Zelda. "If you know someone has a skill, utilise it. The more you can involve people the more they will feel a part of the day and it will make it more personal." Keep a cool head and do not lose sight of what the day is all about. "Even though I work in the industry I learned so much," says Zelda. "I still went down the 'Bridezilla' route and became quite crazy. I could not stop myself going overboard with some of the details and got quite carried away!" Keep on top of guest replies and at least two weeks before the wedding chase-up anyone you have not heard from. Don't lose your grip on the finances and try not to stress or obsess: have wedding free zones in your house and wedding free evenings with your intended. Above all, enjoy it!

BRIDE WITH A BUMP

It might be that your pregnancy has prompted your marriage plans, or you may have been planning your wedding for months only now to discover you are expecting a baby. If the latter, like Zelda Suite–Pedler (our 'Seven Week Wedding' bride) you could be agonising over whether to postpone the wedding or bring it forward to accommodate your new arrival. Whatever your current situation, planning a wedding whilst pregnant is likely to be the cause of some anxiety for you, your partner and your extended family. "When I found out I was expecting a baby Mark, my fiancé, said we'd have to postpone the wedding until after the baby was born as he thought I would not be able to cope. But friends who have done that advised me not to wait, because trying to organize a wedding when you have a baby to take care of makes it even more difficult."

If you discover you are pregnant and have already set the date, what do you do? "Don't panic!" advises Zelda. "If you are in the early stages and feeling really sick, leave it until later in the pregnancy. The first three months you are tired because of the changes in your body. But after that you do begin to feel a bit better."

Only you can know whether going ahead with a wedding whilst pregnant will work for you. You will need plenty of practical and emotional support, not least from your fiancé. Read 'The Seven Week Wedding' (page 23), and take note of the advice. Assess what needs to be done and whether you think you can do it in the time you have available. If you do go ahead with the wedding you need to stay on top of things, ensure you are well organized and get plenty of rest. When weighing the pros and cons of whether to set the date during your pregnancy, or to postpone the wedding until a later date, it is also important to consider that you cannot anticipate exactly how well you will feel a few weeks ahead, or how you will look. Zelda decided to go ahead with her wedding and set a date six months into her pregnancy. "I didn't know what I was going to look like, how I was going to feel, what my skin would be like – it was all unknown. All I did know was that I didn't want to feel that I couldn't be a beautiful bride because I was pregnant. If you are worried about how you will look, make sure you dress appropriately, learn what shapes are good for where you are in your pregnancy and then choose a designer you can work with." For more advice on shopping for an outfit when pregnant see page 114. "Pamper yourself a little more than perhaps you usually do," adds Zelda. "Invest in a couple of nice beauty therapies, and don't wear leather shoes on the day, wear suede or fabric that will stretch – pregnant women do get puffy feet!"

So, does Zelda have any regrets about being a 'bride with a bump'? "No! I wouldn't change a thing. On the day I woke up and thought, 'today is going to be the most amazing day and I want to enjoy and remember every single second of it'. It went by so fast, but it was the most perfect day of my life."

WEDDING ON A TIGHT SCHEDULE CHECKLIST

Contact the registrar or officiant at your place of worship and provisionally secure a possible ceremony date or dates.

Book an appointment with the registrar to Give Notice, or confirm banns with your Minister if planning an Anglican ceremony (see 'Legal Preliminaries' page 56).

Contact family and close friends to confirm their availability.

Establish a budget.

Compile a guest list.

Design invitations and have a printer on standby.

Secure the reception venue (which could also be where you hold the ceremony).

Confirm the date and timings with the ceremony officiant and venue and then mail invitations.

Source a photographer, florist and entertainment if required.

Shop for outfits.

TOP TIP

Don't compromise on service or quality because you are short on time.

THE CHIEF BRIDESMAID & THE BEST MAN

To help steer the wedding love–boat clear of choppy waters, assemble an efficient, reliable and talented crew. Key members of that crew are your best man and chief bridesmaid. These people need to be dependable, responsible, confident individuals who will offer practical support during the lead–up to your wedding and who can relax into their roles on the day. Close friends will want to rise to the occasion or will tell you if they can't. Ensure they understand and accept the tasks delegated to them. Distribute e–mail and telephone contact details of every member of the crew so they know how to contact one another (see 'Wedding Day Contact List' page 248). Close friends and family can also be invited to be bridesmaids and ushers. Ushers do not have to be male. If the groom has close and reliable female friends you may well find they would make excellent ushers. Usually appoint one usher for every forty guests, but there is no official limit. You may decide not to choose adult bridesmaids. If so, appoint your best friend or sister (if you have one) to take on an organizational role. If you invite children to be bridesmaids, involve their mothers early–on so children understand what is expected of them and are not overwhelmed when their big moment arrives.

CHIEF BRIDESMAID'S DUTIES

Attend wedding dress fittings and know how to assist the bride with her dress on the day.

Help choose the bridesmaids' outfits and ensure they know what, if anything, they need to purchase themselves.

Rally the adult bridesmaids and keep them informed of their duties.

Organize a fabulous Hen Party.

Collect and return hired outfits and accessories.

Attend the rehearsal.

Stay with the bride the morning of the wedding and assist with her dress.

Meet the bride at the ceremony and arrange her dress and veil.

Oversee the bridesmaids, flower girls and pageboys.

Take the bride's bouquet during the ceremony.

'Strut her stuff' on the dance floor at the earliest opportunity.

BEST MAN'S DUTIES

Arrange the Stag Night.

Assist the groom with his outfit.

Pick–out the ushers' outfits with the bride and groom and collect them before the wedding.

Act as intermediary between the groom and ushers and ensure they know what elements of their outfit they will need to provide themselves on the day.

Attend the wedding rehearsal and learn how the ceremony will proceed and where the bridal party are to be seated.

Brief ushers of their required arrival time on the day.

Stay with the groom on the eve of the wedding.

Take responsibility for the groom's documents, money and valuables on the wedding day.

Get the groom to the ceremony at least 45 minutes before it starts.

Organize, oversee and brief the ushers.

Distribute buttonholes, corsages and orders of service.

Look after the wedding ring(s) and hand to the groom during the ceremony.

Escort the chief bridesmaid to the reception.

Ensure guests all have transport (if required) to the reception and know their way.

Check for items left behind at the ceremony and take to the reception.

Join the reception receiving line to welcome guests.

Take charge of the gift display and arrange delivery following the wedding.

Act as Master of Ceremonies if there is no official Toastmaster.

Make a speech and read telemessages, telegrams, e–mails and cards.

Hit the dance floor with enthusiasm and invite singletons to dance.

SURVIVE AND THRIVE – DEALING WITH STRESS

You get engaged and suddenly all around you are wedding experts! You are trying to plan your day your way, but find yourselves juggling not only your own expectations, but those of your immediate families. You've not thought about what you'll wear because you've not even set the date, but your mother has earmarked a shockingly hideous dress for you, while your chief bridesmaid's main concern is who you will seat her next to at the reception. As the weeks wear on they may also wear you down. Money, strained relations with close family and differing expectations could begin to take their toll. And you are organizing the biggest party you have ever held. "The biggest day isn't called that for nothing!" says clinical psychologist, Dr Kristina Downing-Orr. "Weddings are a time of joy, but the days, weeks and months beforehand are likely to be stressful. Most brides are working full-time and have to organize this big event during their time off. You might not be able to book your first choice venue, might have a groom who just wants to leave you to get on with it, you may have to deal with the sticky issue of divorced parents. Even without this backdrop, just making sure all the 'i's are dotted and the 't's are crossed for the big moment requires military precision."

Making the 'Big 5' decisions can feel like negotiating a minefield. The trick is to create a day that you both want but that is still an inclusive celebration that family are happy with. Initially, agree with one another what your priorities are. Then present a united front to your families. Be clear from the outset, leaving no room for misunderstanding. "Traditionally, the wedding is seen as the bride's day, but everyone else will want their say! In the early planning stages, I would advise a couple to draft their dream wedding day – taking into account budgetary constraints – but leaving some wiggle room for the input of family. That way, everyone will feel like they've participated and you can pretty much guarantee you'll get your day." Even if you don't agree with them, remember to be sensitive to and respect the views held by your families – particularly if they are of a religious or ethical nature.

Money management is crucial too, and you may need to demonstrate a degree of flexibility if others are contributing financially. Clarify exactly who is paying for what, allow others to tell you what they have in mind for their money, and if you don't agree, negotiate. Then spend wisely. "Weddings are very expensive and it's easy to get carried away and spend more than you intend. You must come up with a budget and stick to it, but have a small contingency fund set aside, just for those important touches," says Kristina.

Behind every blooming bride and gorgeous groom should be an efficient team of helpers. As well as your chief bridesmaid and the best man, other potential members of your wedding dream team are your mothers, best friends, siblings and of course, one another. Have a second-in-command for each key area of the wedding. Many brides-to-be however, find dealing with the mothers tricky! If you know there is an issue bubbling under the surface it's best not to ignore it. "Some people work best when they avoid touchy subjects, others function best when the air is cleared. But planning a wedding is stressful to all parties involved at one time or another, so if you go for the 'clearing the air' option, remember to remain calm when you bring up the subject, otherwise tempers already stressed, will fray. Mothers will have had a dream about their daughter's wedding for years. If there are moments of conflict, take a deep breath, remain calm and try not to let things get heated. Broach the subject again when you're both calm. Your future mother-in-law would no doubt like her say but, as the groom's mother traditionally her role is limited. But invite her to have her say on something, so she'll feel involved," says Kristina. Assess the strengths your mothers have to offer and delegate accordingly. Allocating them jobs will keep them busy!

When things get really heated, you may even start questioning why you are putting yourself through this at all. "Weddings are life-changing events and most people suffer from the odd bout of cold feet. When you do have doubts or second thoughts, remind yourself this is normal and list all the reasons why you love the person you are marrying." Don't alienate your intended just because he can't enthuse over floral arrangements as you do. Being married is all about compromise, understanding and loving one another just for who and what you are.

If you suspect you're becoming 'Bridezilla', reign yourself in! When everyone is telling you that it is your day, it's easy to believe that it is yours alone, so spare a thought for your groom (and your mother). "When we are stressed, we take it out on our nearest and dearest, which means our mother and the groom. Most people understand the stresses of the bride, but be clear in your head what you're stressed about. Is this just 'blowing off steam', or are you stressed because you are frustrated or because others are not doing their fair share?" If you are feeling the pressure get a friend to take some of the strain. You don't have to do everything yourself.

Be clear about your objectives from the start. Remember others who are contributing to your day and allow them their say. Try to keep a sense of perspective: stay organized, delegate and you will enjoy the journey to your wedding day. "Most weddings are spectacular, happy days and that's what everyone tends to remember – even if the food was cold, the band was late or Uncle Charlie got a little too merry at the free bar," says Kristina. "This is your time, so allow yourself to bask in the joy."

TIPS TO SURVIVE & THRIVE AS A BRIDE!

WISE MONEY MANAGEMENT
Plan only for the type of wedding you can afford. Accept what you've got to work with, who you are and always shop with this in mind. Create your perfect wedding, not Posh Spice's.

BE ORGANIZED
Being organized is the biggest sanity saver.

PRESENT A UNITED FRONT
Create your day together and present a united front to your families so they know you mean business, but leave some room for family in-put.

RESPECT & COMPROMISE
Be sensitive to the desires and expectations of your families and respect their views, even if you reject them. Be prepared to negotiate and compromise – especially if they are offering financial assistance.

DELEGATE
Behind every blooming bride and gorgeous groom is a fabulous and efficient team.

BRIDESMAIDS & BEST MAN SELECTION
Have a reliable best man and chief bridesmaid.
If your closest friends are not reliable, give them something else to do.

BRIDES – LEARN TO LOVE YOUR BEST MAN
Become his new best friend, because on the day you need him to be yours and organize the guests.

HIRING & FIRING
Do not hire anyone or anything until you have seen or sampled their wares.

GET EVERY DETAIL IN WRITING
Before signing a contract ask: "is this your best price?"

KEEP COOL, CALM & COLLECTED
Be especially tolerant of your nearest and dearest.
Don't alienate anyone you'll need later on.

WEDDING-FREE ZONES
Have wedding-free zones in your home(s) and wedding-free evenings with your intended.

EXPERTS' WEDDING PLANNING TOP TIPS

4-phase timeline explained

When we at the Wedding Bible Company plan weddings, we break down the process into four phases. We call it the '4-phase timeline':

ideas   decisions   details   event

The purpose of the '4-phase timeline' is to prevent couples getting bogged-down in the detail of the day before the necessary elements have been put in place. Each aspect of your wedding can be broken down like this. For example, your wedding flowers: there would be little point in choosing your flowers if you've not booked a florist, have no idea how much you can spend, have not secured a venue, do not know how many guests you'll invite, when you'll be marrying or what you'll be wearing. It can be useful however, to have two or three florists in mind, know what they can offer and what they charge, and be looking at ideas to see what you like. You'll then be in a position to secure the services of the right florist when you know where and when the wedding will be. The 4-phase timeline for flowers would therefore break down as set-out on these pages.

ideas

UP TO 12 MONTHS BEFORE THE WEDDING

Phase one will involve collecting together your ideas on which florists you might like to consider hiring, what they charge, what style of weddings they have done before and what your flower budget will be. You can also start gathering together magazine clippings of flowers and floral arrangements you like.

decisions

6 MONTHS TO GO

Phase two follows when you have gathered together all the ideas and have made other key decisions about your day (such as where and when it will be). You can then make an informed decision as to which florist to hire and secure the booking. You may not know exactly what flowers you'll choose, but you will have an idea of what the florist will charge for individual items and arrangements. They will be able to indicate whether or not they can work within your budget.

4-phase timeline

details

6 – 4 MONTHS TO GO

Phase three involves filling-in the detail of the day. It occurs later when you have made decisions about other aspects of the celebration (such as what you'll wear, how your bridesmaids will be dressed, what time of day the reception will be held). You can then choose, together with your florist, exactly what flowers are appropriate in your bouquet, buttonholes, corsages, to decorate the ceremony and as table centrepieces at your reception.

event

AND THE WEEK PRECEDING THE WEDDING

The final phase refers both to your wedding day and the previous week. In the case of a florist, this will include contact and delivery details for your bouquets and buttonholes and access to the venue(s) for decorating before and clearing after the wedding.

At the end of chapters where it is relevant we have set out the '4-phase timeline'. If you follow it, it will prevent you wasting time and energy filling-in the details of your day before you are in a position to do so. We believe this process keeps you on-track allowing you time and energy to make the right decisions at the right time and to create your own unique day. It also keeps you organized and leaves nothing to chance.

If you have a long time (a year or more) to plan your wedding then you have more time to consider the 'ideas' phase before making 'decisions'. If you have less than twelve months it is important to secure venues and professionals before they get booked-up. Early in the planning process you do not need to decide on flowers and style of photography, exactly how you'll wear your hair or what you'll eat, you simply need to have booked the professionals. However, once you have set the date, you do not have time to deliberate over venue hire in the same way because it is crucial you have somewhere to get married and to hold your reception. Use common sense and make informed decisions at the right time for you.

wedding planning

Much of the detail of the tasks listed below is covered in later relevant chapters. This is a MASTER '4-phase timeline' to ensure the key elements and aspects of your wedding day are covered.

ideas

AS SOON AS YOU GET ENGAGED

Announce your engagement.

Consider and agree what size and style of wedding you would both like.

Consider the 'Big 5':

How?	Do you both want a religious or a civil ceremony?
Where?	Choose a geographic location to begin your search for a venue(s)
When?	What time of year will the wedding take place?
Who?	Who will you invite to your celebration? Start working on a guest list.
Budget?	Begin working out how much money you can spend. Establish whether financial assistance is likely to be forthcoming. Open a wedding account.

Get organized!

> Create a 'wedding' file on your PC.
>
> Decide how and where you will store your wedding paperwork.
>
> Begin to gather a 'mood board' of ideas.
>
> Label two large boxes: one 'Ceremony' the other 'Reception'. Store everything relating to these events in the appropriate box.

Best man, chief bridesmaid & attendants:

> Write lists of who you are considering as bridesmaids and ushers. The best man and chief bridesmaid must be dependable, responsible and confident individuals.

Hire a wedding planner if desired.

Start wedding gown shopping.

Discuss honeymoon ideas and get travel brochures.

decisions

AS SOON AS THE 'BIG 5' ARE ANSWERABLE

Set the date and book the ceremony officiant and venue(s).

Set the budget.

Take-out wedding insurance.

Decide on final guest numbers . Create a guest spread sheet and compile contact details.

Arrange an appointment with the registrar to Give Notice, or in the case of an Anglican wedding, establish dates for publishing banns.

Choose the best man, chief bridesmaid and other attendants.

Send 'Save the Day' cards if using.

Begin your search for professionals and suppliers (florist, photographer, videographer, hairdresser, cake designer, entertainers, transport, choir, bell ringers, toastmaster).

Start shopping for the groom's and attendants' outfits.

Book your wedding night accommodation and honeymoon.

Check passports and visas are up-to-date and, if required, arrange inoculations.

Register with a gift list service.

4–phase timeline

details

6 – 4 MONTHS TO GO

Ensure suppliers' and professionals' bookings are secured. Start filling–in the detail of the day as appropriate with each one.

Decide menu, choose wine and confirm details in writing.

Compile gift list. Open 6 weeks before wedding and write thank you notes as gifts arrive.

Source a stationery supplier, design invitations, Orders of Service, menu and place cards (as required).

Mail invitations 10 to 8 weeks before the wedding.

Reserve accommodation for guests, if required.

Meet officiant to confirm the order of the service, finalise readings and music. Distribute readings as appropriate.

For hired outfits, ensure booking is confirmed and collection agreed. Inform those concerned how and where they'll receive their outfits. Agree what additional items, if any, they need to provide.

If marrying abroad, ensure paperwork is completed and details are confirmed in writing.

If changing your name on your passport for your honeymoon, send the application to the Passport Office three months before the wedding.

Purchase wedding ring(s).

Book ceremony rehearsal, if required.

Purchase gifts (best man, bridesmaids, ushers, mothers).

One month before the wedding chase RSVPs and begin working on your seating plan and writing place cards if required.

event

AND THE WEEK PRECEDING THE WEDDING

Confirm final guest numbers with venue or caterer.

Confirm access times for suppliers with your venue(s).

Seven to five days before the wedding contact all suppliers to double–check wedding day arrangements and their on–the–day contact details.

Finalise seating plan and arrange for printing.

Check honeymoon arrangements, currency, tickets, passports and transport.

Collect outfits and ring(s).

Collect Orders of Service, menu and place cards.

Finalise attendants' duties and distribute details.

Finalise 'Wedding Day Contact List' and' Wedding Day Schedule' (pages 248 and 249). Distribute as required.

Pack for your wedding night and honeymoon. Arrange how cases and bags will be where you need them.

Wrap gifts.

The day before the wedding go through the 'Ceremony' and 'Reception' boxes (page 249). Ensure everything required is placed in the correct box. Agree who is in charge of them, how and when they'll be sent to the appropriate venue(s) and stored.

At the rehearsal brief the best man about family seating arrangements. Advise of any special instructions for the ceremony.

wedding day venues

Your choice of venue or venues will be important in determining the overall style and mood of your celebration. You are likely to be drawn to venues that you think can create your day in the style and manner you have in mind. If you want tartan and bagpipes, you are obviously going to look in Scotland. For urban chic your search for a venue will be in larger towns and cities. A traditional country garden wedding reception is likely to be in an hotel or country house or perhaps at home in a marquee. You might want to decorate your local village hall or hire a castle. For something more unusual you can celebrate in museums, zoos, sporting stadia and civic buildings – many of which are also 'Approved Premises' where you can actually be married. Or further afield there are Las Vegas love chapels, Bali beaches and sunset safaris.

Atmosphere can be as important as facilities when choosing a venue. A fantastic wedding has as much to do with people as it does with bricks, mortar and beautiful gardens. That starts with those creating and hosting your event. The people in charge must make you feel that your celebration is as important as any they have organized and appreciate that every wedding is different. The *Wedding Bible* experts in this chapter work at some of the country's outstanding wedding venues. They will tell you what to ask and what to expect of those offering to host your dream day; if you are not celebrating in a five-star hotel you should still expect and receive first class service. If you want a reception at home in a marquee then we have advice from the independent marquee inspectorate to ensure you receive a safe, professional, quality structure. If you want to indulge in the fantasy of Lord & Lady of the Manor (or your parents do!) and hire a private country house for a week-end party, we can point you in the right direction. Or perhaps you're considering celebrating within the walls of a grand stately home? Our experts will arm you with the questions you need to ask to be sure you'll get what you want. Much of the advice in this chapter applies to whatever venue you eventually settle upon, whether fit for a prince or a pauper. Remember that fairy-tale days can be created in lots of ways. A beautiful celebration can cost a few hundred pounds or tens of thousands. A cricket pavilion on a summer afternoon set-up with trestle tables and bunting can be as charming as a riverside hotel. A small gathering at a quality restaurant can be as sophisticated as eating beneath a chandelier in a spectacular ballroom. When looking at venues assess their potential: consider what you do and don't like about them, whether they reflect your style and personalities and how willing the people who work in them are to transform your dream into a reality.

what the experts say

STARTING POINTS

When choosing the perfect wedding venue there are two potential starting points: either you will have a precise number of guests and will limit your search to venues able to accommodate everyone, or you will set your heart on a venue and adapt your guest list accordingly. When you have decided how flexible you can be, you have several options. But if you want to secure a popular venue you'll have to see-off the competition in good time!

To help you whittle-down the choice of venues to a manageable number, ensure you have made the 'Big 5' decisions:

HOW?   A religious or civil ceremony?
WHERE?   A geographic location.
WHEN?   Ideal dates.
WHO?   How many guests?
BUDGET? How much can you spend on venue, food and drink?

Set realistic expectations that can be achieved within your budget and confine your search to venues that can fulfil your criteria . Consider what time of day you ideally want the celebration to take place and visit venues at similar times before committing to them.

If you are planning a marriage ceremony at a location other than your reception venue, your search for the latter should ideally be confined to within a thirty minutes' drive from the ceremony. But if you are holding the ceremony at a licensed venue where you can also hold your reception, you have many more options. Licensed venues include restaurants, hotels, country houses, stately homes, castles, football stadia, racecourses, theatres, museums, tourist attractions and monuments. Another alternative is to marry abroad at an exotic location. Remember that in Scotland and Northern Ireland the rules are different and you can apply for temporary approval of a civil marriage to be conducted at a place of your own choice (page 58).

The easiest way to find your local register office is to look in the phone book under 'Registration of Births, Deaths & Marriages'. They will be able to provide you with a list of 'Approved Premises' (the legal term indicating that a venue is licensed to hold weddings). Local brides' guides will contain information and there are several regional venue guides published seasonally and available at newsagents. If you live or want to get married in Scotland, an excellent publication is *The Scottish Wedding Directory* (*www.scottishweddingdirectory.co.uk*). The internet allows you to search for wedding venues anywhere – and you can often see photographs with an indication of costs. Wedding magazines offer inspiration, particularly in their sections on real weddings. If widening the search away from where you live you can also access information on approved premises from the UK General Register Offices' websites:

General Register Office for England & Wales:
www.gro.gov.uk
General Register Office for Scotland:
www.gro-scotland.gov.uk
General Register Office for Northern Ireland:
www.groni.gov.uk

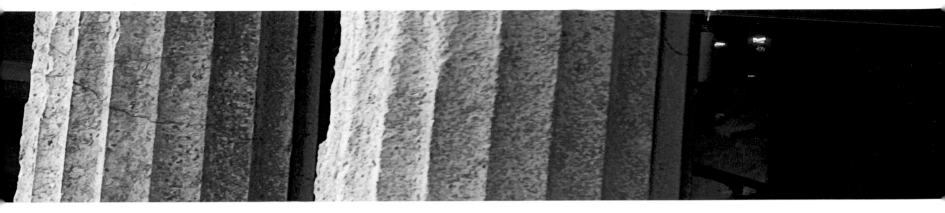

KEY CONSIDERATIONS WHEN CHOOSING A RECEPTION VENUE

In order to have all the information you'll need to compare like with like when selecting reception venues, in addition the 'Big 5' decisions, ask yourself the following questions:

If at a separate location, how far is the reception venue from the ceremony and how accessible is it?

Will you require a pre–lunch or pre–dinner drinks reception?

Will the main celebration be a cocktail and canapé reception, a luncheon, a tea, a buffet style meal or a formal dinner?

Will all your guests attend the ceremony and reception, or will a number be invited later in the day?

If extra guests will attend later in the day or evening, will you provide food? (If planning a late afternoon ceremony followed by a sit–down meal you may not have the flexibility to do this.)

Will there be dancing?

Do you require a venue with a separate area for a drinks reception and/or for dancing?

Will your guests be required to pay for alcoholic drinks after the wedding breakfast?

Do you want to stay at the venue on your wedding night?

Will a significant number of guests require accommodation at or near the venue?

Do you need a venue within easy reach of public transport?

Will a significant number of children be attending the wedding?

If you set your heart on a venue but it can't accommodate your guest numbers, how flexible is your guest list?

Get as much information as you can about venues before visiting them to assess their suitability and whether they can work within your budget. If you are willing to alter your budget or guest numbers to enable you to hold your wedding at your dream venue, explain this when you make the initial enquiry. Consider alternative celebrations if you have set your heart on a venue and it's out of your price range. A cocktail and canapé reception for example, will be more affordable than a sit–down meal. Ask for a breakdown of approximate costs per head for food and drink and whether that price includes venue hire and VAT (see pages 70–75 for more advice on reception food and drink). You will then be able to establish whether the cost of a venue is within your budget.

RESTAURANTS

A restaurant can be perfect for smaller and more intimate wedding celebrations. A few are also licensed as Approved Premises and you can be married in them. On the down side, the average restaurant does not seat more than sixty people, has limited space to move around in and is possibly without an area for dancing. However, many restaurants are situated in stunning positions that can be hard to beat and will be easily accessible if your guests are mostly local. If food is a priority and you know a fabulous restaurant which can meet your requirements within your budget and is available on your chosen date, it is an option well-worth considering.

HOTELS

There are so many different types of hotel, situated in every possible location and at every price range, you are bound to find one that suits your needs. Do you want boutique chic, large and luxurious, intimate, glamorous or grand? Many hotels are used to hosting weddings and are good at it. Most can offer packages so that all you need to do is choose which bits of the package you want and leave the details to them. What a hotel offers is infrastructure: kitchens, waiting staff, banqueting rooms, accommodation and often dedicated events managers who'll take care of everything before and during your wedding day. They can also usually recommend florists, entertainers, photographers, specialist wedding cake suppliers and hairdressers to assist you on the day. The best hotels will also be able offer a bespoke service, managing everything for you right down to the stationery.

The initial meeting at a venue is crucial in establishing whether they can meet your requirements and expectations. But should you expect the same level of service and attention to detail from a small local hotel as you'd expect from a large and luxurious one? James Partridge at Claridge's believes you should, adding that trust and confidence in a venue is the top priority. "The initial meeting should inspire you with confidence. They should establish a rapport with you and illustrate that they are flexible and adaptable." James has organized weddings for as few as four people (when he and another member of staff acted as witnesses) and as many as four-hundred-and-fifty. Who you are, how much money you have to spend and how many guests you'll spend it on is irrelevant. It's service and attention to details that counts. Corina Tibbetts at the Hotel Portmeirion in North Wales agrees with James. "A couple need to be assured that the service they will receive on their wedding day will be five star – whatever the official hotel rating."

When you visit a hotel, start by asking if they have a dedicated events manager or wedding co-ordinator. If it is not the person you are dealing with, when can you meet them? "You must meet them," insists Corina. "They are taking care of the most special day of your life." Does the hotel have a wedding package, if so what does it include? It should include room hire, food, wine and champagne, prices quoted per head and possibly the use of a Honeymoon Suite on your wedding night. If you will be holding your wedding ceremony there too, does it include the use of a room for the bride to get ready in? Are there any additional costs you've overlooked? Can the hotel offer reduced room rates for guests? If you are not being offered a specific package or a choice of packages, you should expect simply to be quoted for each individual component. Always ask if your wedding will be the only event taking place on your chosen day. If not, are the function rooms independent and with their own facilities? "The person you meet must illustrate to you that they are organized," advises James. "They need to have answers and information to hand. You should not be doing all the talking – they should be asking you questions. They should ascertain your likes and dislikes, who is coming, how you want the day run and why you have chosen their hotel." If you are left with any doubt as to the competence of the person in charge, or the ability of the hotel to deliver what you want, search elsewhere.

If you like a hotel, get down to specifics. What is the maximum number of guests they can seat? Is there a minimum charge if you have only a few guests? Is there a separate area for your drinks reception and/or dancing? If not, will they have to clear tables before dancing can begin, and is that acceptable to you? What time must music stop and guests depart? Are there any specific areas for photographs? How flexible is the menu and can you have a tasting? Do not hand over a deposit until you have all the details specified in writing and know exactly how much the event will cost. Consult the 'Ceremony Venue Checklist' on page 43.

EXCLUSIVE-USE HOTELS

A number of hotels, particularly country houses and smaller boutique establishments, are available to hire in their entirety for one or more nights. Although costly, it affords the option of holding your own 'house party' style celebration. Roger Hayward is in charge of weddings at Lucknam Park, a beautiful 40-roomed country house hotel near Bath, where he has organized several such weddings for couples looking for privacy. "What couples especially love about exclusive-use, is that they see only their friends and family wherever they go in the hotel. They are offered an individual and bespoke approach to every aspect of their stay. If they want the ceremony lit only by candles, bacon sandwiches at midnight or a morning of traditional country pursuits the day after the wedding, then it can be done."

Because hotels will be unable to offer exclusive-use if they have already accepted reservations, you will need to secure the booking a year or more ahead. You are also likely to be asked for a significant non-refundable deposit. A country house or boutique hotel will also not want to lose money from the lucrative weekend-break trade. Thus if you only want to hire the hotel for one night it is unlikely you'll be able to do this over a Saturday night. "Be flexible," advises Roger. "Consider having the wedding on a weekday or a Sunday." If you do plan to take over a hotel for two or more nights, check if it is significantly cheaper to do so during the week – which it probably will be. The period of exclusivity will usually run from early afternoon on the day of arrival to lunchtime on the day of departure. Price is normally negotiated by the hotel breaking down the total charge of the bed and breakfast accommodation per night, the cost of the wedding breakfast and additional meals calculated per person, with drinks quoted for by the bottle or measure. The hotel will expect you to settle the account in full whether all the accommodation is used or not. Thus if you are simply planning to reserve the rooms in the hope that guests will choose to book them, exclusive-use is not for you. However, if this is an affordable option you will have an intimate, tailor-made wedding celebration that you and your guests will never forget.

HISTORIC HOUSES, CASTLES & STATELY HOMES

The country homes, grand houses and castles of Great Britain and Northern Ireland are now popular choices for couples looking for a touch of splendour and fantasy on their wedding day. Even properties no longer privately owned and operated by organizations such as the National Trust are sometimes available to hire for weddings and receptions.

Norman Hudson is editor of *Hudson's Historic Houses & Gardens*, the 'bible' of the heritage industry that contains details on every property regularly open to the public. It also lists those licensed to hold civil wedding ceremonies and receptions. "Historic houses offer a sense of unique style. Often they have parks, lakes, trees, fountains, wonderful staircases and grand rooms that you do not find anywhere else. Some offer a complete wedding service with in-house catering and accommodation. Others will advise what you can and can't do and leave you to organize the rest with outside suppliers," says Norman. "Even if a venue cannot offer accommodation, it will usually provide a room for the bride to get ready in and sometimes for the couple on their wedding night. There is a huge choice and range of venues from modest country manor houses to huge stately homes. They are all very special with wonderful photo opportunities."

If you do hire a grand house, or part of one, do not expect to be celebrating amongst items of value where you could, even accidentally, cause irreparable damage. "You will have the splendour of a great house, where often you can enjoy the grand entrance and the beautiful reception rooms, but you'll be moved through them to a stylish area where, although everything looks fantastic, you will not be surrounded by priceless works of art. But you will still have the sense of theatre that is so attractive at our great county houses," states Norman.

Do not assume you will have exclusive use of the venue as many houses are open to the public. Ask what areas you will be able to use, what facilities are on offer there and whether there is a private area of garden. If you are opting for a venue because of its photographic potential, ensure you will have access and use of the areas you have in mind for your photographs. If they are outside, ask to see the wet weather alternatives.

Ardington House in Oxfordshire is amongst a number of privately owned country houses available for exclusive use and with accommodation. You'll see no-one other than their staff and your guests for the duration of your stay. A Baroque house in the lee of the Berkshire Downs, Ardington typifies what is on offer at a family-run country home. You can marry at the foot of a grand staircase or in an elegant drawing room with a huge roaring fire. You can host a champagne reception in a magnificent oak-panelled dining room, or on a beautiful terrace with an unrivalled view. If you want to erect a marquee for a wedding breakfast, you can. If you want croquet on the lawn or lake-side fireworks, it's possible. You can even bring your dogs! The hire charge at such venues is significant, but you are securing exclusivity, the 'wow' factor and the ability to completely tailor-make your wedding day or weekend down to the finest detail. "Weigh that against a hotel!" states owner, Nigel Baring. "We make a point of stating that nothing is set in stone here. So long as it is a reasonable request,

we will do it. A couple's wedding is usually the most important day in their lives so far – it has to be how they want it. Houses like ours offer complete flexibility. Each wedding here is totally unique."

Whether hiring a house such as Ardington or the conservatory of a stately home or castle, find out how the owners recommend the day be run. Take their advice on what does and doesn't work. Other considerations include whether they will provide in-house catering or facilities for you to bring in your own food and drink. Assume there will be some restrictions, even when you have exclusive use of a venue, so ask how much of the house and gardens you can use. Find out who their recommended local suppliers are and ask if they can gather them together for you to meet in one session. Use the advice elsewhere in the *Wedding Bible* to ensure the suitability of suppliers, but appreciate they are probably being recommended for a good reason. "They are tried and tested. They know the venue, the access requirements and what will work within your budget. They will not want to let you or us down because if they do, they will not get our business again in the future," advises Nigel.

If a house can offer accommodation, bear in mind that it is not going to be comparable to a hotel with 24 hour room service and housekeeping. Smoking is likely to be prohibited in all areas, there won't be late bars or satellite TV in the bedrooms. You are in a private home. But you will be living a fantasy and enjoying a celebration beyond compare.

CEREMONY VENUE CHECKLIST

When searching for a ceremony venue, which may also host the reception, consider the following:

How many guests can be accommodated?

If at the same location as the reception, is there a separate room for the ceremony? If not, where can you and your guests go whilst the room is being turned around for the wedding breakfast?

How long will you have for your ceremony and will there be another following yours (especially likely at a register office)?

Can you bring-in flowers (at a register office this may not be possible because of the number of weddings taking place each day)?

Can confetti be thrown?

Is parking available?

Is it easily accessible by public transport?

Where can you take photographs?

Before booking a venue for a civil ceremony, or a religious one where a registrar's presence is required, always ensure you have contacted the local register office. You need to check a registrar is available for your chosen date and make an appointment to Give Notice (see 'Giving Notice' page 58.)

RECEPTION VENUE CHECKLIST

If at the same location as the ceremony, is there a separate room for the reception? If not, where can you and your guests go whilst the room is being turned around for the wedding breakfast?

Is there a facility fee?

Is there a dedicated events manager or wedding co-ordinator?

What is maximum guest number?

Is there in-house catering, or can you hire your own?

What is included in the package and are meals calculated per head?

Does the price include VAT and will a service charge be added to the final bill?

How much is the deposit and when will full payment be required?

Is there a minimum spend?

Can a menu tasting be offered and is there a charge?

How much would an additional evening buffet cost per head?

Are furniture, linens, china and glassware included in the price?

Does the venue have a Honeymoon Suite and is that included in the wedding package?

If accommodation is available, is it discounted for wedding guests?

Is there a baby listening service?

If no accommodation is available, is there any close-by?

Where can the bride get ready and will there be a charge?

Is there a separate area for a drinks reception?

Is there a licence to sell alcohol? If so, determine bar tariffs.

Is there a dance floor or appropriate area for dancing and entertainment?

Is live music allowed?

Do you need an entertainment licence?

What time must the event finish?

Will you have to pay extra for staff overtime if you want the event to end later?

What special areas are there for photographs? If outside, what are the wet weather alternatives?

Is parking available?

Is public transport within easy reach?

Is smoking allowed?

Is confetti allowed?

Are candles allowed?

Do they have a list of recommended suppliers?

Is there a safe area to store gifts?

Will yours be the only wedding taking place? If not, are the function rooms independent?

MARQUEE WEDDINGS

If you are considering hosting your wedding reception at home, a marquee is the obvious solution to the problem of space. Even if you have a relatively small garden, it is a strange shape or on a slope, you might be surprised by what a reputable marquee company can provide. If your only experience of a marquee has been a draughty structure in the middle of a muddy field with appalling lavatory arrangements, then think again. Modern marquees can be magnificent! They can be as simple or sophisticated, traditional or contemporary as you desire. They can be constructed in and around gardens, against buildings, with window walls, twinkly roof linings, transparent ceilings and perfectly level floors. The main advantage of an at-home marquee wedding is that you can put your own stamp on your day from start to finish.

A marquee can be expensive because the cost of extras such as lighting, heating, flooring, linings and furnishings mount up. You will also need to hire-in everything: caterers and cooking equipment, waiting staff, furniture, crockery and linens and possibly mobile washrooms and a separate power supply. But what a marquee provides is an instant aura of celebration and excitement. You can create a quintessentially British wedding celebration and no-one is going to turf you out at midnight. You can make outside features indoor ones, and it doesn't have to be summer. Modern marquees can be provided with thermal insulation, heating systems, suspended flooring, double glazed doors and window panels and draught exclusion (the photograph on the previous pages was taken at a cosy New Year's Eve wedding reception).

When hiring a marquee, safety, not cost, should be a paramount concern. A marquee is more than just a large garden gazebo – it is a complicated structure that poses a serious danger to life and limb if not properly assembled and secured. MUTAmarq (Made Up Textiles Association) is the UK's only independent inspectorate of marquee installations and the top ten percent of marquee companies are certified members. That means they meet demanding and exacting standards of quality, operation and safety. Their spokesman, Stephen Keyes, runs Northampton based The Marquee Company. "If I were having my nearest and dearest gathered together in a temporary structure I would want to know it was safe. The MUTAmarq certification is not something you can buy. Only when a company has passed a stringent set of inspections and requirements are they awarded the marq. They are then subject to random inspections and must conform to a code of practice which is rigorously enforced."

The importance of using a reputable marquee company cannot be over-emphasized. Go to *www.marquee-hirers.org.uk* for a full list of MUTAmarq accredited marquee hirers. They all have public liability insurance and will be fully covered against damage. They'll have someone on-call 24 hours in the event of an emergency before or during the event. Do not hire anyone not offering these basic requirements. Also, beware of a quotation that isn't based upon a site visit. MUTAmarq companies will visit you on-site to properly assess your needs before issuing you with a quote. You will also be offered a choice of linings, floorings and lighting and will be able to hire mobile washrooms and heating and cooling systems. Many can also provide furniture, crockery and linen hire. You will be given a full schedule for the set-up and dismantling of the structure which will guarantee sufficient time for you and suppliers to decorate and set-up for your celebration. Treat with scepticism anyone who claims you can simply have a marquee erected at the last minute.

A starting point when deciding whether to host a marquee wedding is obviously whether you have sufficient space. As a rough guide, a wedding marquee should provide two square metres per guest to include reception, dining and dance areas. "Decide where and when you want the marquee, how many people will be in it and what you want to do inside the structure; and get at least three quotes," advises Stephen. "Once the contractors understand what's required they'll ensure that everything will work on-site, that sufficient access is possible and will provide you with a scale floor plan and a detailed, guaranteed, fixed-price proposal. Everything should be itemised in a menu; you can then pick and choose the things you want and the things you don't. Options range from very basic linings and lighting, to beautiful pleated wall panels with star-cloth ceilings, up-lighters, pin-spots directed at individual tables and lighting on dimmer switches. We can supply chandeliers, glamorous washrooms that can be created with stud wall partitioning, and a huge range of furniture to suit all budgets. We can achieve stunning and spectacular results with very irregular spaces; there are few things that actually fox us!"

Other considerations when hiring a marquee include ensuring an adequate power supply with plenty of sockets, sufficient provision for caterers and their equipment and a safe area for dancing. Do not risk connecting power to an existing supply if the marquee contractor suggests you need a separate source. You do not want to lose power during the event. You'll need to ascertain in advance exactly who will need power and for what. For example, if you are heating or cooling the marquee it will need a power source, a band or DJ will need a number of power sockets for their equipment and amplifiers, you'll need lighting and the caterers will need electricity. Always hire a qualified electrician if you are connecting to an existing power supply. If you are hiring a generator from the marquee company, they will usually be able to provide their own electrician.

Caterers will require their own separate area or tent and it must be large enough. Ask them how much space they will need. In addition to the cooking equipment, space is required for food supplies, crockery storage (both clean and dirty) and food preparation and plating. They may also want to bring-in refrigeration units which take-up a lot of space. Waiting and cooking staff also need to be able to manoeuvre safely around one another. An unhappy kitchen is often a noisy one and no-one wants to hear a 'Gordon Ramsay' competing with the speeches!

Dance floors need to be safe and therefore level; be prepared to pay extra for hard flooring. When deciding where to place the dance area it can be anywhere in the marquee you desire. If you are short on space and are perhaps considering a buffet-style menu, then the dancing could take place from a central or side area of the marquee once the food has been cleared.

The more sophisticated and detailed a marquee, the more time-consuming it will be to erect and the more it will cost. Therefore, if funds are limited, explain this to potential marquee suppliers and ask them to put together the most cost-efficient option. With a marquee wedding the 'devil' is in the detail and the planning. Everything needs to be thought-through and your suppliers will need to liaise with you for timings and access. Remember that nothing can be put in place before the marquee is fully installed. In cooler weather you will not be able to lay tables the night before because the extremes in temperature will result in condensation dampening the linens, crockery and glasses. Thus hire enough help to avoid doing everything yourself on the day. But if you have enough space, with the correct planning and support around you, you will create a very personal wedding celebration – and you can use the marquee again the next day!

THE MADE UP TEXTILES ASSOCIATION'S MARQUEE CHECKLIST

Get at least 3 quotations.

Ask to see valid MUTAmarq certificates from potential suppliers.

Ask what size marquee you will need to accommodate your guests and for a detailed scale plan.

Do quotes include delivery, set-up and dismantling, damage and public liability insurance, 24 hour emergency call-out and VAT?

What kind of floorings are available?

What colour is the marquee and is there a choice of linings?

Can you open and close side doors and windows?

Do you need lighting?

Will you require cooling or heating?

Will you require mobile washrooms?

If additional power is required, can they provide a generator and electrician?

Hire a qualified electrician if connecting electrical power to an existing supply.

Can they supply tables and chairs, crockery and linens?

How much is the deposit and when is the balance due?

When will the marquee be put up (ensure enough time has been left for suppliers' deliveries and set-up) and when will it be taken down? Agree exact dates and times.

WEDDING VENUES ABROAD

Perhaps you'd like to be a bikini bride and tie the knot on a sun-kissed beach? Or maybe you'd prefer to be scuba diving in the Indian Ocean, skiing in the Canadian Rockies, overlooking Sydney Harbour, hanging from a bungee rope or skydiving, at a Californian vineyard or at sunset on an African game reserve? If so, take expert advice from dedicated specialists. All countries require some paperwork and their residency rules vary. In Las Vegas, for instance, you can be married right away, but in France it takes forty days. The British Government advises you contact the embassy or High Commission in England of the country you wish to be married in (see 'Legal Preliminaries' page 56).

In most countries it is possible to organize civil or religious ceremonies, the former usually being simpler to arrange. The major tour operators have dedicated wedding specialists who can assist with almost every detail of the wedding once your booking is secured. If you opt for a wedding package it is likely to include the marriage fees, the service, accommodation and the wedding breakfast. Extras such as flowers, photographers and a cake will cost more. Bear in mind that at many destinations the extras will be basic compared with what is on offer in the UK, so find out exactly what you will get. Also be aware that your wedding may be one of several. Always ask how many other weddings will or could be held at the same place to avoid the conveyor belt effect!

There are specialist top-end tour operators who can offer a bespoke approach at quieter or private destinations. Dedicated 'destination' wedding planners also exist. They have local contacts and can take care of everything both here and abroad offering a tailor-made approach. Specialists advertise in wedding publications and can be found via the internet. First decide what country you'd like to marry in and then approach companies and individuals who specialise in that destination. Also remember to check visa and health requirements as early as possible.

DETAILS

Before securing a venue you'll need to discuss details (food, drink, decorations, access for suppliers and the order of the day). Consult the advice in our 'Wedding Ceremony' and 'Wedding Reception' chapters and, before paying a deposit, ensure you know exactly what you will get and how much it will cost. Agree upon when you will let the venue know the exact guest numbers (usually about 10 days before the event) and how you can contact one another. Keep your venue advised of any significant changes to numbers or details and agree who contractors and suppliers should contact at the venue about the details on the day.

BRIDE ON A BUDGET

If you have set your heart upon a venue but it exceeds your budget, consider either limiting guest numbers or hosting a simpler celebration. The core expense at a wedding is food and drink. Therefore the fewer guests requiring these items the less you will need to spend. A high tea or canapé reception will be cheaper than a buffet or formal seated meal, but can be just as sophisticated.

Consider seeking a venue with a built-in 'wow factor'. A charming room or building may need little spending on decorations other than adding a few simple floral arrangements. Alternatively, hire a restaurant – most require little decorating and will not charge a venue hire fee.

Saturday is the most popular day of the week to marry. Bank Holidays and the festive season are also popular. Many venues charge less for Sunday weddings and can be cheaper still when hired on a weekday. Is this something you could consider? Also ask venues if they lower their hire charge at particular times of the year. To secure a small hotel for 'exclusive-use' it will be cheaper to hire if the overnight stay does not include a Friday or Saturday.

For at-home marquee weddings, marry out-of-season when many marquee hirers will be more flexible with their pricing. Hire a caterer

VENUE TIPS FOR THE BRIDE ON A BUDGET

To secure the venue of your dreams host a simpler style celebration to reduce costs or limit guest numbers.

Search for venues with built-in 'wow factor' which require little decorating.

Consider hiring a restaurant.

Choose a Sunday or weekday to marry when venues can be cheaper to hire.

Marry out-of-season, especially if hosting an at-home marquee wedding.

'Exclusive use' hotels will charge less if the overnight stay does not include a Friday or Saturday.

Consider church or village halls, cricket pavilions and boat houses for charming simpler celebrations. Decorate them to match the season and serve simple, seasonal food.

Avoid Bank Holidays and the weekends preceding Christmas.

who will not charge corkage and buy alcohol at Christmas when you can secure bulk-buy bargains.

Simple venues, such as a church or village hall, cricket pavilion or boat house may lend themselves to particular times of the year when they can be cheaply but beautifully decorated. For instance, silver willow and white fairy lights at Christmas or trestle tables, chequered cloths and bunting during warmer months. Stick to one theme and match food to the time of year. BBQ in the summer, 'bangers and mash' in the winter or festive food at Easter and Christmas (or other religious holidays as appropriate).

TOP TIPS FOR CHOOSING YOUR WEDDING DAY VENUES

The reception venue should ideally be with a thirty minutes' drive of the ceremony.

Assess approximate guest numbers, budget and the form you'd like your reception to take (formal or informal, buffet style meal or sit-down dinner) before visiting venues.

Before visiting venues get as much information as you can. Confirm they can accommodate you on one of your chosen dates.

Be flexible and adaptable – especially if you like a venue but it doesn't conform exactly to your ideas.

If you love a venue but have too many guests, scale-down your guest list or hold a cocktail reception.

Ensure you meet the person who will be in charge of your wedding before securing the booking. Do they appear to be competent and inspire you with confidence?

Will yours will be the only wedding taking place? If not, are function rooms independent?

If hiring a venue that is also open to the public, ascertain what areas will be exclusively yours.

If seeking a venue for exclusive use, establish if there are cost advantages to hiring mid-week.

If choosing a rural location, ensure there is sufficient accommodation for guests close-by and access by public transport.

If a venue has photographic 'wow factor' ensure you will have access to those areas on the day.

If using venue-recommended suppliers, establish their suitability before hiring them.

Put safety considerations before cost when hiring a marquee and go to a reputable company.

If planning an at-home wedding understand you will have to hire-in everything (caterers, waiting staff, furniture, linens and crockery, a florist , mobile washrooms and an extra power supply).

If tying the knot abroad seek expert advice and use a specialist tour operator or 'destination' wedding planner. Establish how many other weddings are likely to be taking place to avoid the conveyor belt effect. Check health and visa requirements as early as possible.

EXPERTS' TOP TIPS ON WEDDING DAY VENUES

wedding day venues

Also consult Ceremony and Reception 4–phase timelines (pages 64 and 88)

ideas

AS SOON AS YOU GET ENGAGED

Will the ceremony and reception take place at the same location? If not, do not search for a reception venue until you are certain where the ceremony will take place.

Decide the 'Big 5' (page 14), ascertain how adaptable your guest list is and confine your search to venues that can fulfil your criteria within your budget.

Search through magazines, the internet and local brides' guides for inspiration and ideas about venues.

See venues at night as well as in daylight if your reception will continue after dark.

decisions

AS SOON AS YOU'VE CHOSEN VENUES

Secure the booking and get all the details, including a detailed breakdown of costs, in writing.

If requiring accommodation for guests, get a reference number for them to quote when reserving rooms and include details with your invitations.

Arrange to view venues with your florist and photographer if they are not familiar with them.

4-phase timeline

details

6 – 4 MONTHS TO GO

CEREMONY VENUE

Establish photography/videography restrictions.

Establish flowers and candles are allowed (if required).

As appropriate, make contact with venue secretary, caretaker, choirmaster, bell ringers.

RECEPTION VENUE

Advise approximate guest numbers.

Discuss menus.

Discuss where official photographs can be taken.

BOTH VENUES

Establish access arrangements and facilities for suppliers.

event

AND THE WEEK PRECEDING THE WEDDING

Confirm final guest numbers 10 days to a week before the wedding.

Ascertain who is in charge on the day and get a contact number.

Confirm access times for suppliers and on-the-day deliveries. Pass details to venue(s) with relevant contact numbers.

wedding ceremony

The heart of every wedding day is the ceremony. It can be performed with just two witnesses present, or before any number of friends and family. Whether or not your vows form part of a religious service, they are more than just a legal undertaking and your guests are more than just witnesses.

There are no experts to offer-up to reveal the formula for the perfect marriage ceremony. That's because every couple commits to marriage for different reasons. Whether you marry in a house of worship or opt for a civil service, a wedding ceremony is a deeply personal, moving and sometimes spiritual occasion. It's steeped in tradition and ritual and every ceremony is unique. Elements can cross boundaries of religion, culture, race and language. The legal definition of marriage in the United Kingdom has not changed for a century and a half: it is a personal union, for better or worse, of one man with one woman, exclusively entered into voluntarily for life. A solemn undertaking indeed, but nonetheless a joyous one. It is a demonstration of love and commitment and before family who have guided you to this point in your lives and friends who have shared part of your journey so far. Their presence supports and affirms your public commitment to one another. It is a statement of hope, confidence and faith in the concept of family.

In ancient Greece children scattered herbs and seeds before a bride as offerings to the gods of fertility. Modern bridesmaids are an echo of that tradition, but they and the other attendants, readers and participants in your ceremony are symbolically chosen by you to honour bonds of friendship and family. The roles you choose to give to those you love on your wedding day and how they fulfil them will also contribute to the tone, atmosphere, style and smooth running of your celebration.

Whether marrying in a religious or a civil ceremony, there are legal undertakings you must fulfil. They are set out here after consultation with the three General Register Offices in UK. Or you may be considering a civil partnership; many same sex couples are treating that ceremony as similar to the one for marriage. If that is the case, you'll need to take much of the same advice to perfect your day. When you have decided where, when and how you will marry, you can fill-in the details of the ceremony. But at its heart will be your marriage vows. When it comes to pledging them, it can be overwhelming. We've therefore sought advice to help you through them and savour the moment. Andrew Wade, a former Head of Voice for the Royal Shakespeare Company, assists some of the world's best known and finest actors to ward-off stage fright. Here he passes-on his top tips for you to carry off your moment on centre stage with clarity, joy and significance. Finally, you have got to get to the ceremony! We'll make certain you do, forgetting nothing and no-one when booking your transport.

LEGAL PRELIMINARIES

The legal requirements for marriage can at first sight be daunting. Within the United Kingdom you can be married at either a religious or a civil ceremony. But different rules apply depending upon whether the ceremony will take place in England and Wales, Scotland or Northern Ireland. You will need to decide how and where you'd like to be married and then seek guidance about the legal preliminaries from those who will officiate at your marriage ceremony. Do this as early as you can. Your ceremony venue will be able to direct you to the appropriate officials. However, the General Register Offices for England & Wales, Scotland and Northern Ireland all have excellent websites (listed on page 36), with very detailed and accessible information about the rules and regulations governing both religious and civil marriages. Alternatively, your local Superintendent Registrar's office will be happy to answer any questions you have. They can be found in the phone book under 'Registration of Births, Deaths & Marriages'.

What follows is not an authoritative statement of the law, but is intended to help guide you through the legal formalities so you know what to expect. Also, be aware that many faiths require couples to attend some form of pre-marriage preparation course which could take several weeks or months to complete.

RELIGIOUS MARRIAGE CEREMONIES

The only religious ceremonies in England and Wales where you do not need to involve the local registrar are Anglican weddings. Church of England ministers act on behalf of the state. Ministers of other religions do not and there are civil requirements for them to fulfil. The minister of an Anglican church or Armed Forces chaplain, if he agrees to marry you, will arrange for banns to be read on three Sundays before the wedding day. Generally, one of you will need to be living in the parish where you want to be married. If you live in separate parishes, banns will need to be read in both. Alternatively, either vicar can arrange for a Common Licence to be issued. This is for those couples temporarily resident in a parish and does not require banns to be published. However, either the bride or groom must reside in the parish during the fifteen days leading to the application for the Licence, and at least one of the them must have been baptised. Finally, there is Marriage by Special Licence, which is rare and must be approved by the Archbishop of Canterbury. If granted, it allows a marriage to take place without a residency requirement. A typical reason for applying is a desire to be married in a parish where neither party is living.

For any other religious ceremony in England or Wales, formal notice, as for civil ceremonies (see following), will need to be given to a registrar before the marriage can take place. Any officiate must be legally recognised to conduct a ceremony; if not, then the marriage must take place in a register office before the service. Many synagogues, mosques and temples have secretaries who are authorised by the state to check that civil requirements are met and who can register weddings once they have taken place. You will need to check. But you may need to have a registrar present at the wedding ceremony to register the marriage. You should first see the person in charge of marriages at your place of worship. That place must normally be within the registration district in which one of you lives. Both your place of worship and your local register office will be able to advise you.

In Scotland and Northern Ireland it is possible for religious marriage ceremonies to take place almost anywhere because the celebrant (minister, clergyman, priest or other person registered as an officiant) holds the licence – not the venue. The officiant should therefore be your first point of contact to discuss your options and whether venues you have in mind are suitable; the venue must not 'compromise the solemnity and dignity of the marriage ceremony'. In both Scotland and Northern Ireland you are normally required to give notice to the Registrar of Marriages for the district in which your marriage is to take place, but the minimum period of notice is not the same in both countries (see 'Giving Notice' on page 58).

CIVIL MARRIAGE CEREMONIES

Civil marriage ceremonies in England and Wales can take place in a register office or any secular building registered for the solemnisation of marriage. The latter are referred to as 'Approved Premises' and include some hotels, stately homes, restaurants and other prestigious buildings. Up-to-date listings of approved venues can be found on the General Register Office websites and from your local register office. Many local authorities (in Scotland and Northern Ireland too) also have these venues listed on their websites, sometimes with accompanying photographs. In England and Wales it is not yet possible to seek temporary approval for a venue such as your own home. However, changes are being considered, so seek advice from your local registrar.

In Scotland and Northern Ireland, as well as getting married in existing approved premises, you can apply for temporary approval of a civil marriage to be conducted at a place of your own choice including your home. In Scotland you apply to your local authority, in Northern Ireland to the registrar for the district in which you would like the marriage to take place. Temporary approval will not be granted for a civil marriage at any venue with a recent religious connection.

GIVING NOTICE

ENGLAND & WALES

In England and Wales you and your partner must attend the register office in person for the district in which you live. If you reside in different districts, you each give notice separately. The notice is a legal document stating that you are intending to marry and where. You can give notice within twelve months of your wedding, but must then wait fifteen days before the marriage can take place. Unless the ceremony is within your district of residence you will be issued with a Marriage Authority to present to the superintendent registrar of the district where the marriage is taking place. For civil marriages, and religious services where a registrar's presence is required, you will need to contact the register office in the district you are hoping to be married before you seek the Marriage Notice. This is to ensure the availability of the superintendent registrar to conduct the ceremony (in the case of civil marriages), and a registrar of marriages to record the details in the Marriage Register. If you are marrying at an Approved Premises the venue will be able to direct you to the correct register office.

SCOTLAND

If your wedding will take place in Scotland, the rules are different. You must complete and submit a marriage notice to the registrar for the district in which the marriage will take place. That applies to both civil and religious marriage ceremonies. Although you need not attend the registrar's office to give notice, at least one of you must attend there before the wedding. If one of you lives in Scotland but the other lives in England, Wales or Northern Ireland, you may be able to give notice to your local superintendent registrar. Seek advice from the register office in the area where you are to be married. You should give notice at least four weeks before the marriage. However, ensure if you are having a civil ceremony that you have booked the superintendent registrar long before this deadline to secure their services on your wedding day. From the information you give, the registrar will prepare a Marriage Schedule. In Scotland no marriage (civil or religious) can proceed without one. If you are having a religious service the Schedule will be issued in person, only to the bride or groom, and not more than seven days before the wedding. It must then be given to the person performing the ceremony. Immediately after the marriage, the Schedule must be signed and returned to the registrar. If you are having a civil ceremony, the registrar will keep the Schedule and register the marriage for you.

NORTHERN IRELAND

Giving Notice in Northern Ireland may be done in person or by post to the registrar in the district in which the marriage is to take place. If you are planning a religious service the officiant must also complete the notice forms to confirm that he or she is willing to perform the ceremony. Notice must be given within eight weeks of the wedding. But if you require a registrar to conduct the ceremony, ensure you have booked them well in advance. As in Scotland, no marriage can proceed in Northern Ireland without a Marriage Schedule. The registrar will ensure they have the Schedule available at the ceremony for signature and will register it afterwards. For religious marriages, the Schedule will be issued in person only to the bride or groom, and not more than fourteen days before the marriage. It must be handed to the officiant at the ceremony and returned to the registrar within three days of the date of the marriage.

LEGAL DOCUMENTATION CHECKLIST

When you give notice to the registrar you will need to produce originals of the following documents:

Current passport or birth certificate (England & Wales, Northern Ireland).

Birth certificate (Scotland).

Proof of address (a council tax demand, utility bill or bank statement).

If you have been married before, a divorce certificate of Decree Absolute (a Decree Nisi is not acceptable) or death certificate of your former spouse.

If you live outside the UK, a Certificate of No Impediment (to establish that you are free to marry).

If any of the documents are not in English, a certified translation must be provided.

Do not delay giving notice if you are awaiting certain documents and risk losing your wedding date. If time is running out, it is better to give notice first and then pass the documents to the registrar when you have them.

OVERSEAS WEDDINGS

Around 10% of UK couples marry abroad. Overseas weddings can be organized by any number of experienced tour operators or wedding and event planners in the UK or at your destination. Contact the appropriate Embassy or High Commission in England of the country you wish to be married in. They'll advise you of the formalities and documentation required. These are likely to include passport, birth certificate, proof of residency, a Certificate of No Impediment (to prove you are free to marry), death or divorce certificates if you have been married before, parental consent confirmation if you are under twenty-one, and return air tickets. When you have all the details, check with your local registrar that your marriage will be valid in Britain and remember to register the marriage when you return home.

CIVIL PARTNERSHIPS

A civil partnership is a legal recognition of a same-sex couple's relationship. It gives you the status of 'civil partners'. A civil partnership can be performed at a register office or at approved premises. As with a civil marriage, it is a legal requirement to give notice of your intention to form the partnership at your local registration authority.

The civil partnership ceremony, like the civil marriage ceremony, is entirely secular and prohibits any religious aspect. However, you will have the opportunity to say a set form of words before you sign the schedule. Two witnesses will need to be present to sign the Civil Partnership Schedule. If you wish to arrange a non-religious ceremony in addition to the registration, this is allowed.

If you are hoping to form a civil partnership abroad, contact the Embassy or High Commission of that country. You might be required to obtain a Certificate of No Impediment to confirm you are free to enter into the partnership. Your local registration authority should be able to issue you with one. If you are required to produce an Apostille, which is a confirmation that a signature, seal or stamp appearing on a document is genuine, you will need to contact the Foreign & Commonwealth Office (*www.fco.gov.uk*) in London.

With the legal preliminaries out of the way, the organisation of your event can be just like a wedding! Take what advice from us and our experts you feel is appropriate, but be informed. We want you to have a fabulous day!

SECOND TIME AROUND

The acceptability of second marriages where one or both parties are divorced varies among the different faiths. Many denominations will not consider marrying a person who is divorced and whose first spouse is still living. But this is not the rule. If you are not able to have a religious ceremony, but would like your marriage blessed, this might be possible. A marriage blessing does not have to occur on the same day as the civil ceremony. If you are inviting a large number of guests to a blessing it can be easier to hold it a day or more after the official marriage.

One or both of you may have a child or children from a previous marriage or relationship whom you want to give a significant role to. In a civil ceremony the registrar may consider it inappropriate for a younger child to act as a witness, because the witnesses must be of an age to understand the gravity of the marriage vows. But younger children could be bridesmaids, pageboys, or read a poem. An older child could be best man or best woman, or your children could give you away. There's also no rule prohibiting a bride have a best man!

PERSONALISING YOUR CEREMONY

It is up to you how much or how little you influence your wedding ceremony. Within religious ceremonies you are confined to what is appropriate, but that does not mean you can't usually add some individual or personal elements to the service. But you must consult your officiant and be guided by them. By law, civil marriage ceremonies cannot include any music or words with religious connotations. If you marry at a register office the ceremony is usually restricted to about twenty minutes. But civil ceremonies at approved premises can be more elaborate and you have a great deal of freedom to stamp your mark and personalise the ceremony with secular readings and music – you can even add your own vows. We all enjoy different music, readings and poems and use them on our wedding day in different ways to express our emotions, gratitude and hopes for the future. There are thousands of websites and publications you can consult to get ideas about such music and words, also browse among the shelves in bookshops and libraries.

How you decorate your chosen venue, photograph it, film it and how you prepare for your day is covered in the relevant chapters. But ensure you have liaised with officials and caretakers, that you understand what fees are payable and when, and that you thank everyone after the event. If you have any special requirements, such as a choir or bell ringers, ask your officiant whom to contact. Assume that there will be a charge for these services. Find out about parking restrictions and always telephone in advance of taking suppliers to visit the ceremony venue.

Before finalising and printing the order of service, send a copy to the Registrar or officiant to confirm it is correct and that your choice of readings and music is acceptable.

Ideally you should organize a rehearsal a few days or the evening before the wedding, dependent upon when the main participants are available. Registrars do not usually require a rehearsal, but you can still hold one to familiarise yourselves with the venue and the order of service. For a religious wedding the celebrant usually takes the wedding party through the service and advises who stands where, does what and when.

EXCHANGING WEDDING VOWS

Wedding vows are a series of statements that bind us; they are words that we will act upon and stand by. Exchanging these vows, and in public, can be a nerve-wracking and emotional experience. "That is because in life nothing is quite as real as when it is spoken," states Voice Coach Andrew Wade, formerly Head of Voice for the Royal Shakespeare Company. Many of us can attest to the fact that the reality and enormity of the meaning of the commitment we were taking hit us full force as we exchanged our wedding vows. This is not a moment to wrestle with other emotions – such as fear, tears and embarrassment – it is a moment to savour. In North America it has become increasingly popular for couples to have voice tuition before their weddings. Andrew has long been in demand the world over by stars of screen and stage, but now his services are also called upon by the occasional bride and groom. If voice coaching sounds a somewhat drastic measure, fear not – Andrew will now share the advice he has offered such couples.

"When exchanging our wedding vows, the person to whom we are speaking is normally someone we relate to privately and intimately. Most of us are not used to speaking such thoughts and feelings publicly – actors train for years to perfect this craft. But on our wedding day, we are bringing a new sense of reality to our thoughts and feelings by speaking them aloud, and with the weight and importance of what we say and how we say it never truer," says Andrew. "Add to this that we are being heard not just by the person we are directly addressing, but by others too. No wonder the act of speaking at such an occasion can be a tense and emotional one!"

There are a few easy steps you can take to help you on the day. Most important of all, advises Andrew, is to keep your breathing under control. "Take a full and deep breath before speaking, form the words with the outgoing breath and make sure you hear them. Secondly, focus on the person you are speaking to. Be consciously trying to convince your partner of what you are saying – putting the focus outside yourself will help you be less self-conscious. Thirdly, smile! The voice reflects how we are physically and our facial muscles affect the sound of our voice; when we smile we are more vibrant and alive. This is a serious occasion but not a sombre one."

It is also important to acknowledge the congregation as witnesses to your commitment and include them. "Too often the couple stand with their backs to the guests. This makes both speaking and hearing more of a challenge. Try and turn to the side and open yourselves out so that the congregation are part of the experience. If you include them physically you will be more effective vocally. Practice makes perfect, so begin as soon as you can! Doing so will demystify the act of speaking publicly. Most of us dislike saying our own names, so start by saying them out loud around the house. When you have got used to hearing yourself speak your names, start practising the rest of the marriage vows. Say them louder than you normally speak. Next, try singing them – it's not about how well you sing but about being more extravagant and elongating the words, which singing helps you do. When you return to speaking the words they will be firmer, stronger and have more colour. Then, by contrast, whisper them, and be aware that you are making the air define the words. Again, when you return to speaking them, because you have employed more muscularity in whispering than you are used to, the words will be fuller and the consonants sharper."

If you are nervous or overcome with emotion on the day, don't panic. Just try to keep your breathing under control. "When we are nervous we forget and lose the ability to breathe properly. Breathing deeply is a form of relaxation and will have a calming influence. It's the key to breaking the cycle of feeling out of control." So breath deeply, speak slowly and clearly focus on your partner. Pause and take a deep breath as often as you need. Even if you are nervous and emotional the words will still flow. "But above all savour this opportunity to share with others your commitment to each other," says Andrew. "Some cultures believe that once something is said, it remains out there forever. Remember this as you verbally commit to one another. It is a lovely sentiment to leave in the air."

THE VOICE COACH'S TIPS FOR FEARLESSLY EXCHANGING YOUR WEDDING VOWS

PRACTISE
Get used to hearing yourself say your own name(s) out loud. Speak, sing and whisper the vows.

THE WEDDING DAY
Keep your breathing under control.
Turn sideways-on to your guests.
Focus on your partner.
Smile!
Take a full deep breath and form the words with the outgoing breath.
Listen to the words as you speak them.
Don't panic if you are nervous or overcome with emotion – pause and breathe deeply as often as you need.
Enjoy and savour the moment!

ATTENDANTS' DUTIES

As well as the best man, ushers and bridesmaids there are other roles you can give to important friends and family at your wedding ceremony. Young children can be flower girls, pageboys or can simply carry baskets of petals or confetti to pass among guests at the end of the ceremony. Friends and family can be invited to read poems or readings, and the musically-gifted invited to sing or play musical instruments.

On the day, delegate to your attendants. Ensure you have briefed your groom and his best man about the role the ushers need to play. Don't assume they'll know what to do. It is the best man's job to get the groom to the ceremony. They and the ushers need to arrive at least forty-five minutes before it is due to start to allow enough time for photographs. Ask the best man to bring umbrellas in case of rain. The ushers responsibilities include seating guests and distributing orders of service. Traditionally, the bride's guests are seated to the left and the groom's on the right with family occupying the front rows. If you have significant family numbers to seat you might want to roughly allocate seats or pews and jot a seating plan down on a piece of paper. You could also print some RESERVED signs. Keep some seats near the exit for any couples with young children or babies who might want to leave in the event of their offspring becoming noisy. (A child crying during the wedding ceremony, however, is meant to be lucky!) The groom and best man greet guests until the bridesmaids arrive and then take their seats. In case she is alone, an usher should be on-hand to escort the bride's mother to her seat. If the venue is adjacent to a road and the bride is not arriving on foot, an usher should be appointed to ensure the approach to the venue is clear for the bride's car.

The bridesmaids wait for the bride before the ceremony and if necessary, arrange her train. Traditionally the bridesmaids, pageboys and flower girls process behind the bride, but some couples are opting for the North American alternative, particularly at civil ceremonies: ushers each escort a bridesmaid and process before the bride and her father. The bride's father (or whoever is giving her away) slips his right arm through her left (see 'How to Carry a Bouquet' page 191). The bride is always on the right for the procession and recession, an echo from the days when gentlemen carried a sword on their left. However, she stands on her groom's left during the ceremony, freeing his right arm to fight-off unwelcome suitors or challengers!

If you are hoping to avoid a formal receiving line later in the celebration, consider greeting your guests as they exit the ceremony to ensure you manage to speak to everyone. If moving to another venue for the reception, guests traditionally delay their departure until the bride and groom leave, so be considerate to their needs, especially if it is cold or wet and you have stopped for photographs. The departure from the ceremony is the usual time to throw confetti, but check that the venue will allow it. One or more ushers should remain until last to ensure all the guests have transport to the reception and know where it is. It is useful to supply a few photocopied sets of directions for any guests making their own way there. Ushers should collect and remove any Orders of Service and lost property and tidy-up ceremony room/venue once guests have departed.

CEREMONY CHECKLIST

Ensure the legal preliminaries are fulfilled.

If required, confirm the registrar's availability on your chosen day at your chosen venue.

If required, book the organist, choir or bell ringers.

Has the officiant approved readings, music and the Order of Service?

Supply copies of readings to participants.

Arrange for the Order of Service to be printed.

Arrange a rehearsal if required.

Advise photographers and videographers of any restrictions during the service.

Establish whether confetti is allowed.

Establish to whom fees are payable and when they are due.

Agree access arrangements for decorating the venue the day before the wedding and on the day of the ceremony. Confirm details with your florist.

TRANSPORT

How will you arrive at your wedding ceremony? On foot, in a vintage Bentley, a stretched limousine, a classic car, Cadillac, helicopter, boat, balloon, motorcycle and sidecar, pony and trap or a modern 'mean machine'? Consider the distance you have to travel when choosing transport to the wedding ceremony. A slower vintage car, a horse and carriage or open-top sports car might not be the best choice for a long, wet or cold journey. Your mode of transport needs to be clean and comfortable and must get you there unruffled!

Other considerations in addition to budget include who else might need a lift. If you and your groom each have short distances to travel to get to the ceremony the same car could be used. Similarly, if the bride has only a short journey, a car could return for her when it has dropped-off her mother and the bridesmaids. In addition, the groom's parents also need to get to the ceremony and might appreciate being remembered when transport is being booked. If the reception is at a separate location, everyone who has been provided with transport so far will require transport to the next venue. If a significant number of guests need ferrying to and fro and if the budget will stretch, you could consider hiring a coach or bus (perhaps a red or white double-decker bus suitably attired with ribbons, or a 1950s coach?). Guests will love this gesture! And members of the wedding party may again require transport at the end of the day.

Before hiring wedding transport see and check the condition of cars – reliability is crucial. Ask if chauffeurs will be uniformed and if they carry umbrellas. Get a detailed written quote with a full schedule of pickup points and times. Ask what the back-up plan is in the event of a breakdown. Add the telephone numbers of local taxi firms to your 'Wedding Day Contact List'. Also, don't be afraid to ask friends with smart cars for assistance.

WEDDING TRANSPORT CHECKLIST

Who needs transportation from the following list?

Groom & best man

Bride's mother and bridesmaids (is one car enough?)

Groom's parents

Bride & bride's father

Does anyone else need transport?

Do you need transport from the ceremony to the reception?

Do you need transport from the reception to other locations at the end of the event?

Will cars be decorated with ribbons and flowers?

Will champagne be provided in the car for the bride & groom following the ceremony?

What is the back-up plan in the event of a breakdown?

Is there easy parking for cars at the venue and a place for them to wait if required during the ceremony?

Ask for a detailed breakdown of costs per car with pickup times and locations.

Ask for on-the-day contact numbers for drivers and add them to your 'Wedding Day Contact List' (page 248). Give transport companies a copy of the list indicating your preferred contact in the event of an emergency on the day.

wedding ceremony

ideas

AS SOON AS YOU GET ENGAGED

Decide whether you would like a religious or civil ceremony. If the former, establish that it is permissible.

When the venue is confirmed, secure the date and book the ceremony with the registrar or officiant.

Arrange appointment(s) with your local registrar(s) to Give Notice.

decisions

UP TO 3 MONTHS TO GO

Choose your witnesses and readers.

Book transport.

Book organist, choir and bell ringers if required.

Choose readings and music.

Visit the venue with your florist.

4-phase timeline

details

2 MONTHS TO GO

Finalise the Order of Service with the registrar or officiant and arrange for it to be printed.

Supply copies of readings and music to performers.

Practise your wedding vows aloud!

Confirm Banns Certificate (Anglican ceremonies).

Collect Marriage Authority if required (England).

Book rehearsal if required.

Book additional transport for VIP guests.

Confirm requirements with florist.

event

AND THE WEEK PRECEDING THE WEDDING

Collect Marriage Schedule (Scotland and Northern Ireland).

Prepare a list of attendants' duties with their on-the-day required arrival times and distribute it to them with the 'Wedding Day Schedule' and 'Wedding Day Contact List' (page 248).

Confirm transport details.

Ensure ushers will have umbrellas in case of rain.

Confirm with your florist buttonhole and bouquet delivery address(es) and times.

Check 'Ceremony Box' (page 249) and delegate delivery.

Brief best man at rehearsal about seating arrangements. Check he has ring(s).

Ensure groom, best man and ushers know their required arrival time for photographs before the ceremony.

wedding reception

Wedding celebrations are among life's highlights – none more so than your own. Of all the parties you will ever attend, your wedding reception will be the most memorable. It's the party of a lifetime!

Much of the detail of your wedding day and the part of it that requires the most planning is the wedding reception. And it is the aspect of your wedding you have most control over. It is fun to plan and offers plenty of scope for imagination. It is also where most of the money will be spent. Up to a quarter of your overall budget is likely to go on food and drink. Sticking to your budget when planning your reception is therefore crucial to ensure costs don't escalate out of control.

Lavish celebrity weddings featured weekly in glossy magazines have left the average bride-to-be with the impression that it is money that creates those magic moments. It is not! There are countless ways to make your celebration gorgeous and unique without it breaking the bank. Your venue might lend itself to a theme that ties-in with its history. The season may dictate a theme or a simple colour scheme. Creating the right mood and atmosphere will probably require thought and careful planning, but style is a matter of taste, not budget. A simple, understated and glamorous celebration need not cost the earth.

If you don't know where to start, our Wedding Bible experts will steer you in the right direction. We'll leave it to the magazines for inspiring ideas on how to set tables, design favours and tell you the latest trends. What we have to offer is fundamental no-frills advice: where

to start, what to consider, how to negotiate and how to plan your day within your budget. Before you can plan the detail of your reception you have decisions to make, and lots of them. Our Wedding Bible experts have organized every style of wedding reception, on every budget and with guest numbers ranging from two to several hundred. Claridge's in London is one of the world's finest hotels. It's been hosting weddings since it opened in 1898. The House Manager, James Partridge, has over twenty years experience organizing weddings for anyone and everyone from Joan Collins to European royalty and girls and their grooms who scrimp and save to realise their wedding day dream. Portmeirion in North Wales is a stunning private resort. With a fairy-tale backdrop, the Traeth Bach Estuary and Mountains of Meirionnydd beyond, it really is the perfect place to celebrate the perfect day. Noël Coward wrote Blythe Spirit at Portmeirion in the 1940s and it continues to host both big bash celebrity receptions and small modest weddings with style and panache. We at the Wedding Bible Company have organized weddings to suit every purse: from celebrity couples looking to fulfil the expectations of the magazines who will photograph their celebrations, to members of our own families hoping to realise their dreams on a limited budget. We know that planning a wedding is partly about managing expectations. We aim to enable you to do that here. Many of the moments that will define your day and be talked-about for years to come will not be the elements you have planned. They will be the spontaneous stolen kisses, poignant embraces, tearful toasts, heartfelt expressions of joy and renewal of friendships and family bonds. Our job is to help you create the atmosphere that will promote the magic that is a wedding day celebration.

what the experts say

STARTING POINT

Once you have decided upon a venue you can get down to the details of your wedding reception: how you want it to look, what you will eat and drink and how you will be entertained. Start with a 'Wish List' of what you want to do and achieve and agree a plan of action with the venue that includes timings.

Plan the reception around what people would normally be doing at a specific time and replicate it so if it is a meal time or example, serve food. Creating a 'Wedding Day Schedule' (see page 249) is the key to a smooth running wedding reception. It will leave you free to celebrate, confident in the knowledge that the day will run without a hitch. The following is the 'traditional' format for the day. Personalise it by adding, removing and switching events around as you desire.

WEDDING RECEPTION WISH LIST

PHOTOGRAPHS
Where, when and if necessary, a wet weather alternative.

DRINKS & CANAPÉ RECEPTION
Where and when.

RECEIVING LINE
Where, when and who will be in the line-up.

TOASTMASTER
Professional or amateur? You could ask a friend, an usher or the best man to act as Master of Ceremonies.

WEDDING BREAKFAST
Formal or informal, canapé reception, buffet or silver-service meal.

SPEECHES
When, who and how long.

CAKE CUTTING & EATING
When.

FIRST DANCE & ENTERTAINMENT
When, where and stop time.

TOSSING THE BOUQUET
Details and time.

BRIDE & GROOM'S DEPARTURE
When and how.

CARRIAGES
Official stop time.

THEME, STYLE & ATMOSPHERE

Will your reception have a theme? That could be as simple as co-ordinating flowers and bridesmaids' outfits, or as specific as a medieval banquet set in a castle with jousting, jesters and mead served in pewter tankards! Your venue must be the starting point. You may have chosen one specifically because it lends itself to the theme you have in mind, or you may be starting with a blank sheet of paper. If you're looking to create something adventurous, think carefully about every aspect. "Work with a company or venue that can pull it off for you," says James Partridge of Claridge's. "Meet and discuss your ideas and if hiring an outside company, ensure they and the venue talk to one another and everything is agreed between the parties."

Assess your venue's potential. What are it's good points and what don't you like? A contemporary building will lend itself to a minimalist theme with cool colours and no frills. A plain, uninteresting venue may need you to be bold with colour and detail. A traditional country house, a building with specific architectural detail or a stately home will require you to be sympathetic and to emphasize the existing natural charm, character and grandeur. A marquee is a blank canvas.

Lighting is an important contributory factor and can make a considerable difference to the mood of a celebration. Avoid harsh lighting – keep it soft and flattering. If you plan to use candles, plain night lights are an effective way to create an atmosphere and holders can be bought very cheaply. But purchase 'night lights' that burn for eight hours rather than 'tea lights' which only last four.

The focal point of a reception room is likely to be the dining tables, dance floor and cake table. How they are arranged in relation to one another and how they are lit are integral parts of the decoration. Very often, stunning flower arrangements strategically placed and matched to the table centrepieces are all that is required to decorate a room. Seek advice from your florist and the person in charge at the venue.

If possible visit the venue when it is set-up for another celebration. Ask to see photographs of other events held there.

Consider weddings you've attended as guests. "At the last wedding you went to, what were the things you least liked about it?" asks James. "Did your feet ache because the pre-dinner drinks went on too long? Did you have to wait around because the photographer took an age? Were you thirsty because it was a hot day and you had travelled a long way but there was nothing to drink before the ceremony? Decide straight away not to plan your wedding that way. Next, think about what you have enjoyed at other weddings and parties. A good venue will be flexible and adapt to accommodate reasonable requests so you can do things your way."

Let the celebration evolve and the atmosphere build and be flexible. "Avoid making the reception too structured, that's when guests start to feel uncomfortable," advises James. "A wedding day starts quietly, you build-up to the party and guests leave on a high. Limit the time you set aside for photographs and if you can do them in front of everyone, all the better. Work out your timings around people's usual eating habits – if your ceremony is at 1 o'clock the guests will not have had lunch, so go heavier on the canapés and lighter on the meal. Get the glasses topped-up at the beginning and have someone formally welcome everyone. Keep building the day. Move to the meal and don't interrupt it with speeches at least until after the main course or you'll stop the flow of conversation. Once the first dance is underway, don't stop the music – you can make it softer or louder but don't interrupt it." Always end on a high and don't be the last to leave – however tempting it is to stay.

James's top tip for smaller gatherings is to be indulgent. "Eat what you like to eat, drink what you love to drink and do things you like to do! Again, don't make the day too structured. Keep it an intimate, sociable gathering over a good meal."

THE FOOD OF LOVE

Guests will remember good or bad food forever, so ensure it is delicious! Cost might determine the form of the meal – seated or standing, a buffet or silver-service. If you don't want a formal three course meal you could serve brunch, afternoon tea, a canapé and drinks reception, a finger or a full self-service buffet. Discuss cost alternatives with your venue or caterer. If working with in-house kitchens you'll have to be guided by what they are prepared to offer. Simple seasonal food is likely to be the most affordable unless they specialise in a particular style of cuisine. If hiring outside catering (page 74), you have more flexibility and can specify your requirements at the start. Perhaps a sizzling BBQ cooked in front of you, a Moroccan banquet or posh fish and chips.

Draw-up a list of foods you don't like and a list of those you love. Show it to your chef or caterer. Most venues and companies will offer a free tasting once you've secured the booking – keep an open mind and see what they come up with. If you'd like to serve your wedding cake as dessert, you could suggest a cheese course instead of pudding within the quoted price. Usually a quote will be costed per head and exclude drinks. If serving pre-dinner canapés, establish whether they are included in the price. Budget permitting, extravagances such as a chocolate fountain, an ice cream van in summer, a vodka luuge, a champagne fountain or an oyster bar can also be worked into wedding receptions as appropriate.

When considering what time of day you are to be married, it is worth bearing in mind that an event later in the day will mean you can move straight into a drinks reception followed by dinner and dancing. This removes the need to serve additional food and drink later in the day and keeps the cost down.

MENU CHECKLIST

What sort of meal would you like to serve (brunch, lunch, afternoon tea, hors d'oeuvres, dinner)?

What style of service are you seeking (canapé reception, fork buffet, self-service seated buffet, silver-service meal)?

What kind of food would you like to serve (traditional, ethnic, seasonal, vegetarian, themed)?

Will you be offered a free tasting?

Will you need to provide food for additional evening guests?

What prices do packages start from and what is included?

Can specific dietary requirements and children be catered for at no additional cost?

Can wedding cake be served as dessert?

Can you provide your own wedding cake and will they cut and serve it free of charge?

Can you supply your own alcohol and is there a charge for corkage?

When will the venue/caterer require final guest numbers?

Will a service charge be added to the final bill?

BUBBLISHIOUS!

The traditional wedding tipple is of course champagne. However, there are hundreds of alternatives in addition to this. Bucks Fizz, Bellinis (peach juice and sparkling wine), Pimms, cocktails, Pim-Poms (Pimms and pomegranate juice – delicious!), mulled wines and punches. If serving champagne, will you want it instead of, or as well as, the toasting champagne? Will you serve red or white wine with the meal or both? Will you provide bottled or tap water? Perhaps you'd like a pudding wine with cake or dessert?

Most venues will allow you to provide your own alcohol, but in most cases will charge you corkage. Unless you are planning to serve fine wines and champagnes you are unlikely to save a significant sum of money by bringing-in your own alcohol. If hiring outside caterers, for a marquee wedding at home for example, ask if they'll charge corkage – some don't. It's therefore an important consideration when assessing which company to choose. If buying direct from a wine merchant, ask for 'sale or return' on unopened bottles or cases. If you've access to storage, remember Christmas is a great time to secure good deals on champagne and fake fizz. If time permits, don't forget the 'booze cruise' option.

Never underestimate the amount of alcohol you'll require and don't forget a plentiful supply of water and soft drinks. When calculating how much to budget for, there are roughly six glasses to a bottle. On average guests drink two glasses per hour over the course of a wedding reception. Then add 10–15% to the calculation you've made.

If your reception is at an hotel or restaurant, will you be paying for guests' drinks following the wedding breakfast? James Partridge at Claridge's advises you to carefully consider the bar prices and who your guests are before requiring them to pay. "Prices at, say, a top London hotel may not be what you or your family and guests are used to paying. So you need to work out not only what you can afford, but what they can afford. You should be able to offer free drinks all day if you stick to wine, beer and soft drinks. Forget about the champagne if you are on a tight budget and men always like bottled beers." Do the calculations so you don't under-budget. Ask to see a bar tariff and decide what you will and won't provide; you don't have to offer a full bar, even when you serve more than just wine and beer. Seek advice from your venue's banqueting manager who will be able to advise the 'average drinks spend' for previous weddings they've catered and how the costs broke down.

DRINKS CALCULATION CHECKLIST

PRE-DINNER DRINKS RECEPTION:
1/3 bottle of champagne or wine per person, or 2 cocktails
Soft drinks for 25% of the guests.

MEAL:
1/2 bottle wine per person
2/3 bottle water per person
1 glass champagne per person (for the toasts)

AFTER DINNER BAR:
2 drinks per person
1/3 bottle of water per person

Order or calculate an extra 10–15% and allow for guests drinking more in hot weather.
Remember beer and soft drinks.

HIRING OUTSIDE CATERERS

Use a caterer who has cooked in your chosen venue before or, in the case of an at-home wedding, one who is recommended to you. Other suppliers, such as your photographer and florist, work closely with caterers and private dining companies and may be able to offer a recommendation. Always see more than one company and ask for testimonials and a menu tasting. You will need to have an idea of guest numbers and the style of meal you'd like to offer.

If you are constructing a temporary kitchen, adjacent to a marquee for example (see 'Marquee Weddings' on page 46), be realistic about what can be achieved in it. A six course meal for two hundred guests is not a viable option for a chef working in a small area with limited catering equipment. Consider too that the more complicated the meal, the more equipment you'll need to hire, which adds to the cost. Also, temporary kitchens do not have the same facilities as purpose-built ones, such as large warming plates to get the food out piping-hot. At recent Wedding Bible weddings we've been able to serve some delicious and fun meals at marquee receptions to large numbers of guests catered in small kitchens. Because space has been limited we've created menus that require little pre-plating in the kitchen. This also reduces the number of waiting staff required and therefore staff costs. We've served joints of beef or lamb, individual Beef Wellingtons or salmon-en-croute to each table. One guest is allocated as carver and provided with a chef's hat and apron (search on-line for reasonably priced linen aprons and paper chef's hats). This also breaks the ice and encourages cross-table talk. If the idea appeals to you, ask your caterer what other similar dishes could be served at the table.

When hiring outside caterers, establish exactly what is and isn't included in the price. The majority offer a flexible service allowing you to tailor-make your event. Most provide the cooking and catering equipment, crockery, linens and glasses. But many will require you to source and hire tables and chairs. Ask if waiting staff costs are included and whether they can provide chilling equipment and ice. Companies have different ways of charging, so you need all the information up front in order to make a like-for-like cost comparison. As already stated, corkage will make a significant difference to the overall catering costs, so establish early-on if there is a charge and what it is.

An important consideration when hiring crockery and glasses is whether you can return them unwashed. Always go for this option if catering at home - it will only be a few pence more per item. Also establish that your caterer will lay and clear tables and pack the dirty crockery and linens away after the event. It's worth paying extra for them to do so because it is hard, time-consuming work. When hiring furniture and linens ensure the cloths are larger than the tables and the same shape. Always place a lining cloth on each table that reaches almost to the floor. Remember to order a smaller table and cloth for the wedding cake. Don't lay tables up in a marquee the day before an event in damp or cold weather because linens will crease. If the budget allows, hire linen napkins - people will notice if they're the disposable variety.

OUTSIDE CATERING CHECKLIST

Are the following included in the package price:

  Cooking and catering equipment?
  Crockery, glasses and linens?
  Tables and chairs?
  Waiting staff?

Will you need to be present for delivery and collection of any of the above items and when?

If sourcing crockery, cutlery, glasses and linens yourself, can they be returned dirty?

Does the caterer charge corkage?

Can the caterer provide chilling equipment and ice and is there a charge?

Does the cost include laying and clearing tables and packing used crockery and linens?

THE RECEIVING LINE

Many modern couples balk at the idea of a formal receiving line – usually because at weddings they've attended it has not been thought through carefully and guests have got bored waiting in line. A receiving line affords the opportunity for you to talk to every guest and thank them for coming. It's also a great way to make parents and older children feel included and important. It can be at the entrance to your reception, in a separate room or before you go into dinner. However, it takes on average thirty seconds to greet each guest, therefore it can take a considerable amount of time if you have a significant number of guests. Think carefully about where and when you'll do this and what else will or could be going on at the same time. Try and position yourselves where guests can be offered a drink

and canapés. If there's an available side room at a formal reception you could greet guests there, they then don't necessarily need to wait in line, but can come forward a few at a time. In that event a Toastmaster could announce each guest, or appoint a friend or the best man as Master of Ceremonies to do the same. If guests are announced, everyone in the receiving line will know who they are.

The traditional line-up (see below) is based upon the notion that the bride's parents have paid for and are hosting the day. Since that is no longer the norm, the receiving line can be reconfigured as you desire. If the chief bridesmaid or best man are family members, it is traditional to include them at the end of the line-up. Go through the

TRADITIONAL RECEIVING LINE: BRIDE'S MOTHER   BRIDE'S FATHER   GROOM'S MOTHER

guest list with everyone in the receiving line in advance, so they have an idea of who is who.

If you decide not to opt for a traditional receiving line, allow enough time elsewhere during the reception to circulate among your guests. Make the effort to find and speak to everyone. Encourage your parents, or older children in the case of second marriages, to do the same. At some point during the meal you can circulate among your guests visiting their tables. However, decide in advance if you'll do this together. Once you've separated it will be difficult to break free. Remember this throughout the reception if you want to spend it together!

GROOM'S FATHER   BRIDE   GROOM   CHIEF BRIDESMAID (IF FAMILY)   BEST MAN (IF FAMILY)

TABLES & PLACE SETTINGS

The modern wedding does not require professionals to plan and do everything. Many brides take great pleasure in sourcing and making decorations and favours, and some couples partially or wholly decorate venues themselves. The mood and theme of the reception are likely to dictate the style of the table decorations. Pretty place cards, table names or numbers and menus co-ordinated to match your theme or colour scheme might be all you need in addition to a beautiful arrangement of flowers at each table. But when considering the styling of your wedding breakfast room, first decide where in it you will sit.

For a seated celebration, round tables seating eight or ten guests are increasingly the norm. Alternatively, you could opt for a banquet style formation, as used to be traditional, with long rows of seating based upon a 'U' shape, the middle section being the 'top' table. You will need to bear in mind the shape of the room or marquee, how level the floor is and how traffic will flow. Ensure enough elbow-room when working out the number of guests per table, and do not position tables so close together that waiting staff will be unable to move comfortably around them.

The traditional top table is long and rectangular, positioned at the head of the room, with the bride and groom seated in the centre flanked by their parents (see opposite).

Traditional rules of wedding etiquette sometimes don't fit with the modern couple and the make-up of the contemporary family. Nowadays, with divorced parents, step-parents and newlyweds with their own children, anything goes! The traditional top table layout is not especially conducive to conversation and can leave one feeling somewhat exposed. Increasingly couples are choosing to sit at round tables, often positioned in the centre of the room at the heart of the action. "If the guests are positioned around you it makes it feel more intimate," says Claridge's James Partridge. "We sometimes put-in a larger or a different shaped table, such as an oval." It might be considered rude for the bride and groom to be seated in such an arrangement with their backs to guests, however, neither I nor the *Wedding Bible* experts consulted here have ever heard this complaint at the hundreds of weddings we've hosted between us. A round or oval table can also solve many potential problems if you have step-parents or children - it means no-one is left seated at the end of the table.

Indeed many couples invite their parents to host their own tables, thus avoiding placing estranged couples together. However, if you are going to do this warn those concerned in advance. For more advice about your seating plan see page 242.

Next decide what, if anything, you need in addition to flowers to decorate your tables. "Keep everything as simple as possible and it will look far more elegant on the day. Simplicity is the key at most wedding venues," states Hotel Portmeirion's Corina Tibbetts. James Partridge agrees. "Crisp, clean linens, beautiful flowers, polished silverware, simple crockery and sparkling clean glasses - you can't go wrong with that." However, we don't all have a reception salon in Claridge's hotel or sunset over the magical Portmeirion village as a backdrop to our weddings! Nevertheless, simple, understated elegance is a good starting point: no balloons (unless they fit with the theme), no hearts or horseshoes and definitely no table clutter! That doesn't mean there is no scope for a few frills and details. But keep it simple - less is more.

You could name rather than number tables for a formal seated meal. You'll also need a seating plan (page 242) positioned somewhere accessible. A smaller seating plan could be taken among guests during the drinks reception by children - it's a good way to make them feel important. Table names and numbers and place and menu cards can be printed to match your stationery. Or there are a hundred and one creative alternatives from hand-painted dried leaves to chocolates to indicate where guests are seated. Consult any bridal magazine for the latest ideas. If the chairs are shabby, consider hiring more elaborate ones or slipcovers. But the costs can soon mount up if you have more than a few guests.

Wedding favours are now replacing the more traditional five sugared almonds (signifying health, wealth, fertility, happiness and longevity). If you are on a tight budget dispense with favours. "I've seen some nice things, but I've seen some horrible things too!" says James Partridge. "I've broken my teeth on them, thrown them out six months later and often we find favours left on tables when clearing them or in guests' hotel rooms after they've checked out." Guests don't expect a gift when attending your wedding. Favours can be beautiful and offer an opportunity for you to express your gratitude, but they are an optional extra.

ENTERTAINMENT

Often the catalyst for a great wedding is the soundtrack that punctuates it. Music establishes the ambience and enlivens the event. But it needs to be in harmony with the surroundings and style of the celebration; a one-man band on the terrace of a grand stately home for instance, might feel somewhat out of place. To entertain at a drinks reception, in addition to the usual string quartet or harp (give careful consideration to the latter because at larger weddings the sound can be lost among the noise) there are steel bands, jazz trios, barbershop quartets, solo pianists and a whole host of live musicians you can employ. For dancing there are cover bands, jazz bands, salsa and samba specialists, and ceilidhs to name but a few ideas. And there are of course, mobile DJs. If you've begun the event with live music you might want to consider it continuing through dinner, culminating with a big band to dance to, but a good disc jockey is always preferable to a bad band who can ruin the atmosphere. Budget is likely to dictate your options. The more live musicians involved, the more it will cost because they all have to be paid. If music won't be live at the start of your celebration, you could explore what options are available at your venue for piped music via a sound system and build up to a band or DJ.

When hiring musicians always hear them first, preferably live, and ask for testimonials. Similarly with disc jockeys. If you are unable to secure a recommendation for a musician or band, consider going to an agency. Most have a variety of acts and artists on their books and will select only those they think suitable for your event, saving you valuable time. You will be required to sign a contract; standard Musicians Union contracts stipulate musicians must be paid before they perform. Remember that musicians will need breaks, so consider what will happen when the music stops so that the atmosphere is not lost. Arrange for CDs to be played, or for a disc jockey to entertain between sets once the dancing has begun. Many bands can provide their own DJ for a small additional charge. Bands and disc jockeys should carry-out a sound check before guests arrive. When booking, they'll usually suggest you provide them with a play list in advance which includes the first dance. Your guests' tastes in music will differ dramatically. Therefore, select a mixture of styles which will appeal to a variety of age groups. Our 'Seven Week Wedding' bride (page 23), Zelda Suite-Pedler, asked guests to indicate on her reply cards what their three favourite tunes were. "We compiled a list for the disco around those songs. It was bizarre because it was like a competition with people arguing that particular numbers were theirs and not someone else's. Indeed during our first dance we actually had to tell people 'Leave us some room – it's our tune!' But every song that was played was someone's so there were always people dancing." Give a live band your play list well in advance to see if they would be willing to perform some of your favourites. Don't assume popular numbers are part of their standard repertoire.

Establish in writing exactly when musicians, entertainers and disc jockeys will arrive, who they'll liaise with at the venue, a dress code, what changing facilities they might require, what options there are between sets and whether they can provide a microphone for the speeches if required. If you have taken dancing lessons and learned to tango to wow your guests, ensure the band can strike the correct tempo. Also remember to give musicians and entertainers refreshments and arrange this with your venue or caterer in advance. During the reception ensure music is not so loud it is overpowering.

In addition to music, there is a whole host of entertainments you can provide for your guests: a close-up magician, mime artists, fire eaters, tightrope walkers, staffed casino tables, fortune tellers, a cartoonist or artist to capture the event on paper, a bucking bronco and in good weather a bouncy castle, croquet or boules. Don't lose sight of the fact that you are planning a wedding celebration, not a corporate event. But do consider children – you want to enjoy their presence and not worry what they are up to, so incorporate some child-friendly activity and entertainment. To keep them busy during dinner and the speeches, make up children's fun activity bags (there are companies who'll custom-make these for you). You could hire a clown, a face painter or a children's entertainer. You could even section-off an area to provide your younger guests with their own party and food away from the adults.

Ending an evening with a blast of fireworks is a guaranteed winner! Specialist companies can even set displays to music. If the weather is suspect, provide rugs or space blankets for older guests.

SPEECHES – THE GREAT DEBATE

Speeches usually occur at the end of the meal, or before the cutting of the cake at a cocktail reception. It's considered bad form to interrupt conversation for the speeches between individual courses – it also interrupts the natural flow and build–up of events. But it is now acceptable for the first speaker to begin once pudding has been served. Many a heated debate among families before a wedding concerns when the speeches will ideally occur! Social norms and traditional etiquette are partly there to offer guidance. Speeches are delivered at the end of the meal precisely because that is the best time for them to occur – guests will be relaxed and more receptive. They'll be looking forward to the speeches, will know what to expect and how they are expected to respond.

The reason usually given for speeches occurring earlier in celebration is that one of those delivering them feels the prospect will prevent them from enjoying themselves until the ordeal is over. Only you can decide whose comfort zone will have to be stretched! If doing things your own way, let your guests know. The Master of Ceremonies, the groom or the father of the bride could formally welcome everyone at the earliest opportunity – preferably when they have been served a drink. When weighing–up the pros and cons, remember it is easier to speak publicly to a receptive audience, and hard to win over a hungry one! If the speeches will occur before the meal keep them very short – especially if everyone is standing. Direct a nervous speaker to voice coach Andrew Wade's advice (page 60) for tips on public speaking.

Check if your venue has a microphone. If not, ask your band or DJ to lend you one. Ideally, speeches should not last more than ten minutes. A Toastmaster or Master of Ceremonies (this can be a friend) introduces each speaker by name. Traditionally the speeches open with the bride's father welcoming guests. He gives timely advice to the newlyweds and ends by proposing a toast to the bride and groom. If the bride is going to speak, following her father is an opportune moment. But it's optional and her prerogative to change her mind either way at the last minute! Next up is the groom who compliments the bride, highlights the things the couple have particularly enjoyed about the day and thanks both sets of parents, children (if you have them), friends and anyone who has contributed to the event. He might present gifts to his best man, bridesmaids and the mothers. The groom finishes his speech thanking and toasting the bridesmaids. Finally the best man replies on their behalf. His job is to be humorous with a tasteful and light–hearted speech about the couple's history, particularly the groom's! He should also read any messages – these days they are more likely to be received via e–mail than by telegram. There is no formal toast, but guests are invited to raise their glasses to the bride, groom and absent friends.

ORDER OF SPEECHES & TOASTS

Bride's Father (toasts the bride and groom)

Groom (toasts the bridesmaids)

Best man (invites guests to raise their glasses to the bride, groom and absent friends)

To avoid a lull in proceedings and keep the momentum building, the best man/Master of Ceremonies/Toastmaster should immediately invite the bride and groom to cut the cake, or if they have already done so, to take to the floor for the first dance. Ensure each event flows seamlessly to the next. If the first dance is a slow number, follow it straight away with something more upbeat which will encourage guests to join in. Remember James Partridge's earlier advice not to interrupt the music once it is underway.

BRIDE ON A BUDGET

If you are working with a limited budget there are lots of cost-saving devices you can employ. Initially bear in mind that guests are your core cost – you have to offer them food and drink. Therefore the fewer guests you invite the less you'll be spending. "Have a long, hard think about who you are inviting. You could always have a party at a later date and limit wedding guests to close friends and family. Choose a weekday in London or a Sunday in the country. And consider lunch which is usually cheaper than dinner (so long as you are out at a certain time)," advises James Partridge. You could even hold an old fashioned tea dance. When creating menus keep food simple and seasonal.

If you want an evening reception, start your service later in the day so you can move straight from a drinks reception into dinner, or throw a fabulous cocktail party. A canapé and drinks reception will be cheaper than a buffet which will be cheaper than a sit-down meal. Serve wedding cake instead of pudding and don't invite extra guests to arrive later in the evening who will expect to be served food.

Alcohol: do you need champagne or can you serve sparkling wine? "If your speeches are delivered at the end of a meal, you don't have to offer champagne, simply top-up the wine glasses," states James. Do the sums – if you have invited a lot of guests, assess how much you could save by buying your own drink. But first ask the venue if they'd consider lowering their price. If you purchase from a wine merchant, buy on a 'sale or return' basis. If you travel to France you won't be able to get your money back on unused bottles, so factor that into the equation. Always negotiate when buying a significant amount of alcohol – many suppliers will reduce the price on a bulk order and include free delivery. If you can, purchase around the festive season when the best deals are available.

When decorating the venue, keep it simple. If you have not got a lot of money don't waste what you have got to spend on favours and table clutter. You can save hundreds of pounds on menus, seating plans and place cards by making them yourself. The 'real weddings' sections in wedding magazines offer great insights into how other couples personalised their days. Copy ideas you like.

If funds are limited keep remembering the 'Wedding Bible Golden Rule' (page 15): weddings are about people, about family and friends, about affirming our relationships with one another and about sharing and witnessing a moment. How much money you spend celebrating your commitment to one another is not a measure of it's strength. A beaming couple in love make a happy wedding! At the Wedding Bible Company we've photographed and organized hundreds of weddings between us and we agree that the best and most enjoyable ones have not always been where large sums of money were spent.

THE GREAT GETAWAY

Having danced the night away, as stated earlier, leave on a high. Photographer Pascal Plessis of Contrejour, suggests you plan in advance when and how you'll depart. "This is the last image your guests will have of you and the last you will have of them and your wedding. So leave with some sparkle in your eyes!" You need not depart half way through the evening, as often used to happen, but plan to leave about half an hour before the official finish time.

Modern brides have dispensed with the traditional 'going away outfit', preferring instead to spend all the cash on their wedding gown. And it's the best dress you've ever owned, so why remove it a moment before you have to?

As you prepare to depart, gather everyone around you, toss the bouquet and allow your guests a fantastic last glimpse of you – maybe another blast of confetti, some fireworks, sparklers or a grand getaway in a fast car.

RECEPTION TIPS FOR THE BRIDE ON A BUDGET

Marry early-afternoon and host a fabulous tea dance.

Marry later in the day and move straight from a drinks reception into dinner, or hold a gorgeous cocktail reception instead.

Keep menus seasonal and simple.

Serve your wedding cake as pudding.

Don't invite additional evening guests who will be expecting food.

Consider sparkling wine or cocktails instead of champagne. Don't serve champagne for after-dinner speeches just top-up the wine glasses.

When purchasing alcohol from a wine merchant, buy on a 'sale or return' basis.

Keep decorations simple, avoid table clutter and favours.

Consult wedding magazines for inspiration on home-made menus, place cards and favours.

TIPS FOR CREATING THE PERFECT WEDDING RECEPTION

Plan your reception around what people would normally be doing at a given time and replicate it.

Draw up a 'Wedding Reception Wish List' (page 68) to help plan the structure of your day.

If creating an adventurous theme, ensure you and your venue can pull it off or hire professionals.

Assess your venue's potential and accentuate the good.

Consider what was good and bad at other people's weddings.

Serve delicious food!

In addition to alcohol, ensure a plentiful supply of water and soft drinks.

If organizing a pay bar, top venues charge top dollar and guests may be shocked at their prices. Could you afford to offer free drinks all day by limiting the choice to wine, beer and soft drinks?

Be realistic about what can be achieved in a temporary kitchen. Consider dishes that do not require pre-plating, but which can be served at the table.

When hiring crockery and glassware ensure it can be returned dirty.

Provide refreshments for photographers, entertainers, musicians and suppliers present at the event. Arrange in advance with your venue staff or caterer – avoid sandwiches if you want to be appreciated!

Hire a Toastmaster (or appoint the best man or a friend as Master of Ceremonies).

If available, consider a side room for the Receiving Line, where guests can avoid queuing in line.

If there will not be a Receiving Line ensure you make the effort to speak to everyone.

Stick together! If you separate it will be difficult to break free and find one another again.

Consider a round or oval top table positioned in the centre of the room.

Invite estranged parents to host their own tables if they'll be uncomfortable placed close together.

Seek inspiration from bridal magazines for alternatives to traditional reception stationery and favours.

Do not interrupt the wedding breakfast with speeches.

Limit speeches to ten minutes each and ensure the availability of a microphone.

Ensure entertainment is in harmony with the surroundings and the style of the celebration.

Consider hiring a child minder or children's entertainer and purchasing activity packs to keep younger guests occupied.

Let the day build momentum – move seamlessly through events avoiding a lull between the speeches, the cutting of the cake and the first dance. Never stop the music once it has started and plan how you'll cover between live musicians' sets.

A blast of confetti for the first dance is very romantic!

Always leave on a high and give your guests a fantastic last image of you.

EXPERTS' TOP TIPS FOR A PERFECT RECEPTION

wedding reception

ideas

AS SOON AS THE VENUE IS CONFIRMED

Break down your reception budget into categories: venue hire, food, drink, entertainment, flowers and decoration.

Assess your venue's potential and consult your 'Wedding Reception Wish List' (page 68).

Gather together information and pricing about food, drink and facilities for guests.

If hiring outside caterers, book appointments with at least three. Secure a booking as soon as you have made a decision.

Consider your entertainment options – consult an agency if required. Provisionally book musicians, entertainers or a DJ as soon as possible.

decisions

6 – 4 MONTHS TO GO

Confirm menu options and advise the format of your meal (canapé and drinks reception, lunch, tea, buffet or silver–service meal).

Assess whether you can afford to offer free drinks throughout the reception.

Book a Toastmaster if required.

Arrange to visit the venue with your florist.

4-phase timeline

details

4 –1 MONTH TO GO

Arrange a tasting and select the menu and wines.

Establish who will be overseeing your event on the day and take contact details.

If purchasing alcohol, source a supplier and place the order.

Confirm timings with musicians and entertainers and give them on–the–day contact numbers for the venue and best man.

Give a play list to band and/or DJ.

Confirm details of flower and table arrangements with your florist. Give on–the–day contact numbers for the venue and best man.

Purchase a guest book and pen.

Chase unanswered invitations two weeks before.

Begin a table and seating plan.

Compile your 'Wedding Day Contact List' and 'Wedding Day Schedule' (pages 248 and 249).

event

AND THE WEEK PRECEDING THE WEDDING

Confirm final guest numbers with your caterer or venue.

Complete seating and table plan, write place cards and take to printer.

Complete and distribute 'Wedding Day Schedule' and 'Wedding Day Contact List'.

Confirm first dance with DJ or band.

Write instructions for the Toastmaster or Master of Ceremonies with names of speakers.

Confirm suppliers and musicians access and delivery arrangements.

Delegate tasks – ensure sufficient reliable help on the day for last minute tasks.

Check 'Reception Box' (page 249) and delegate delivery.

wedding gown

What you wear on you wedding day is a serious statement of personal style and is likely to be among the most costly clothing you'll ever buy. The good news is that as never before the modern woman can truly be the bride she wants to be: sleek and modern, sexy but simple, refined, decadent or demure – the choice is yours. Bridal fashion today is an exciting blend of old and new that reflects the diversity of contemporary culture and the various ways we celebrate marriage. Today's bride can choose classic designs that are daring in detail. Everything from the traditional Cinderella fairy-tale gown to the funky fashionistas trouser suit is available and can be tailored to any budget.

The trend for the traditional white gown was set by Queen Victoria in 1840. When she walked down the aisle to marry her prince she wore a rich, white satin gown adorned with orange blossoms, trimmed with yards of lace, finished with a flowing veil and an eighteen foot train. Bridal fashion has never looked back. Although brides had been wearing white since ancient times it wasn't the norm. Henceforth it was the choice of most society brides and those who could afford such luxury. By the 1900s clothing manufacturers were producing elaborate, ready-made, white wedding gowns for the affluent middle classes. Although through the decades styles have come and gone and been revived, hem lines have crept up and down again, bodices worn tighter and then looser, the classic white gown endures. For the modern bride it's available from couture houses and top designers, made-to-measure and ready-to-wear off-the-peg. It can be made from the finest silks, most luxurious fabrics or man-made fibres. You can pay a few hundred pounds or a few thousand. It's even available on the high street and second-hand . But you don't have to marry in white and it doesn't have to be a gown!

For this chapter we consulted some of the country's leading bridal designers and couturiers. They will first assist you to navigate the minefield that is designer jargon. 'Couture', 'designer', 'made-to-measure'; these terms are bandied about and sewn into labels, but you need to know what they mean and what you will get. 'Couture' may be placed after a designer's name, implying you'll get a couture service - but you might not. A 'designer' gown might also be a made-to-measure garment, but that's not couture. A dress that is tweaked to your measurements is not couture or made-to-measure, even when it is designed by a well-known designer! Our *Wedding Bible* experts explain exactly what the different bridal services involve. An understanding of this is a good place to start, whatever your budget – it's not only the exclusive couture service that is expensive. We also offer advice on how to begin your search, give shopping tips and advise how best to manage weight loss so your dress still fits you on your wedding day. We've some tips on securing a fabulous nearly-new outfit, hiring one or using a dressmaker. If you are seeking something a little out-of-the-ordinary we've an interview with Britain's leading vintage specialist. Additionally, the Queen's corsetière offers her tips on shopping for your wedding day underwear. Finally, because this chapter is also relevant when shopping for bridesmaids' and mothers' outfits, there's a section for them too.

what the experts say

The 21st century bride has inherited an incredibly diverse dressing-up box. She can draw on styles from any age and made of any fabric, and can complement her look with shoes and accessories chosen from a huge array of designs from around the world.

What you wear on your wedding day can set the tone of your celebration, but to a certain extent is also dictated by the type of wedding you are hoping to have. If you are not having a religious ceremony then almost anything goes. That being said, a gown with a flowing veil and huge train might feel a tad out of place in a register office. But that's not to say you shouldn't wear a traditional dress – just something in keeping with your chosen venue. Indeed you may be having a civil ceremony in a grand location and want a grand gown to match.

Our wedding gown experts have dressed brides from all walks of life who spend as little as a few hundred pounds and as much as several thousand. Most of them are among the country's few true couturiers. Even if you can't afford their clothes, take their free advice! Amanda Wakeley is one of Britain's most successful fashion designers. Her A-list clientele includes Jennifer Lopez, Elizabeth Hurley and Queen Rania of Jordan. Her bridal collection includes an internationally available and affordable ready-to-wear line. Basia Zarzycka designs for foreign royalty, international pop stars and some of Hollywood's biggest names. She also specialises in bridal accessories and you'll find her quoted in our 'Stepping Out' chapter too. Multi-award winning designer Caroline Parkes trained under the world renowned Hardy Amies couture house. She sells her gowns through a limited number of bridal wear outlets across the country as well as her London studio. "It's important that the dress makes you look your best," she says. "People need to remember you at your wedding because you looked beautiful, not because the dress did!" Catherine Walker began her business selling children's clothes from a basket on the Kings Road. She's a self-taught designer who is now one of the country's foremost couturiers. Not all her dresses are as elaborate as the gown she designed for Countess Guerrini Maraldi on which a staggering forty-four-thousand pearl and crystal beads were meticulously hand embroidered! Christina Marty is the winner of numerous fashion awards. She offers a couture service from her London boutique, Christiana Couture.

She also designs two collections annually, available to order from selected bridal boutiques world-wide. Christina designed the gown our front cover bride is wearing (that photograph was not staged, it was taken at a real wedding). Neil Cunningham opened his Piccadilly salon over a decade ago and has been discreetly dressing some of the richest, most powerful women ever since. Self-owned and independent (as are most of our experts) his bridal wear is expensive but among the best. Phillipa Lepley is one of the country's most savvy bridal designers. She's been creating critically acclaimed wedding gowns for almost two decades. She's a hands-on designer at the forefront of her industry. Sharon Cunningham has also won a slew of fashion awards. She's worked with and learned from top names such as Ben De Lisi and Catherine Walker. It was when she got engaged that her bridal collection was born. Designing not only beautiful wedding gowns but outfits for the bridal party too, we've sought Sharon's input for your bridesmaids, mother and mother-in-law. Because vintage clothing is more popular than ever before, we've advice on wedding day vintage wear from Virginia Bates of Notting Hill's vintage emporium Virginia. That's your outerwear taken care of – for your underwear there was really only one place to go: London's Rigby & Peller. The company's director, Jill Kenton, offers her advice on completing your wedding day wardrobe.

At this point you may have no idea what you want to wear on your wedding day, or you may have a clear image of the dress of your dreams. Either way, where do you start? If you've set the date and you've more than nine months to go then you won't be rushed into making a choice. For couture you need around six months, the made-to measure outlets like on average six to four months. Off-the-peg is obviously easier, but only if the shop carries the stock – don't assume because you've seen an outfit in January it will still be available in April. If you are planning a wedding in the next few weeks don't panic, you'll simply need to call around and see who can do what for you. Even couturiers may be able to help, especially at quieter times of the year. Naturally, your budget will go some way towards dictating what you will wear. But you might be surprised to discover what you can afford if you know not only where to look, but what to look for. There is considerable overlap in terms of cash outlay between the main bridal gown services that most brides use.

left to right

Christina Marty, Jill Kenton, Phillipa Lepley

Basia Zarzycka, Neil Cunningham, Virginia Bates

Catherine Walker, Amanda Wakeley, Caroline Park

COUTURE

Most women have never purchased a couture gown. It is therefore not surprising that many brides don't know what the term means or what is involved in making such a garment. Couturier Catherine Walker states that only the terms 'off-the-peg' and 'made-to-measure' are obvious and many brides are confused before they've even started the search for their outfit. "There are many, sometimes confusing, bridal services on offer. Even off-the-peg dresses are sold with an alteration service so that they are 'made-to-fit'."

Neil Cunningham says the word couture has been 'bastardised', especially in the wedding business. "Now it can just mean expensive and made for you. I'm appalled by what some people call couture. There's a common misconception that it can mean 'made by a dressmaker', and simply see how it turns out in the end, or designed by a name but is made-to-measure."

Amanda Wakeley agrees that there is confusion over what the term actually means. "The word 'couture' gets so overused," she says. She knows because she offers couture gowns, a made-to-measure service and designs a ready-to-wear collection. "As far as I'm concerned couture is the making of a gown from scratch for the client, and true couture is by hand. People should be very, very careful how they use the term."

If you can afford a couture service what should you expect? A couture garment, as Amanda states, is one that is made from scratch, exclusively for you and to your exact measurements. Mostly crafted by hand, the end result will be a gown that is a perfect fit down to the last stitch. Along with the design and the fabric, this is essentially what you are paying for because the process takes many, many hours. Your dress may be chosen from an existing design from the couturier's collection, or it could be a gown that has been designed uniquely for you (and will therefore cost more, a lot more). If the term *couture* has been used you should expect a toile to be made, which you'll try on at the second fitting. This is essentially a test garment and pattern, usually made from muslin, and upon which any modifications, fine tuning and adjustments to size and detail are made. The fabric of your gown (which from a couturier you should expect to be of the highest quality) will be cut by an experienced pattern cutter, it will be sewn together by an experienced seamstress, and the detail added by expert embroiderers and beaders. The designer will see this process through and liaise with you at up to six fittings which are likely to last an hour or more. It's a time-consuming process, but it's also a highly skilled craft for everyone involved in making the garment. Thus it comes at a price. But if you can afford it – if only this one time – it will not only be the experience of a lifetime, but the end result will be a perfect and unique wedding gown that fits like a glove.

"Definitely, if money is no object, then don't even consider anything else," says Phillipa Lepley. "Off-the-peg and made-to-measure is never going to fit *perfectly* in just the right places. But if you have a couture toile made it is going to be accurate in the right places and to your exact measurements."

Another popular misconception is that couture means a one-off garment exclusively designed for you. This is not the case. "A bride can have that, but she has got to pay for a lot of processes," says Neil Cunningham. "The beauty of coming to a couture designer and seeing a dress that you like is that it has gone through those processes and is tried and tested. It is finished, it is perfect and the design is faultless. But if you want something you have in your head it has to go through a number of prototypes to get it right, and that costs a fortune. I don't generally recommend it."

It is possible a designer will make changes to the original design – such as a neckline or a sleeve, swapping some detail, adding beading or embroidery – but only if the design still works. After all, they're the designer, that's what they do. If there was a better way of designing a particular dress they probably would have spotted it themselves during the design process.

If you are being offered what is described as a couture service ensure there will be a toile. If there won't be it is not couture, even if it's a one-off. Ask who will be present at the fittings. You would usually expect it to be the designer, but if it won't be, who will it be and will it always be the same person? If you want to alter some of the detail from the original design in the sample garment, check that the designer is happy to do this. A few won't, and if they will, it might depend on what you want to change. Will there be an additional charge for any changes? Watch out for the additional costs involved with alterations as you go along. They can result in a lot of extra work and add significantly to the final bill, especially if you are simply changing your mind about a detail. This also applies to extra embroidery and beading which is time-consuming and therefore costly.

MADE-TO-MEASURE

'Made-to-measure', 'designer', what do these terms mean? Many good bridal designers offer a made-to-measure (or made-to-order) collection available either at their own shops, or through department stores and bridal boutiques, or both.

You'll choose a dress from the collection which will be available in standard sizes for you to try in the shop. The essential difference between made-to-measure and couture is that the dress will be cut from the nearest pattern size to your measurements at the designer's studio, and then altered to your size, but before the garment is sewn together. There is obviously no toile. Usually you'll require three fittings; the first to take your measurements, the second to try the dress, and if it needs any adjustments you'll return for a final fitting. Those adjustments could be made at the store, or the dress might be sent back to the studio. If you have chosen a more intricate gown an extra fitting might be required before the fine detail is added.

In addition to the design, which from a reputable designer will be tried and tested and will work, you are paying for the personalisation of the service. It is not factory made. A well cut made-to-measure gown will be a good fit and you can be assured that it will be beautifully cut, expertly constructed, and made from high quality silks and fabrics. If you choose a design with embroidery or beading, or with a bodice and boning, much of the detail will also be finished by hand,

as will buttons and laces. Many good designers are quite choosy about where their gowns are sold and you'll only find them at the quality department stores and better bridal boutiques. Shopping at the right out-of-London store or boutique is an extremely good way of acquiring an exquisite, well-made designer dress. Multi-award winning designer Caroline Parkes, for example, sells through a limited number of bridal wear outlets across the country as well as her London studio. Check designer's own websites for information as to where you can find their collections.

The danger for the unsuspecting bride-to-be is that anyone who designs dresses is theoretically a designer. But they are not all in the Amanda Wakeley or Caroline Parkes league, although their dresses may sometimes be sold in some of the same outlets. In addition, tweaking a size 12 dress and letting out a seam is not a made-to-measure service, it's a tweak. Ensure that your made-to-measure dress really is made-to-*order*. The advice from the experts is go to a reputable store or boutique and examine the gowns close-up. Look at the fabrics, the cut and the finish of a dress. Check there is no tension at the seams. Are there loose threads and evidence of machine sewn buttons that could pop off under pressure, when for example you are leaning to get out of a car, or are dancing? Does the quality match the price tag? What exactly are you getting? Be absolutely sure it's made-to-order and not a gown altered when it arrives in the store.

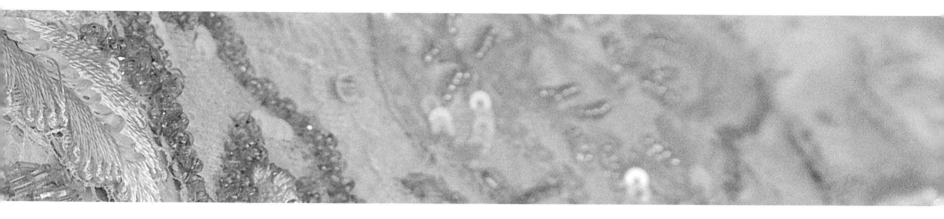

OFF-THE-PEG / READY-TO-WEAR

Off-the-peg and ready-to-wear are the same thing. Nearly all bridal departments and boutiques will offer an alteration service. If they are reputable they won't charge a fortune for this or confuse you into thinking it's made-to-measure; as Catherine Walker stated earlier, this service is 'made-to-fit', and that should be reflected in the price. Be really sure what you are being offered. You can find beautiful dresses among these ranges, and a few with top-ten bridal designer labels. The lesser known labels are where you need to exercise caution; for some inexplicable reason you have to pay a lot more for an off-the-peg bridal gown than a ready-to-wear ball gown of similar design and fabric. You can pay several hundred pounds more for a plain machine sewn cream or white gown with a train. It may even be made of a cheaper fabric than a traditional ball gown. As with the made-to-measure gowns, examine the garment close up and with a critical eye. If it looks cheap it is; don't waste your money.

DRESSMAKER

If you know a good dressmaker, fantastic! But just because a friend of a friend can knock together a Hallowe'en costume doesn't mean they can design and sew a beautiful wedding gown or outfit. It doesn't make them a good seamstress. Be sure you know someone who has used the services of the dressmaker before, and that you both like the result. Don't take their word for it. You must have total confidence in your dressmaker's abilities. Don't simply take a magazine clipping of a dress you like the look of and ask a dressmaker to copy it. How do you know the style will suit you? Read the advice in this chapter; know what image you are trying to create and what shapes and fabrics suit you. Be in a position to make an informed decision about the service the dressmaker is offering, the raw materials they are using and the quality of the results.

A good dressmaker may not necessarily be a good designer: "The worst thing you can do is go to a dressmaker who draws something for you, and you say 'Yes. That looks nice. I'll have that!'," says Neil Cunningham. Check out the many patterns available in the shops, at department stores and via the internet. You may find something you like and be able to try on garments of similar design in the shops. In all likelihood the dressmaker will not have a selection of shapes and designs for you to try on. You still need to know what suits you, and need to try on different shapes. You may never have worn the type of outfit you want for your wedding day before. Be sure you do know what suits you and are confident about the design – whether it's yours, the dressmaker's or from a pattern. If yours, what questions is the dressmaker asking you? Does he or she have the expertise to tell you if a design is flawed? Ask if there will be a toile? If not is there a pattern? If neither, how do you know what you are getting until you try it on? Are you in a position to judge the quality of the fabric and the finish of the garment? If not, acquire the knowledge. There are many fine dressmakers out there, but be sure it's a fine one you've chosen.

BREAKING WITH TRADITION

There are all kinds of reasons why you may not want a gown – traditional or otherwise. Those reasons may be cultural, religious or simply logistic. You may of course be rejecting the traditional look because you don't like it. The possibilities now are numerous. Much of the advice our experts are offering in this chapter however, is still highly relevant. Tailor it to your needs. When it comes to fashion they are the qualified experts. They know about designing beautiful clothes, making them and shopping for them.

Wherever you shop the basic services you can find are the same: couture, made-to-measure, off-the-peg and dressmaker. Whichever service you choose you are likely to get more for your money if you're not seeking a white wedding dress.

Personal shoppers in the larger department stores are a great place to start. They know their stock. Tell them your budget and what type of outfit you are looking for. If, for example, you were to spend the day in London and booked appointments with the personal shoppers in, Harvey Nichols, Harrods or Selfridges, told them you had several-hundred pounds to spend on an evening gown or tailored suit, they'd find you something! If you are not concerned whether you wear a pale evening gown or simple white wedding dress you'll also find this service much better value for money. Similarly, there will be a major department store near you, wherever you live, that will be able to offer this service. (This is also a route the bride's mother can take when shopping for an outfit.) On the high street there are also plenty of independently owned boutiques and dress shops that will be only too happy to help you. In addition there are shops like Monsoon stocking very pretty and affordable outfits for your wedding day. If you are concerned you'll look 'high street' then shop around for something different with your accessories. You could also consider vintage clothing (page 112).

You may be among the ten percent or so of British couples marrying abroad. If saying "I do" on a sun-drenched beach, you may feel comfortable in a bikini! (You could have fun accessorising that.) More appropriate might be a simple strapless dress and shoeless feet. Or taking your vows at sunset on safari could mean you've set your heart on a simple ivory evening gown. You'll find that a lot better value than a white wedding dress.

'Wedding' and 'dress' do not have to go together. Not opting for the traditional western look does not mean you can't look like a bride. If still seeking 'the look' then create it with your accessories.

SETTING A BUDGET

You will know whether you have a few hundred pounds, a few thousand or an amount in between to spend on your wedding gown. As already stated, if money is no object go couture; make that decision right now. If you've seen a stunning dress, fallen in love with it, but it is beyond your means where else in your budget can you make savings or cuts and steal for your gown? We'll go into purchasing second–hand or at sales later, as well as hiring. But let's assume for now you want a new dress.

"Unless you have pots of money, put the cash in the dress and not into £300 shoes," is Caroline Parkes advice. "No-one ever remembers the shoes and most don't even see them!" We're not sure if we agree with this advice – but for some it will be pertinent! You can certainly pay hundreds of pounds for designer shoes, or less than fifty on the high street.

Bridesmaids and pageboys: how many are you having and do you need them all? Do you need any? If you are not walking down a church aisle – and even if you are – there is no rule stating you are required to have them. You can save hundreds of pounds, thousands even, by cutting down their number or eliminating them altogether. "You don't have to have them," states Caroline Parkes. "Don't spend a fortune on young children, either, because they may refuse to wear the outfit on the day."

There's more advice on shopping for your bridesmaids on page 122. It is also worth considering that an older bridesmaid, particularly a family member, might be happy to pay for their outfit leaving you more money to spend on yours. But if you expect this of a bridesmaid you need to establish it with them early on.

Accessories – what can you borrow? Has a friend recently married, and would they lend you their veil or tiara? Who has got jewellery they could offer? You could save a substantial sum by begging and borrowing and put it all towards your gown.

The top tip from Amanda Wakeley, if you are having trouble finding something beautiful within your budget, is to explore purchasing a simple dress which costs less to make. "I've always believed in quality, so would aspire to have the best I could get," she says. "Just because a gown has got 'bells and whistles' on it doesn't mean it is the best. Simple but beautifully cut is better value."

To follow this advice, do your homework. Find out what simpler made–to–measure gowns cost in comparison with the all singing all dancing off–the–peg dresses. Similarly, instead of paying for an intricate made–to–measure design, consider what you might get at a comparable price from a couture collection. You might be surprised by the price designers and couturiers such as Phillipa Lepley, Caroline Parkes or Amanda Wakeley charge for one of their simpler gowns. Compared with the more expensive made–to–measure dresses they are affordable – just! Mention you are on a tight budget when you phone to make an appointment. Don't be embarrassed, if they can't work within that budget they will tell you. If they can, then when they see you, they won't waste your time, or theirs, showing you dozens of outfits beyond your means. And wherever you purchase your dress, if they care about what they are doing, they will want you to be happy with both the service and the end result. No-one wants an unhappy bride!

STARTING POINTS

This is probably the most important clothing purchase of your life so it is crucial you get it right. Your gown or outfit should be a reflection of who you are: your personality and your style. You may already have a strong sense of that style, or you may not. Your religion or nationality may be something you want reflected, for example. Your ethnicity may even be a dictating factor. What image do you have in your mind about how you'll look on your wedding day? Is there an 'inner-bride' in there who can help you? Who are your style icons?

Do you imagine yourself in a full gown with diaphanous layers of tulle, lace, organza and chiffon? Will the dress sparkle with crystals or shimmer with pearls? Will it be a dress at all? It could be a tailored suit or an evening dress. Perhaps sleek, simple but sexy is how you imagine your look. Do you envisage you'll wear long or short? Do you want a veil and a train – if so how long will they be? Off-the-shoulder, sleeves, a shrug or jacket? Perhaps if it's winter you've a burning desire to wear fur. Maybe you've a penchant for feathers. Will you wear white? If taking the designer route this is all food for thought as each designer has a 'signature look'. If you want retro with a twist, you'll recognise it when you see it, so that designer will be an excellent starting point. Check designers' web sites to see if they are designing clothes in styles and fabrics you like. Browsing through magazines will also give you a good idea of the latest bridal fashions and of what is available and where. You may also find yourself drawn to particular styles.

Christina Marty of Christiana Couture suggests you assess what's already in your wardrobe and works for you. "I have a T-shirt and I know the neckline really suits me – it makes my bust look good," she says. The 'queen of bias-cut' also advises you keep an open mind and don't have too many preconceived ideas about styles and cuts, especially if you are having a dress made for you which can make a huge difference to what will suit you. "Bias, for example, when it is cut for you rather than off-the-peg in the high street, will look great. That's one of the reasons I do it because the seams skim in all the right places."

There are also a few practicalities to take into consideration that will help you narrow-down the search. These include the venue, the type of ceremony and the time of year. "Think about how long you will be in your wedding dress, and what it has to go through," says Caroline Parkes. "What will the temperature be? Will you be getting into a boat, into a helicopter or stepping up into a horse drawn carriage? Will you be dancing and how vigorously?"

You might be taking your wedding vows in a special venue or location and want this reflected in your gown. You may also have family jewellery that you know you want to wear. Whether having something exclusively designed or choosing from an existing collection these are factors to take into consideration. Catherine Walker designed Lady Helen Windsor's wedding gown and looked into such details for the design. "I spent many hours in St. George's Chapel studying the shapes of the windows. Together with the motifs of the Kent tiara, they were worked into the design and embroidery." You may not be a member of the Royal Family or taking your vows in such a grand location, but if you are going to the trouble and expense of having a gown designed, such special attention to detail can be a source of inspiration to both you and the designer or dressmaker. If you are purchasing an existing design you could find similar inspiration for your accessories.

"You could also ask your groom to look through magazines," suggests Caroline Parkes. "He can tell you the gowns he likes and hates and thereby give you an idea of how he might like to see you." This is great advice. Your intended might hate laces and frills or dream of a Cinderella bride. He may love the idea of lifting your veil for your first legal kiss, or think that naff. It would be good to know now!

THE HUNT – PRELIMINARIES

If you are hoping to wear a traditional wedding gown, bear in mind that there is a finite number available. If you go to dozens of shops it is likely you will simply be seeing and trying on the same dresses. Therefore do some research and select just three or four boutiques and/or department stores who carry a large and varied stock. Do your homework on the internet and see which designers you like. Their websites will state where their gowns are sold. Phillipa Lepley also points–out that going to too many shops can be overwhelming and confusing. "Go to four or five different places and ensure they know what they are talking about and offer good advice."

On your first outing in the quest for your outfit, go with an open mind and plenty of time. Couturiers and designers will see you by ap-pointment only, and the same usually applies to stores and bridal boutiques if you want to try dresses on (which you do!). "Don't shop when you are too tired," advises Christina Marty. Pertinent advice. You don't want to be searching for the perfect look when you are not feeling one–hundred percent. Take it easy the evening before and get a good night's sleep. You'll be sharper and find it easier to remain focused on the task.

Should you take someone with you, and if so, who? If you usually prefer to shop alone do the same now. You can always take someone with you before you place an order, or to help you choose when you've narrowed the selection. "I much prefer they come alone," says Neil Cunningham. "But if you have got a bossy mother bring her early on, not at the end. There's nothing worse than a mother coming at the last fitting and saying: 'Oh, I don't like that'."

If you want to take someone with you choose carefully and limit the number you take. "Listening to too many people can be confusing," says Phillipa Lepley. "If you really trust your mum and she's got great taste then fine. But if you also take a friend there can be too many opinions."

Neil Cunningham suggests you consider shopping with a man: "Bring a male friend or your dad. Don't bring your mum or best friend unless you really trust them. Mums often have an idea about how they think their daughters should look, and how they want them to look. But a man will see things totally differently."

Christina Marty advises you to think carefully about what type of person the individual you bring with you is. "Make sure it is someone who is not a 'me' person, but someone who can listen and understand what you like. Someone who is not going to tell you to pick something because they would wear it."

Amanda Wakeley agrees. "You have to be careful, as people have different agendas. Someone else might have quite another idea of what they want for you. A quiet hour by yourself with a really trustworthy and expert sales advisor can be more helpful."

IN THE SHOP

First, allow plenty of time both to look and to try on. Wear white or flesh-coloured underwear and ensure you are wearing a well-fitting bra (page 118); it cannot be overstated what a difference this will make. Do not wear heavy make-up, and if possible don't wear any at all. If you can, shop on a weekday. The consultants will be able to give you more time; on a Saturday they are busier with back-to-back appointments, and there are often browsers in the shop needing attention. If there's something specific you want to wear on your wedding day, such a special piece of jewellery, take it with you and let the sales consultant know. It could affect or limit your choice of design and fabrics. Arrive with an open mind and be prepared to try-on different styles. Many outfits do not have hanger appeal and you need to see them on you. "Most people come in with an idea of what they want, but when they try it on all their preconceived ideas are not really what will suit them. I usually advise people to try on loads of shapes," says Phillipa Lepley. Refer to magazines for ideas but don't get too bogged-down in detail. This can unwittingly be what confuses you. "The problem is that you can end-up with too many ideas, saying 'I like this, I like that', and over-designing a dress with six completely different details," adds Phillipa Lepley.

Put your preconceived ideas behind you. "You must try on shape, after shape, after shape, to get an idea. You'd never buy a pair of trousers without trying them on," states Neil Cunningham. "The most fundamental thing is try the shapes. It's no more complicated than buying an ordinary dress – it's just a bigger and whiter one!"

Think of your starting points. As already discussed, the overall image you have in your mind – not specifics, just basic ideas. For example, the silhouette you are looking for, and whether you'd like a romantic, traditional, sexy, simple or demure look. This gives the sales consultant a reference point and saves a lot of time: "It really helps if the bride-to-be has a strong idea of what she likes style-wise. We then take a look through the collection and try and see what looks good," says Neil Cunningham. "A good sales consultant or designer will know and say what is a good shape for you."

But how do you know if you are in a good shop or boutique with a sales consultant who is good at what they do? "Do you feel comfortable with them?" asks Caroline Parkes. "Do they convey that they know what they are doing? Are they getting to know you? Are they asking pertinent questions? You would expect them to ask you what type of ceremony you are having, what type of venue the reception will be in, the time of year, and if there are any special considerations."

A good consultant will be able to assist you with shapes and styles that suit your height and build. You can then start eliminating. Together you can begin to build-upon and modify the look. You may prefer a particular neckline from several that work for you. Some fabrics, textures and shades will suit your hair colouring and skin tones better than others. If you reject a dress or outfit what is it that you don't like about it? Perhaps the neckline is too high or too low, a skirt too full or figure-hugging. You might want long or short sleeves. You may prefer to keep your flesh covered up. Gut instinct will also help, and shouldn't be ignored. Even if an outfit looks fabulous do you feel comfortable in it? Is it you? "I'm a big believer that a bride should stay true to the styles she normally loves to wear," says Amanda Wakeley. "I think it's a great mistake when a bride walks down the aisle and her husband-to-be does not recognise her. I think that is sad."

"If you know it's not you then don't choose it," says Christina Marty. "No matter how much or little a gown costs you should feel happy and comfortable in it. You should know when you put the dress on that it is right for you." However, Christina adds that this is the one time in your life when you can go that one stage further – if you are comfortable with it. "Do not be afraid if it feels right to go that little bit more over-the-top. If it feels exciting, do it!"

Catherine Walker agrees. "It's fun to try on a few styles, but the main thing is to be true to oneself and a little daring," she says. "The outfit should be an extension of the bride's own style. She should not let the latest fashion trends dictate her choice unless she is always wearing the latest fashions."

If you find a gown or outfit you like do not allow yourself to be pressured into making a decision immediately. A reputable shop or boutique will be happy for you to go away and think about it. If they tell you the price is going up tomorrow, shop somewhere else. And if you've plenty of time, don't hand over a deposit and book a dress too far in advance. There are all kinds of reasons why you might later change your mind. The longer the wedding planning process, the more likely it is there will be major changes to the event. Neither do you need to buy the first dress you like for fear of not finding something better. Know what your options are and explore them.

When you think you have made a decision, book an appointment and try on the dress or outfit again. When you have made a firm decision you need to ask some questions. At the top of the list is what is included in the cost? What should you expect to pay for alterations if it is not made-to-measure or couture? What are the payment terms and what is the deposit? You will want to know the time schedule and how many fittings you need. If you work Monday to Friday, can they see you on a Saturday? And ask if you will see the same consultant or fitter at each stage. Only hand over your deposit when you are comfortable and confident with the decision you have made.

WEIGHT LOSS

As soon as they get engaged to be married nearly all women claim they'll lose weight! It's a fact. "We get very used to it," says Phillipa Lepley. "At the very beginning they all say they want to lose weight. Some gradually lose it along the way, others shed masses in the last two weeks." This can be a nightmare for those selling your outfit, and especially for those making it. If what you ordered does not fit, and it is because you have changed your body shape, you may not be able to do anything about it at the last minute. If your dress requires extra alterations you may well be charged for them. If you really do need to lose weight and you've not sufficient time between now and ordering your outfit to shift it, then make this known when placing your order. Ensure this can be accommodated, and if there will be any additional charges. If there are constant alterations along the way expect to be charged. Set realistic and achievable targets for yourself. "Be honest at the beginning," advises Christina Marty. "If you are setting realistic goals it can be worked around, but we need to know in advance."

"Tell the store or designer," agrees Caroline Parkes. "And don't lose any more weight after the final cut. If the bride states at the start that weight loss is a goal, if at all possible we don't cut the dress until six weeks before the wedding."

Women come in all shapes and sizes: tall and willowy, small and petite, big and busty, wide-hipped, slim-hipped, long-armed and short-legged. Few of us can identify with the tall, slim, perfectly proportioned models with no lumps and bumps we see in magazines and on billboards. But some of the world's sexiest women are not the slimmest! There are right shapes for every body type, it is just a matter of identifying them. Refer to our previous advice: try everything on and find the shape and design for you. A well-cut dress that fits and hangs properly will do far more for you than covering yourself up. But if you are big, you'll still be big inside the dress! It must be flattering. Be realistic, don't choose an outfit that fits with how you'd like to look. "Choose a dress according to the weight you are now (when ordering) and not your envisaged three stones lighter – it won't happen!" says Amanda Wakeley.

Be comfortable with who and what you are. Neil Cunningham's advice is if you've got it, you flaunt it. "It's amazing how much more daring a big, busty, curvy bride can be!" he states.

It is safe to assume that your fiancé likes you the way you are. However, it is not unreasonable for you to want to look your best to marry him. If it is important to you to lose weight, and you have some to lose, listen to what our experts have said: set realistic goals that you can achieve. If you've time, get rid of the weight before you order the dress, and keep it off. If you haven't time, negotiate with the shop or designer. And if you've more weight to lose than time available to lose it, don't let that be the excuse to do nothing. Work with the time you have. Remember that crash diets wreak havoc with your hormones and complexion. Eat healthily and exercise. But above all be realistic, don't end up with the outfit you wanted for the thinner you.

NEARLY NEW

A once-worn outfit is another way to secure a bargain bridal gown. There are many specialist shops selling-on used, once-only worn gowns and ex-hire dresses. Couturiers and designers will also sometimes have a dress that was made for a client who did not need it in the end. It's rare, but worth asking. But when seeking a top name, second-hand dress, your best friend is the internet. There are new sites popping-up regularly, and a few well-established ones selling second-hand designer dresses. Often a picture of the dress will be posted along with a description including the size, the designer and the name of the design. The more navigable sites allow you to search by the designer's name. So if you know you want a Christiana Couture gown for example, you can type in the name and see what comes up. If there is no picture of the dress, but the designer and the design name are there, you can cross reference with the designer's website where there might be a photograph. You can expect a price tag of fifty percent or so of the original cost. And, if a girl has shelled-out a small fortune for her wedding dress, she is likely to have treated it with respect whilst wearing it. But NEVER purchase a gown over the internet without first knowing its condition. Ask about stains and damage and assess the likelihood of being able to remove, repair or conceal. Get a written description as well as photos. Ask as many questions as you can.

If you find a gown via the web, the danger is that you probably won't be able to try it on before purchasing it. It's therefore important you get as much detail about the dress and the original wearer before you part with money. It won't be an exact fit so can it be altered? Standard sizes are not a good indicator of how similar you are in shape or height to another person. Find out how tall the first bride is and what her vital statistics were. That may be enough of an indicator to you that it will not be a good fit. If this information is promising, get some more detailed measurements. In addition to the bust, waist and hips ask for the following: the measurement from the centre of the dress, at the back, to the hem; the same measurement at front; the measurement from the underarm to the cuff, and the shoulder seam to the cuff (if there are sleeves); if there are shoulders to the dress get the measurements and ask where they were measured from and to, similarly with straps if they are fixed; if the dress has a bodice or corset get the measurement from the underarm to the waist, and the skirt from the waist to the hem. You can then ascertain if your upper body is of a similar length. Depending on the style of the gown you may also need the original bride's breast cup size. You can't squeeze into her dress if she was tiny; there may be some material you could let out, but you need to know. Once you have all these measurements you could try them against yourself, or against a dress you already have that fits well. It's then up to you to assess the garment's potential.

Another route worth investigating are charity shops. Oxfam has a number of bridal departments across England selling second-hand dresses, some discontinued styles and samples from leading designers. They have a regular turnover and also stock accessories, bridesmaid and pageboy outfits. Go to *www.oxfam.org* for more information. Some savvy brides have looked a million dollars in a charity cast-off!

HIRING

There are many hire services available, mostly for the traditional-style white wedding dress. In most big towns and cities you can also find privately-owned hire boutiques offering high quality bridal and evening wear. Specialist hire shops often have an extensive, ever-changing collection to suit all pockets. What you can't always expect when you hire an outfit is an alteration service. Many will be willing to make minor alterations, but not always. As when shopping for any article of clothing, getting something that you like and is a good fit can be difficult.

If you decide to hire your wedding outfit, you still need to follow the advice already given in this chapter; your starting points remain the same. The preliminary considerations are still relevant. Once in the hire shop you must feel comfortable and confident with the advice you are given, and try-on as many shapes and designs as possible to see what suits you. Having made a decision, check the small print: Is the outfit available on your chosen day? Will it be clean? When can you collect it, and when must it be returned? Do you have to clean the dress or outfit before returning it, and what will the penalty be if you damage it? Most hire shops will insist you take out insurance with them to ensure you are adequately covered. Get all this information in writing before handing-over a deposit. If you can, and certainly if you are in any doubt, call into the shop two weeks before the wedding and inspect the dress. It may have been hired-out, more than once and not be in the same condition. If it's not, you want to know what they are going to do for you.

BRIDE ON A BUDGET

In addition to the 'Nearly New' (page 109) route, bridal sales also offer an opportunity to get your hands on a fabulous designer dress at a knock down price. Most couturiers have sample sales where they sell-off the clothes potential clients try-on in their salons, and which are made to standard sizes. These sales also offer discontinued designs, and the samples loaned to the press and used in shows and photo-shoots. It is cost-effective to sell them off cheaply rather than get them professionally cleaned. The quality, however, will be the same as their couture clothes. These are the garments that sell their service, so they're usually near-perfect. A lady shopping at a couturier's boutique is spending big money. She doesn't want to try-on soiled, lipstick covered clothing, so the samples are regularly replaced. Many of the samples are sold at up to one-third cheaper than the couture version. Some salons will also offer an alteration service at an additional cost. Others won't, and you'll have to find a good seamstress. In either event you'll be responsible for the cleaning costs. Read the advice on professional cleaning services on page 115.

Similarly, department stores, bridal boutiques and hire shops have regular sales. These will include end-of-lines and bad sellers as well as samples. Again you can save a third or more of the original ticket price. These outlets can usually offer an alteration service at a fixed price.

If you find an outfit via this route, examine the clothing close up. Look for flaws and potentially difficult-to-remove stains. If they won't come

out will they be noticeable? If there are rips and tears how easily can they be repaired and disguised? If there are buttons and beads missing can the shop source matching replacements? You are unlikely to be able to return an outfit if you've bought it in a sale, so be absolutely sure it is suitable and can be altered to properly fit you. Don't buy it just because it's a bargain. Buy it because you love it!

TOP TIPS FOR THE BRIDE ON A BUDGET

Visit sample sales.

Check what's available nearly-new at bridal salons, on the internet and in charity stores' bridal departments.

Look at hiring from a specialist store.

Consider a gown or outfit that is not from a bridal department or boutique.

Seek the assistance of a personal shopper at a top department store.

Consider vintage clothing.

Look at simpler designs from great designers rather than 'bells and whistles' gowns from cheaper ranges.

Seek the assistance of sales staff and advise them of your budget – don't look at what you can't afford.

Accessorise a simpler dress or outfit.

VINTAGE BRIDE

There are several specialist retailers throughout the country selling vintage clothing, including wedding gowns. You can also, of course, go to antiques markets and fairs as well as searching the internet (see the advice on page 109 when purchasing gowns on-line).

The 'Vintage Queen' is Virginia Bates, one of the country's leading antique clothing dealers who has been in the business for thirty years. Her discerning clients include Hollywood actresses, supermodels and international designers. "I do have a few genuine antique wedding gowns, but on the whole the dresses I'm selling for weddings were originally made for 'coming out', when a debutante was presented at Buckingham Palace. A girl had to wear a white or cream gown with long gloves and all the accessories. Many so-called vintage wedding dresses were not designed and made as such." Virginia's most popular genuine wedding gowns date from the 1930s, earlier than that the dresses are very small. Women have developed larger frames than their Edwardian counterparts. Additionally, ladies then wore very tight corsets making them even smaller. The tiniest bride today would have trouble squeezing into an Edwardian gown.

A genuine antique wedding gown from a dealer will cost anything from £1200. But the dealers are buying items with a good provenance. They'll be clothes that were originally hand made, maybe as part of a girl's trousseau. They'll have been well-looked-after and stored. Someone of Virginia's reputation will be offering you a garment robust enough to withstand all that a wedding day entails. She will have restored it to a clean, wearable condition. She'll also be offering you a service: perhaps three fittings with her expert seamstress to make alterations and

repairs and even additions – like a slip or extra detail. Virginia advises not to be afraid to alter antique clothing. "I'm not a purist or a museum. I love the fact that these pieces are to be worn again and are being given another life."

From a fair or market, or even a charity shop, you could be lucky enough to pick-up a garment for a few pounds. Virginia advises you to closely examine it as old fabrics weaken and deteriorate. "First look at the armpits to ensure they have not rotted. You cannot get out orange stains. Check for marks down the back, which is another area that can get damp with sweat which damages the fabric. Loose stitching is not too bad because you can repair it, but if you find a horizontal tear it's too risky. If there's anything wrong with it then don't buy it."

Virginia also says not to "go all the way" with vintage clothes. "It starts to look a bit 'folky'. My advice is get a nice pair of modern, classy shoes and see what you can do with contemporary accessories."

You could of course go the opposite way: dress up a modern gown or outfit with vintage accessories. Designer Basia Zarzycka says that this is a wonderful way to create a vintage look. As well as her one-of-a-kind gowns, her Sloane Square shop is full of accessories and shoes she's designed inspired by vintage items. She also carries a large stock of the genuine articles. She too advises you to scour antique fairs and markets like London's Portobello. "They have vintage flowers, shoes, bags and parasols, as well as laces and trimmings you could use on a new dress. It's not just the look of vintage clothing and accessories, it's the quality."

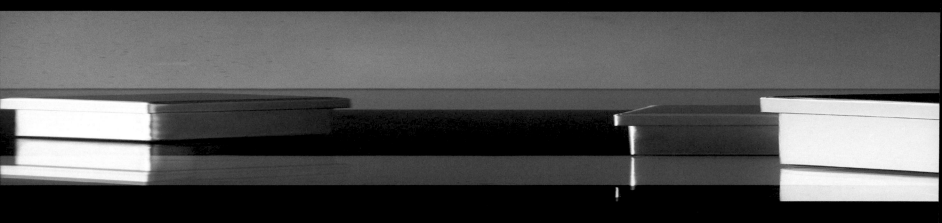

BRIDE WITH A BUMP

Bumps can be accommodated! You may even want to accentuate the fact that you are pregnant. As with weight–loss, weight–gain requires your shop or designer to be flexible. "We have to consider how pregnant they are," says Amanda Wakeley. "After four months they can balloon in just two weeks!"

As soon as you know you are expecting a baby you need to inform those who may already be making your outfit. And the more pregnant you are, the more urgent is their need to know. If you are having a couture gown, the couturier will be able to work around your growing figure with you. Made–to–order services are more tricky because of the lead time, which is usually four months. If you are able to tell the shop you are pregnant before placing your order, however, they may be able to help you. They can try negotiating with designers and suppliers several weeks or months ahead, who, if you place the order, may be willing to cut the dress nearer your wedding date. But they will only be able to schedule this with advance warning. You may even find they won't charge extra for this. It's alterations because you have unexpectedly changed shape that are costly.

As with the advice to larger ladies in the previous section of this chapter, a pregnant woman is still pregnant, even when you attempt to cover her up. It's usually difficult to disguise the fact that

you are expecting a baby, even by just a couple of months. Search for and choose a style that suits you, is comfortable and well cut. "Even with a six or seven month bump a bride can look really sexy," says Christina Marty. "Bias is a great cut for pregnant brides," she advises. Amanda Wakeley agrees. "A bias cut dress is quite forgiving and gives some leeway. It's also comfortable."

Comfort is crucial, especially when you are pregnant. Do not be tempted to squeeze yourself into an outfit you found before you fell pregnant, especially if you are more than six to nine weeks. It won't only be your tummy that is swelling. You do not want to spoil your day because you are physically uncomfortable. And remember, you are likely to be spending several hours in your wedding outfit.

SECOND TIME AROUND

If you've been married before, are there any hard and fast rules dictating what you should, and should not wear? "No!" states Neil Cunningham. "Second-time-around brides are great and often the best."

"A veil on someone who is getting married for the second time gets a bit silly," says Amanda Wakeley. "But then it's your wedding, so do what you want. I'm not into rules. 'What do you want?' and 'Does it feel right?' are what I'd ask."

"Just because you may be older, don't feel you can't do what you want," agrees Caroline Parkes.

Choose an outfit following the advice in this chapter and that you feel is appropriate to your age and the style of your celebration. "If you want the white wedding 'look', and feel comfortable with it, then go for it," says Christina Marty. If however you'd feel more comfortable in an evening gown, a smart suit or a dress with a hat, then do that. There are no rules!

CLEANING & STORING YOUR GOWN

Every designer in this book emphasized the importance of properly cleaning and storing your gown after the wedding. When you take your dress or outfit off, hang it on the original hanger and store it in the garment bag it came in. As soon as you can, get it professionally cleaned by a reputable dry cleaner. "Clean it straight away," says Christina Marty. "Even marks that don't show-up immediately oxidise and stain eventually. The longer you leave it the less likely it is the stain can be removed."

Look for a dry cleaning specialist offering a hand-finishing service, preferably one that specialises in formal wear. Ask for a recommendation from the person who sold you the dress. Alert the dry cleaner to any stains and loose threads and seek their advice on beading or pearls (some crystals can dull or pearls melt in the cleaning process). Identify any rips and tears so there's no further damage done during the cleaning process. A good cleaner will return the dress wrapped in acid free tissue paper either boxed or in a breathable garment bag. If you opt for the latter ensure the bag is breathable. Most of the designers we spoke to did not like the idea of vacuum packing because you can't easily get your gown out and look at it again!

Store the dress in a temperate dry place, out of direct sunlight. "Keep it accessible," says Phillipa Lepley. "And once a year wear it again!"

WEDDING GOWN SHOPPING TIPS

When making an appointment check samples are stocked in your size. If you have a particular designer or dress in mind check they have the samples in stock.

Inform sales staff before you visit of your price range to ensure they can work within it.

Inform the assistant of time of year and style of your wedding.

Show the sales advisor clippings of designs you like (it may prompt them to show you something you have not selected to try on).

Take any special jewellery or accessories with you at the start of your search.

Examine garments close–up. Look for flaws. Does the quality match the price?

Ask the right questions about the service you are getting. Ensure that the service is what it says it is (e.g. couture as opposed to made–to–measure, or made–to–measure rather than an alteration service).

Advise now if weight loss is a consideration. If it is, be realistic. If they can work with you, what additional costs will there be? Similarly, check additional charges if you are pregnant.

When you have chosen a gown or outfit ask for the payment terms:

  How much is the deposit?

  What is included in the cost?

  Will there be a charge for alterations?

Read and check the disclaimer before signing it – check and double check – especially the dates.

How many fittings will there be and will the same advisor look after you at each visit?

What are the delivery and collection dates?

Secure a date for your final fitting for at least 2 weeks before the wedding.

Ask for a fabric swatch of your material.

TOP TIPS FOR SECURING A FABULOUS OUTFIT

Know the difference between the services available (couture, made-to-measure, ready-to-wear).

Browse through bridal magazines and keep clippings of dresses and outfits you like. Also look at designers' websites.

'White wedding or not?' This a good starting point!

Who are your style icons?

Seek the advice of your groom. Show him magazines and ask what he does and doesn't like.

Think of what will be appropriate to your occasion and the time of year.

Research a few stores and salons and see who stocks designers you like.

Make appointments at three or four outlets – don't assume they'll fit you in if you turn up.

If you can, shop on a weekday – you'll be given more time and it will be quieter.

Only take someone with you whose judgement you trust, or go alone.

Purchase a good bra.

Keep an open mind. Try on shape after shape after shape, eliminate and know why you have done so.

Remember some outfits have little or no 'hanger appeal' – you have to try them on.

Be comfortable with the sales assistant or designer and don't allow yourself to be bullied or pressured into making decisions.

Don't purchase anything for the trimmer, thinner bride you hope to be – unless it is realistic.

Don't limit yourself by trying to find an outfit you could later alter to wear again. If that's a requirement then widen the search from bridal wear.

After the wedding, professionally clean your outfit and store it in acid free tissue.

EXPERTS' TOP TIPS FOR A FABULOUS OUTFIT

the bolstered bride

WEARING THE RIGHT UNDER WIRE

"Don't spend a fortune on your outerwear and neglect your underwear." That's the advice of Jill Kenton, who knows because she is a director of Rigby & Peller, corsetieres to Her Majesty the Queen. Bras are her business. Basques, bodies, bras, g-strings, panties, backless strapless corsets, skimpy lacy briefs, camiknickers, functional body-shrinking long leg supports, off-the-peg and made-to-measure – Rigby & Peller sell it all. Mrs Rigby and Mrs Peller founded their now internationally renowned corsetry businesses in 1939, and Rigby & Peller have been giving ladies a lift ever since. A staggering 75% of customers walk through their doors wearing the wrong size bra. That can cause back ache, neck ache and headaches, can promote cysts, lumps and sores, and means we are not making the most of our assets – whatever their size. Following the advice Jill gives here can change your life!

"The most important thing when buying underwear for your wedding day, or any other day, is to get your bra size right. If you don't you'll look like you have four or six breasts, and what you want are two neat bosoms!" states Jill. Dressmakers normally ask you to bring your bra or basque with you to about the third fitting. Don't! Have it with you from the start.

So how do you know if you are wearing the right bra? "The trick to finding a good-fitting bra is that if you can feel it, you are not wearing a properly fitting one. You should not be able to feel it. If you touch the back of your bra around the rib cage, and the front in the centre, and it is one line around the side, then you are wearing the right size. If you feel that it is riding up then it is the wrong size. What most women do wrong is they buy bras that are too big in the back and too small in the cup. Many women get fitted for their first bras as teenagers, are told they are a 34B, and think that they have stayed like that for the next ten years! Often they will have gone up at least in

the cup. I see women coming-in with their under wire half way down their bust, and all they need to do is go up a cup size or two. The under wire must lie underneath the armpit."

Rigby & Peller have offered a list of common problems and their solutions in the 'Bra Problem Solver' on page 121, but how do you go about finding the right underwear? As with clothes and shoes you need to try a bra on – we are not all standard shapes and sizes. "Every manufacturer cuts their bras and basques differently," says Jill. Because of this no-one can ever tell you that you are categorically a certain size. Always, wedding day or not, try a bra or a basque on before buying it, and go to a shop offering an expert fitting service and an extensive range of manufacturers and styles. "Check you go somewhere where they know what they are doing. But remember, if you have been wearing an ill-fitting bra, at first the right one will feel tighter, but it will wear-in and feel a bit snugger around the rib cage." And do not be concerned if the fitter does not use a tape measure. "Some people believe in tape measures, but I've tested it and it does not work. It's trying on until you get the right fit that works."

If you have not been for a bra fitting before it can be a daunting prospect. You can be forgiven for feeling anxious and thinking you'll be embarrassed. Don't be. The ladies in the fitting room will be sensitive to this and have seen it all before! It's unlikely that it will be a big bosomed Brünnhilde with a tape measure around her neck; she won't need to touch and feel you, she is there to assist.

Other considerations when choosing your wedding underwear are what shape and size you are. "A bride must always check before she buys her dress what is available in her size in underwear," states Jill. "A backless, strapless dress is no good if you are a 34G. You cannot wear

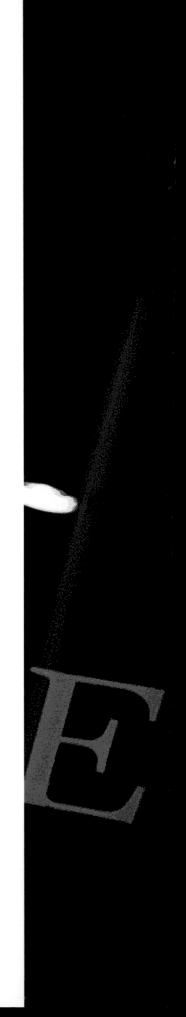

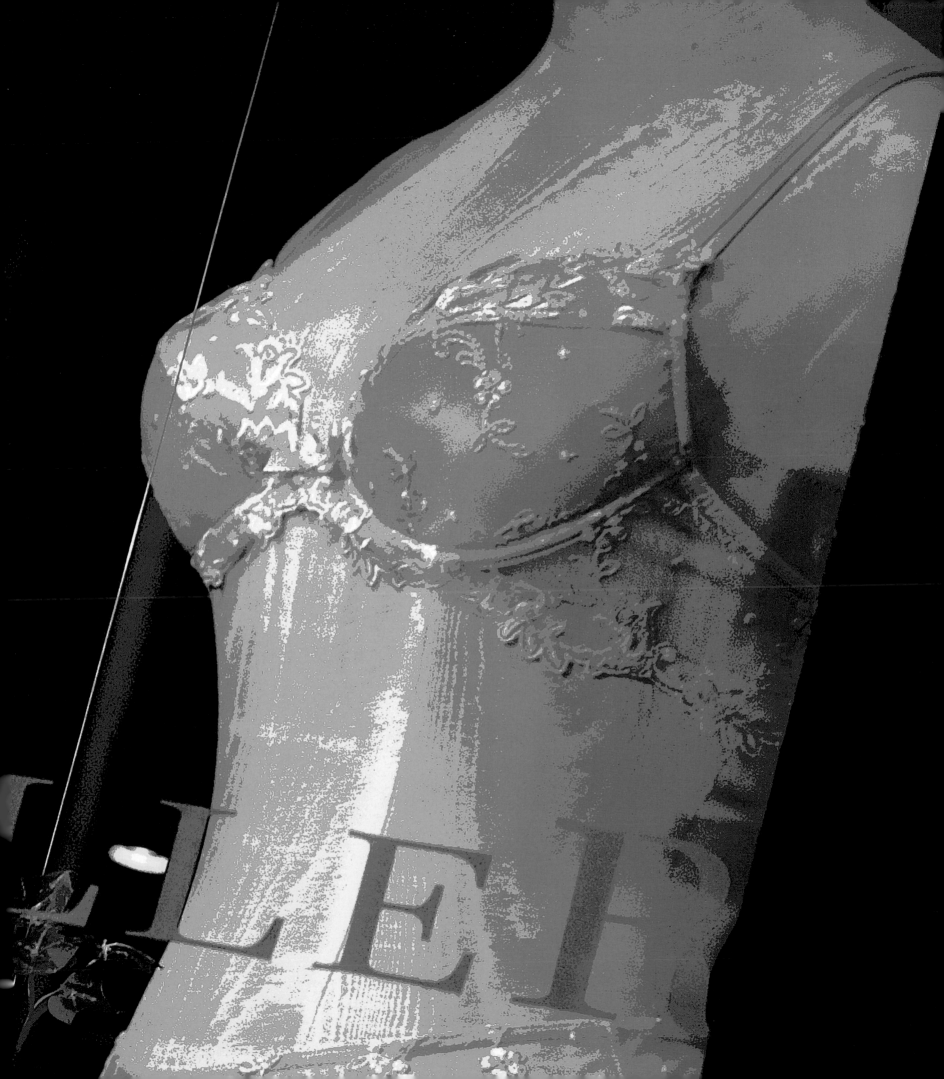

a regular strapless bra in larger cup sizes because you will just fall out. You need some support from underneath to hold you in. Bring in a picture of the dress, let us see how the back is, where the straps are, how low it is cut." And if you are thinking of wearing gels or stick-ons: "Fine up to a C cup, otherwise forget it!"

If you are small-chested and slim you can wear practically anything. A bra and sexy knickers, a body or a lacy basque. You can wear strapless and backless and you'll be able to find underwear that lifts, supports and enhances. But take into account how figure-hugging and sheer your dress is because you don't want your underwear to show through. "You need to look at the lining of the dress and check that it is thick enough if you want to wear something frilly underneath," advises Jill. If you are smaller and are looking for a plunge bra, according to Jill the most common mistake women make is buying one that is too small. This results in the appearance of four bosoms – two of which are bulging over the top of the bra! This does not achieve a good silhouette or cleavage. "When you buy a plunge bra in a smaller size it doesn't mean 'push out plunge' it means 'fitting you plunge'. You don't want it too tight, you want a good fit."

Rigby & Peller's experience is that the majority of brides favour wearing a basque. These can be long line, backless and with or without straps. In specialist stores they come in sizes up to FF cup and a 44" back. "Backless, strapless basques are fine if you are large in the cup but slim. But if you are bigger you don't want to be hanging out under or over it, you need support. If you are quite full you may also be larger in the bottom; the manufacturers forget this, and a basque can be too tight," warns Jill. So if this is the case you may not want to opt for a strapless dress, but have something that allows you to wear either a bra or basque with straps. You'll then be supported correctly without any flesh spilling over. Again, try things on, and keep trying until you find underwear that fits properly.

If you want to be 'scaffolded-in' there are plenty of options – and it might be that you just fancy a laced-up corset and don't actually need to wear one for extra support. If you are trying to achieve a slimmer silhouette you can reduce your waist line with the correct underwear – but be sure you are comfortable in it and can breathe! You are going to be wearing your wedding outfit for several hours, will have to both sit and stand in it, and often dance, too. There are various options, including panty-controlled, long-legged supports (a bit like bicycle shorts), basques and bodies. "We don't believe in strapless bodies," says Jill. "You can get them but we won't sell them because they offer no support." And can you still wear sexy underwear if you are a larger lady? "Yes," says Jill. "Years ago, no. G cup and above would have been the 'over shoulder boulder holders'! But now there are FF bras and basques in fantastic styles." If you are larger you don't have to be tightly laced-in. Properly fitting underwear will not only support you, but will assist you to achieve a better shape and silhouette. As for colour, Jill's top tip is: "Never wear white under white – wear skin colour. It's a fantastic colour to wear under white."

The author of this book took TV's Trinny and Susannah's tip and invested in a pair of 'Magic Knickers'; she can testify that they are indeed magic! There are many manufacturers who produce these slimshorts, and if you are a little on the plump side they shrink you around the middle at the same time as ironing out the lumps and bumps.

At the very least, when you shop for your wedding dress be wearing underwear that fits properly. If you have been wearing the wrong bra, the right one will alter your body shape, whatever your size, for the better. If you are smaller in the bust, the correct fit can offer you a better shape and lift. If you are larger, the right fit can make you appear slimmer because your bust is not spread out over the rest of your upper body, but is lifted and supported and is not spilling out. Either way you will feel like a new woman! You can then choose a dress that really suits and enhances your body shape. If you do this you will need no convincing to buy the right colour or a strapless version of your correctly fitting bra (or basque) if that's what the dress later dictates. "And have matching underwear," says Jill. "You never know when you are going to get knocked down!"

PROBLEM	EXPLANATION	SOLUTION
The band at the back of the bra rides up	The band is too big	You need a bra with a smaller back size
The under wire digs into the armpit	The cup size is too small	You need a bra with a larger cup size. The under wire should encase the breast, not dig into it
Indents in the shoulder where the straps dig in	Bra too big in the back and too small in the cup causing you to pull the straps too tight for support	You need a bra which is smaller in the back and bigger in the cup
Breasts falling out of the bottom of the bra	The band of the bra is too big and the cup is too small	You need a bra which is smaller in the back and bigger in the cup
Bumpy silhouette under clothes	Cup encasing the breast is too small and causes the breast to overspill	Increase the cup size until the silhouette is smooth

RIGBY & PELLER'S
BRA PROBLEM SOLVER

BRIDESMAIDS AND MOTHERS

"For a really stylish wedding it is important that the bridesmaids and the mothers, particularly the mother of the bride, complement the bride's look," says award-winning designer Sharon Cunningham. "The golden rule for the bridal party is not to outshine the bride. Therefore the bride should select her gown first. Confidence in clothes is about how we wear them and how we feel in them. As with a wedding gown, one can never underestimate the power of having a dress or something special designed and made for bridesmaids and mothers. Even the simplest shapes, when made well and fitted correctly, will look stunning. Cleverly thought-through accessories can really make an outfit too. Fabulous hats, jewellery and shoes worn in the right way will complement the bride, and the whole wedding party will appear really well turned-out."

BRIDESMAIDS

The modern bridesmaid is glamorous and sophisticated – if you let her be! So pay attention to your bridesmaids' likes and dislikes. For young bridesmaids and pageboys there are companies specialising in made-to-measure outfits and several chain retailers offer ready-to-wear lines. "There are some beautiful dresses and outfits on the high street for under a hundred pounds. So be clever and shop around," advises Amanda Wakeley, who knows because she designs some of them! With adult bridesmaids you have the same options as you have with your wedding gown: couture, made-to-measure, ready-to-wear or dressmaker. For most brides, budget is likely to dictate for their bridesmaids either something ready-to-wear or a design made by a dressmaker. If money is no object, go to a designer for something special.

Whenever possible, shop with all your bridesmaids present and ask them to try-on a variety of shapes and colours. "Usually, bridesmaids should all wear the same colour or shade," says Sharon. "Keep the outfits flattering but simple, and pick up an accent of the bride's gown. Very clean, well-cut gowns in a striking colour will flatter and look great in the photographs and the bridesmaids will not outshine the bride. If there are several bridesmaids with different proportions I often encourage varying the design slightly to suit each one, but they should all wear the same length. If you want a classic look you could opt for a shorter version of the bride's style and shape of gown. Or you could dress your bridesmaids in tailored suits."

SHARON CUNNINGHAM'S TOP TIPS FOR THE BRIDAL PARTY

Sharon Cunningham

The golden rule is not to outshine the bride.

The bridesmaids and mothers should complement the bride's look.

Listen to bridesmaids' ideas, but ultimately it is the bride's decision what they wear.

Shop for young bridesmaids' and pageboys' outfits on the high street.

If possible, shop with all bridesmaids present. Try a variety of designs and colours and see what suits them.

Stick to outfits of the same colour or shade.

If the design varies, keep lengths the same.

Mothers should stay true to their own style and not wear clothes or accessories in which they are uncomfortable.

Seek the assistance of a personal shopper in department stores.

Always consider how outfits will look in photographs.

Hats add glamour, but avoid those too big to kiss in!

If a hat is not an option, wear a stylish headpiece.

EXPERT'S TOP TIPS FOR THE BRIDAL PARTY

MOTHER OF THE BRIDE

"I like to think that the days of the lilac suit are gone!" states Sharon. "There are so many fabulous alternatives. Mothers can wear anything from full length evening gowns for black tie weddings, to simple cocktail length dresses with lace jackets, or velvet coats with fur collars. I'd advise veering towards ensembles that will be cherished, not just a suit that will never be worn again. Mothers should stay true to their own style and not wear a colour they are uncomfortable with or a hat they're unsure of. Don't match everything – it will be overkill. Seek advice from professionals. If shopping for something ready–to–wear, ask for a personal shopper."

The mother of the bride picks her colour first and advises the groom's mother what she'll be wearing. Both should think really carefully about how they will look in the photographs. A large ruffled collar that makes a great statement in the flesh or hat that hides your face will not be flattering in the pictures. "There is nothing more unbecoming than a big hat on an unconfident head! We love hats in the UK however, and they definitely add to the glamour of a wedding day. But the mothers will spend a lot of time kissing the guests so they must feel comfortable. Without any headpiece at all, the mothers can look a little underdressed, so if a hat is not an option go for a feathered headpiece or a sculpted net. Above all, mothers should be themselves and be stylish. They shouldn't feel guilty for buying something really fabulous as the photographs will be around for generations to come!"

wedding gown

ideas

AS SOON AS YOU GET ENGAGED

Until you've decided the date, the venue and the style of your celebration, simply curl-up on the sofa with a pile of wedding magazines. Look at what you like and don't like and start to gather a collection of clippings.

Arm yourself with information. Digest the advice from our experts on the different bridal services on offer. Be sure you truly understand the difference between the couture, made-to-measure and ready-to-wear services.

Know where you can get what. Use magazines, the internet and local guides for brides.

Think of who your style icons are and why.

Start budgeting and realistically assess how much you'll have to spend.

decisions

SIX MONTHS TO GO

Select three or four stores and/or boutiques and follow our 'Wedding Gown Shopping Tips' (page 116)

When you think you've found your dream dress leave it a few days and try it on again with someone you really trust.

Place the order, pay deposit, get final fitting and collection dates in writing.

When you have placed the order, turn to the details.

4–phase timeline

details

UP TO A MONTH TO GO

Unless you've selected a couture service then the detail is all in your shoes, accessories and how you'll wear your hair.

If you are fortunate enough to be having a couture gown made, your designer will take you through the process and assist you with every detail (including accessories and shoes). Listen to them, they know what they are talking about.

At the final fitting have your shoes and accessories with you and confirm the delivery and collection dates.

If you need assistance getting into your dress take someone with you to the final fitting who will be able to assist you on the day. Make sure this is the right person, someone calm and helpful.

If there's anything wrong do not panic, that's what a final fitting is for.

event

AND THE WEEK PRECEDING THE WEDDING

When you've collected your gown, hang it somewhere clean and safe.

Don't let inquisitive house guests take a peep – they might have dirty hands.

On the eve of your wedding take the cover off your outfit and steam or press if necessary. If you have transported and stored it correctly you will not need to do anything with your dress except look gorgeous in it!

Don't spend any time during your wedding day worrying about your dress getting dirty. It will – this is the day it was designed for.

stepping out shoes & accessories

Wedding attire is often a departure from the style a bride is used to wearing. You will want to feel comfortable and confident in your wedding gown and the same applies to your shoes, jewellery and other accessories. The purpose of these accessories is to adorn and enhance your outfit. Therefore your starting point needs to be that outfit. Don't get carried away trying on dozens of pairs of shoes, headpieces and jewellery until you have chosen your dress. It is time-wasting that gives brides-to-be a bad name! Your accessories, however, are an essential part of the ensemble. The wrong shoes, gloves, veil or headpiece could detract from, or even ruin your look. So do not leave shopping for them too late.

To assist you with that shopping our team of *Wedding Bible* experts includes Basia Zarzycka who, in addition to a wedding gown collection, designs individually made tiaras, head-dresses, shoes, hair accessories and handbags. "A wedding day is a special day," she says. "The bride doesn't want to look like one of the guests – she wants to look and feel special." Maria Merola has been assisting brides to feel special for nearly three decades. She designs, sources and sells a range of new and old wedding day accessories to suit all budgets from the London jewellery boutique that bears her name. Our footwear experts, Elizabeth Rickard and Olivia Morris, design shoes that give Choos and Manolos a run for their money. We've information on choosing a veil from the experts already introduced in the 'Wedding Gown' chapter. Internationally-renowned British glove manufacturer and Royal Warrant holder, Genevieve James, offer words of wisdom on how to select and wear gloves. Finally, if you wear glasses don't choose your wedding day to show people how you look without them – that's spectacle-frame designer, Jason Kirk's advice in 'The Bespectacled Bride' on page 140.

The accessories you wear on your head and neck will be in every photograph, so it is important they look right. Try on a variety of accessories and see what suits you. Ask for help from sales staff. Often your hairdresser will have a tiara you can experiment with; similarly, bridal boutiques and departments will have accessories you can try-on with your dress to give you ideas. Bear in mind that it is not the occasion you are dressing, it is you. As with your outfit, ask yourself how your 'inner bride' looks. Do you want a traditional or contemporary look? Do you want to add a touch of drama or glamour? Is there something about your ethnicity that you want to highlight? Or perhaps something in your husband-to-be's background or religion that you'd like to acknowledge? You could embellish or adorn a family heirloom or add vintage buckles to a new pair of shoes. If you are marrying in high summer or in warmer climes you could carry a parasol. Is there any special detail on your dress that you would like to highlight or enhance? Perhaps you would like a simple understated look and will opt for diamond stud earrings and a single flower in your hair. Or you could choose one simple accessory, such as a pair of long evening gloves, that will completely change your look.

Start with the basics: shoes are your first priority after you have chosen your outfit. Next look at your head and neck. Other accessories then follow. You don't need to spend a fortune; indeed a large budget is no guarantee you'll get it right. It's all about style, so seek advice from those you trust and those you buy or borrow from.

what the experts say

SHOES

Will you wear killer or kitten heels? Will they have chiselled or pointed toes? Will they be ivory satin, metallic sling backs, round–toed pumps, strappy sandals, cowgirl boots or saucy stilettos? Shoes are the area for you to express your own style for your Cinderella moment. You can have some fun! Once you've chosen your outfit your shoes are your next stop – you'll need them at each fitting. Ultimately comfort is crucial. "You have got to stand up in them all day, make an entrance in them, walk, sit or stand through some form of eating and dance non–stop in them!" says Olivia Morris. A graduate of country's premier shoe design college, Cordwainers (where Patrick Cox sponsored her graduate shoe), Olivia's award–winning designs make her shoes coveted accessories among the funky and fashionable. If ivory satin is not an option she's your cobbler.

As with all your accessories, your outfit must be your starting point. Your shoes need to suit its length and style. Our *Wedding Bible* footwear experts state that what you wear on your feet is as important as what you dress the rest of your body in. "A shoe can transform your outfit," says Elizabeth Rickard of Rickard Shah. "The shoes need to speak to you. Buy ones that will make you look and feel fabulous." But

do you have to compromise on comfort for style when stepping–out on your wedding day? "Absolutely not!" says Elizabeth. The first shoes she made were her own wedding shoes. Her now internationally sought–after designs state timeless elegance, stylish sophistication and are the mark of supreme quality. Before starting Rickard Shah with her husband, Binith Shah, Elizabeth worked with Sonia Rykiel in Paris, Giorgio Armani in Milan and Emmanuelle Ungaro in New York. She says three things make a good shoe: style, balance and comfort. "If the balance of the shoe is correct you can go as high as you like and it will be as comfortable as a flat shoe. People always think that heels equal pain but it isn't so. Heels can be comfortable."

Your wedding day, however, probably isn't the time to experiment with very high heels if you are used to wearing flats every day, so get some practice in if you do decide to wear them. "If you are not used to wearing high heels be warned that after a few hours your feet might feel sore – not because the shoes are uncomfortable, but because you are not used to putting that kind of pressure on your feet," says Olivia Morris. "But if you put on a high heel you stand better and feel sexier." Olivia's shoes have extra foam padding on the ball of the foot to aid comfort.

Binith Shah &
Elizabeth Rickard

Her top tip for those of you not fortunate enough to wear a pair of her shoes on your wedding day are silicone foot pads. "Everyone should have a pair," she says. These non-slip, reusable, clear gel pads (Scholl call them 'Party Feet') provide cushioning for the ball of the foot and are available from high street chemists, supermarkets and shoe-shops.

Bespoke shoe services will allow you to choose a style and match it with a variety of leathers and fabrics in different colours, often dyed to your own requirements. You may also be able to mix and match heel heights. Basia Zarzycka makes all her shoes from scratch and they can be as simple or ornate as you desire. "We measure your feet and make a toile to check you are happy with it. Then we make the shoes from either our own fabrics or one of the bride's. We can flower them, bead them, I can write poems on the sole – something to make them really special and individual. Or I can adorn a pair of shoes you bring to me." Rickard Shah will stamp the date of your wedding on their bridal shoes. Olivia Morris can decorate hers with vintage buckles. If such services are beyond your means the high street is getting in on the act and producing great styles at affordable prices. But on no account squeeze your feet into the last pair of shoes in the shop, because you have left it too late to order a pair in the right size. Similarly, don't let your heel hang over the back of a strappy sandal or your toes poke out over the front of the shoe.

When you have bought your shoes, break them in at home, indoors and on clean floors. If appropriate, spray with fabric protector and scuff the soles with a bunch of keys to prevent you slipping on freshly cleaned floors on the day.

If you are concerned that wet weather on your wedding day might spoil your shoes on your way to the ceremony, get some throw-away shoe slipcovers (the kind they give you as a spectator at swimming pools). After your grand entrance don't worry about your shoes, if they are ivory satin they will get dirty. Remember regular pedicures, especially if you are wearing toeless strappy shoes, and on the day gracefully totter about looking glamorous! "A pair of gorgeous shoes can make you look and feel beautiful. You don't have to spend hours working-out in the gym to get great feet, you just need a fabulous pair of shoes." says Olivia Morris. "They will change the way you walk, can elongate your legs and make you feel fantastic. Don't skimp on your shoes (and you can wear them again)!"

THE VEIL

The veil has a long legacy and women have worn it as a symbol of their purity and chastity since biblical times. At weddings in ancient Rome the veil, which was yellow and wrapped around the body, held more significance than the dress and was a symbol of devotion to Hymen, the Goddess of Marriage. If the Vestal Virgins in the same city broke their vow of chastity they were buried alive in theirs! In some cultures, if a woman's face was covered with a veil it implied she was spoken for. In others it was used to disguise the bride so she would not be recognised by evil spirits. In early arranged marriages of many faiths and cultures, the groom was not permitted to see his bride until he committed to her at the wedding ceremony – only then could he lift her veil and see her face. For the majority of western women today it is questionable that the veil represents purity and chastity, but it can be said to be a symbol of fidelity. In terms of symbolism however, for many 21st century women the veil is as important as the dress and represents the transformation from woman to bride.

As with almost everything in brideland, when you delve into the subject it is more complicated than you expected! Veils can be long, layered cathedral length, short and simple or anything in between. They can be plain or ornate, heavy or light, beaded, sequined, pearled, covered in crystals, embroidered and edged in ribbon or lace. A veil can be made of expensive, luxurious silks, or simple man-made affordable fabrics. They can be worn at the nape of the neck or so they completely cover the face. They can be secured with a simple plastic comb or anchored with an antique tiara. The veil could even be omitted altogether – the choice is yours.

For a dramatic, romantic entrance the wisp of chiffon, tulle, silk or lace is hard to beat. "It's nice to add a bit of ritual and sexiness," says Neil Cunningham. "And the chaps like it too!" Amanda Wakeley agrees. "There's something very romantic and mysterious about a veil." If you don't know whether you'd like to wear a veil consider whether in your overall look your hair is more important. If it is, you've more options if you do not wear one. But remember, a veil can be secured so as to be easily detached. If you think it might not be appropriate because you are an older or a second-time-around bride, ask yourself if it is appropriate both to your outfit's style and the location of your ceremony. "There are no rules for second-time around," states Christina Marty. "Don't hold back. If you want to wear a veil go ahead and wear one."

A word of caution if you are hoping to wear a family veil. "The fabric of your dress may need to be matched to it and that can be very difficult," says Caroline Parkes. Lace, silk and tulle can fade very quickly and discolour badly over time. "It can start to take over and even wreck your look," warns Amanda Wakeley. If you really want to wear a family or vintage veil, you need to have it professionally cleaned in advance of purchasing your outfit, and take it with you when trying-on gowns.

Veils can vary widely in price from off-the-peg to hand made. Consult with whoever has sold you your outfit as well as your hairdresser before making any decisions on your veil and/or head-dress. Try on as many different styles and lengths as you can and with your dress on (or a similar sample of it). Your veil should complement your outfit, not compete with it; it's an ensemble. "You are better not to break up the length of your dress," advises Caroline Parkes. Also choose a style that suits the shape of your face and your body type. For example, a full round face could benefit from a single layered veil that falls down the sides of the face thereby narrowing it. A thinner-faced bride could opt for a layered veil that adds width. Similarly, a shorter or fuller figured bride could choose a long, narrow cut veil that creates a vertical line and adds height. The choice of veil will largely be dictated by the outfit, but even then there are several styles and lengths to choose from (see page 132).

VEIL LENGTHS

SHOULDER length veils are contemporary, but can add an element of tradition to a less formal outfit. Usually it will be made of between one and four layers of the same length of tulle, silk or lace. The more layers, the more dramatic the effect.

ELBOW and FINGERTIP are as their names imply. Usually made of four layers adding volume and movement as they cascade down the back. These are flattering lengths worn with empire or princess–line gowns. But beware of the length cutting you in half – especially if you are short.

THREE QUARTER or WALTZ length falls somewhere between the knee and the ankle. Up to four layers of material can be used either of one or varying lengths.

FULL or CHAPEL length is a more formal veil that extends to the floor creating a puddle effect where it falls at the back. Traditionally made of three tiers – at the shoulder, the waist and the floor – this is a good length to wear with straight gowns and will add volume at the hem line.

CATHEDRAL length is the most formal and spectacular veil with the material flowing romantically behind the bride. It can look fantastic with bias–cut, full and princess–line gowns.

MANTILLA is a traditional Spanish–style circular veil usually made of lace, or lace–edged tulle, secured with a comb and which frames the face. This style is very popular with continental brides.

BLUSH or BLUSHER this is the optional part of a veil that covers the face. To dispense with it will create a less formal effect and is a good compromise for the second–time–around bride who still wants to go the whole way.

ATTACHING YOUR VEIL

How you wear and attach your veil is an important consideration. Early brides secured theirs with crowns of flowers or herbal wreaths. Now they can be simply and discreetly kept in place with a small transparent comb anchored to the veil. They can be worn alone or with other accessories. If wearing a tiara or other headpiece, will it be used to secure the veil in place? If so, can you remove the veil but leave in the hair accessory? This need not be complicated, you just need to decide in advance and talk it through with your hair stylist.

If you decide to wear a veil covering your face, at what point will you lift it? Tradition dictates after exchanging your vows, but many brides choose to allow their father or groom to lift it at the start of the ceremony. Also ask the person officiating if they have a preference.

TOP TIPS WHEN CHOOSING A VEIL

A veil should not compete with your dress. Embellishments, such as pearls, crystals and embroidery, don't need to match the details on your outfit – they need to complement it.

Does the veil flatter your body shape? If you can afford to, consider having a veil hand-made to ensure the correct proportioning to your shape and height.

Beware of how shorter-length veils are trimmed. Although a ribbon trim looks cleaner close-up than unfinished tulle or lace, with a shorter veil the trim could create a horizontal line cutting you across the middle and making you appear shorter.

Check the quality of the fabric and embellishments. Look for a clean finish close-up. Examine for loose threads and how securely beads or crystals are attached. Does the quality match the price?

If you want to wear a longer-length veil consider a multi-layered version where the longer layers are detachable allowing you to keep a fingertip or elbow length layer on during the reception celebrations.

Crystals and seed pearls add a touch of glamour and romance as they shimmer when the light catches them.

If you plan to remove your veil during the reception consider whether you want it on during the photographs of the cake cutting. (There is no rule that states you have to.)

Do not allow a gap between your veil and your head dress.

TIARAS & HEADPIECES

Tiaras, floral headpieces, bejewelled combs and diamantè grips can all be worn with or without a veil. Your hair accessories are probably one of the most important aspects of your outfit as they will be in every photograph. It is therefore worthwhile spending time trying-on as many styles as you can to see what will really suit you. Tiaras have become very popular, are affordable and can look fantastic with any style and length of hair. For tens of thousands of pounds the real thing is available and, like many Royal tiaras, can convert into a necklace. We are talking the kind of money, however, that most don't even get close to spending on their entire wedding wardrobe and celebration combined! Vintage tiaras can be found at auction, but they usually go under the hammer for considerably more than the guide price. Some are available to hire from specialist stores and bridal boutiques. Basia Zarzycka's for-hire collection includes pieces dating from the Napoleonic era up to the 1940s.

Is a tiara suitable for all women? "Most women can wear them, but not all," says Maria Merola. "The thing you need to watch is the height with the proportions of your face. Usually the moment a woman tries on a tiara her neck instantly goes up and she looks very regal. I'd advise any bride to try one on and give it a go." Shops like Merola sell one-off creations, usually handmade and with prices starting at little more than a pair of designer shoes. Most bridal retailers stock more affordable versions and they come in various shades of gold and silver. They can be adorned with crystals, pearls, diamantè and be of traditional or contemporary design that sit either high in the centre of the head or are of more shallow proportions. If you are short and would like to look taller, a high-set tiara can help create that illusion. Conversely if you are concerned about looking too tall, especially if your groom is similar in height to you, don't choose a tiara or headpiece that adds inches to your own height.

Milliners also have fabulous hairpieces and can tailor these to suit your shape of face, head and silhouette. They have feathers, beads, pearls and ribbons and there are many ready-to-wear stunning sculptural creations available. These are all options for you to consider for your bridesmaids too.

Hair jewellery is another alternative. "There's lots available and we sell tons of it – it is so romantic!" states Maria Merola. "Little sprays with crystals, sometimes in configurations of flowers or leaves. On pins so that you can dot them around your hair. Grips and combs and feathers too. These can take the 'grown-up-ness' out of a hairdo and make it look really pretty. But it is very important you take these hair accessories to your hairdresser ahead of the wedding. They might suggest something a little different you could do with them. You may also need more of whatever it is you have chosen."

HOW TO WEAR A TIARA

The correct way to wear a tiara is in the middle of the head at a 45-degree angle. If you have long hair, it should ideally be worn up, allowing the tiara to be incorporated into your hairstyle. If you are also wearing a veil, it is safer to have that secured separately, and essential if you'll want to remove the veil before the end of the celebration.

JEWELLERY & HANDBAGS

Jewellery: do you or don't you wear it? "Jewellery can make you feel absolutely fabulous!" states Maria Merola. "It can make an outfit, but it can also ruin it." You cannot make any decisions about what jewellery you'll wear until you have chosen your outfit. (As stated in our 'Wedding Gown' chapter, however, if you have a special piece of jewellery you want to wear on your wedding day, you'll need to have it with you when you choose your dress.) "I always start with the neckline and establish how the hair is going to be worn. Is the bride wearing a veil? Is she also wearing a tiara? If she is, we start by complementing that with earrings and a bracelet. Some women can go for the choker, tiara and earrings, but for most it's too much. Usually it will be earrings and a necklace, or a tiara and earrings, or a tiara and a little necklace, but rarely all three. I always advise women to think about a portrait of themselves. If the head and shoulders are correct when you put the jewellery on, the rest will follow."

Remember that you are accessorising the person not the occasion. Although a wedding is a celebration, you don't want to be decked-out like a Christmas tree! You must be able to carry your jewellery and neither over- nor under-do it. "Sometimes if you have got a very busy dress you also need rich jewellery. It doesn't necessarily need to be simple because that could be too much of a contrast, but it must not overtake the dress either. It must complement and balance it," advises Maria Merola.

Basia Zarzycka adds that jewellery is a great way to make a statement. "A dress could be very simple, but worn with a fabulous pair of chandelier earrings. You can bring your personality to a wedding day outfit by adding these different accessories." And you don't have to stop with jewellery. "I love parasols, gloves with pearls and jewels, feather fans, silk fans, handkerchiefs with a little puff on the end. And every bride should have a little handbag handy to keep a lipstick, a small mirror and personal things in."

Specialist stores like Merola and Basia Zarzycka carry a vast selection of jewellery and accessories in most price ranges, including specially-commissioned pieces. "Only buy from people you trust," advises Maria. "You can only do that by establishing a rapport with them. So go to a friendly shop with a good selection and tell them what you are trying to achieve. It's a huge occasion in your life. Your wedding day is a departure from what you are used to doing and wearing. This can make you feel insecure because you want to get it right. So it is important you really relax. You've found your dress or outfit, so now stay calm and have fun accessorising it. Jewellery is great fun – and you get to wear it again!"

far right Maria Merola

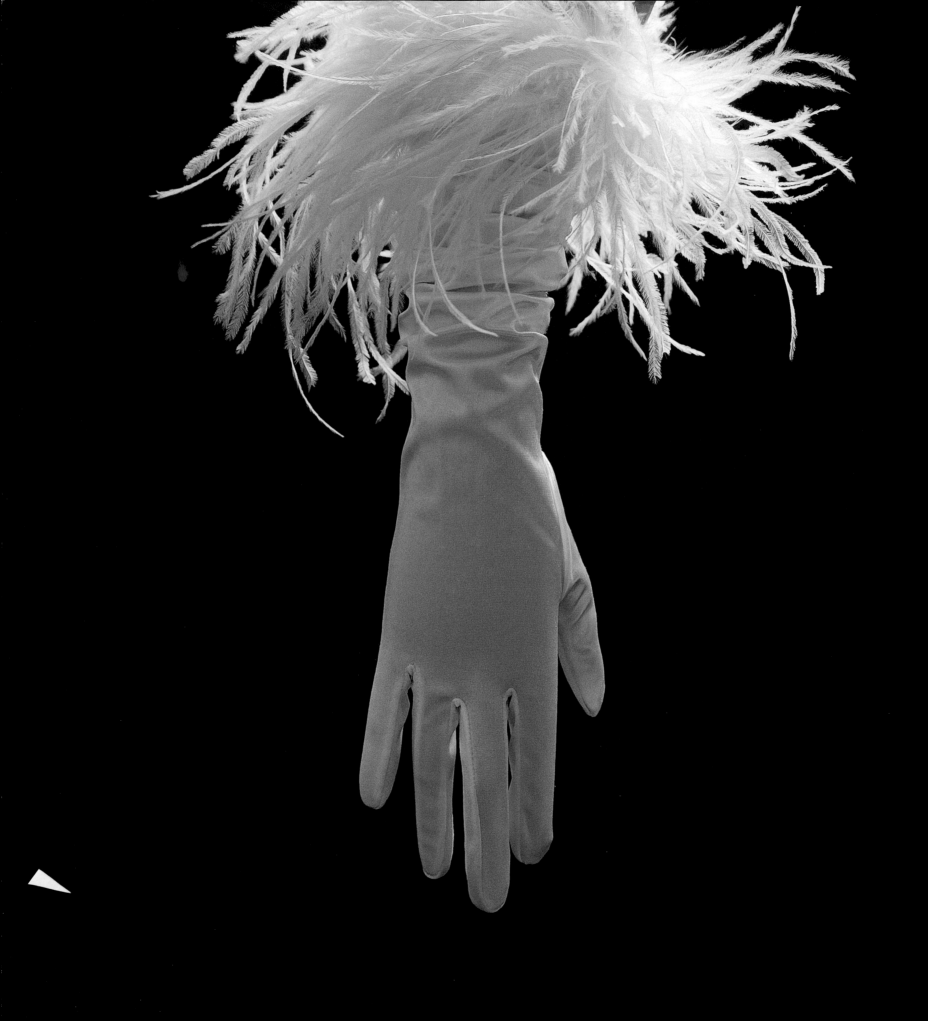

GLOVES

Gloves state glamour, elegance, style and sophistication. They add the finishing touch and there was a time when a lady was not considered properly-dressed without them. The good news for brides, their mothers and bridesmaids is that gloves are back! They never went out of fashion for Genevieve James, whose mother, Cornelia, founded the famous British glove company in 1946 that still carries her name and holds the Royal Warrant. "Elegant things never date," she says. "We make gloves for all sorts of people: the weird, the wonderful, the famous and the wacky, and for every occasion." As well as dressing Her Majesty the Queen (her going-away outfit on her wedding day included a pair of Cornelia James gloves), the company supplies the Empress of Japan, West End shows, Hollywood sets and the world's most fashionable department stores. Remember Nicole Kidman's fabulous and sexy, long evening gloves in Moulin Rouge? Well you too can have a pair of these exquisite handmade evening gloves made from a fabric of your choice and dyed to your exact colour requirement – and for less than the cost of a handbag. "You are spending a huge amount of money on your outfit, your hat, your shoes and flowers. Finish it off with a lovely pair of gloves. They add a touch of class," says Genevieve. "Have them trimmed with ostrich feathers or marabou, have them encrusted with Swarovski jewels, beaded, buttoned or ribboned up the arm, or just plain simple cotton." Gloves can also cover a multitude of sins (like bitten fingernails) and will elongate short stubby fingers!

As well as being plain, ornate or something in between, gloves can be wrist length, to the elbow or extend to the bicep. If you are wearing a dress with a considerable amount of detail, opt for a simpler glove, perhaps plain cotton with a button at the wrist or made of lace. But a pair of full-length evening gloves worn with a simple off-the-shoulder gown could complete and really finish-off an outfit. "We try and guide brides towards a style and material that will work," says Genevieve. "For example, a very long glove with perhaps bows going right up the arm will probably look better on a slimmer arm. We can't work on pure silk because it has no 'give' in it. Often we'll suggest a knitted silk, duchess satin or silk with lycra, all of which give a much better fit. We can suggest colours and fabrics that will go with what the bride is wearing and that can be dyed to whatever colour she wants. We've made gloves to match the bouquet and the ribbon used to tie and trim it. But bear in mind that gloves should enhance your outfit, not kill it."

HOW TO REMOVE GLOVES

If you decide to wear gloves you'll need to slip them off during the ceremony for the receiving of your ring. Gently tug the glove at the tip of each finger, starting with your little finger, then slowly slide the glove off in one movement. Choose an appropriate moment (perhaps during some congregational singing) and either keep the gloves with you, or pass them to a bridesmaid to carry. If you want to put them back on, a good moment would be whilst one of the witnesses is signing your Wedding Certificate or the Marriage Register.

THE BESPECTACLED BRIDE

Do you wear glasses? If so your wedding day might not be the best opportunity to let everyone see you without them for the first time. You don't want the first impression you give to be that you are not wearing your glasses. So consider not using this day to start wearing contact lenses. "Why would you do that?" asks Jason Kirk of Kirk Originals, the Covent Garden based designer of some of the sexiest frames available. "If you want to do that then you are wearing the wrong glasses!"

Consider this: you will spend money on your dress, your shoes and your hair – why not your eyes? "People don't think of glasses as being a sexy accessory, but actually they are the most sexy accessory because they work around your eyes. For most people, eyes are the sexiest part of the body," says Jason. Ask yourself how you want to feel in your glasses. Do you want them to say that you are interesting, sexy, demure, fun or exciting? The right pair of frames can suggest all this and more. "Say you are working in the City and you want to use your glasses to say 'Yes, I am professional, but when you get me out of work you are going to have a lot of fun with me!' You can say that by hinting it with colour and shape. What does a bride generally want to feel? She wants to feel beautiful, glamorous and special. It's the biggest day of her life. Glasses can do that for her." And glasses don't have to be loud, they don't have to dominate or scream at you (unless you want them to). "When you have got a beautiful gown and shoes you don't want people to say 'I like your glasses'. They have to fit–in with and complement your look. We need to examine what is going to work and look nice with certain colours. In the same way as you apply eyeshadow, the colour should enhance the eyes. Then the shape of the frame enhances your bone structure as blusher does when added to the cheek bones."

How do you choose a frame that is right for you? "You might want to think about going to an independent optician for advice," says Jason. If you won't be creating the rest of your wedding day look on the high street but will be going to specialist stores, then spectacles are no different. "I can't imagine many brides want to look 'high street'. They want to look special, individual, unique and fantastic. You have to find glasses that offer that opportunity."

Be open to advice when choosing your frames, but be clear about what you are trying to achieve and what your look is communicating about you. If you are gregarious and can get away with something startling – maybe upswept and Dame Edna–ish frames – and that's you, then go for it! But if you are looking for a more sophisticated glamorous look then choose something that fits with that. You can opt for frames more opulent than usual, but feel comfortable and confident wearing them.

And what about a groom in glasses? "Grooms often neglect this area," says Jason Kirk. "For them it's a special day too, and that sometimes gets overlooked. Guys often wear terrible glasses because they see them as just functional. Again, ask how do you want to portray yourself, how do you want to be seen? Who do you want to be? Are you a strong dominant character? Are you interesting, funny or perhaps you're reserved? Do you want to tell people that you are a complete character? Do you want to look like Woody Allen? All these things are possible and your glasses can say so much about you and who you are."

If you are both bespectacled you could opt for a bespoke service such as Jason Kirk offers. Perhaps a matching theme? But be careful about matching frames, the odds that you'd both look good in the same style are stacked against you. You could have a name or some text engraved on the frames, jewels can add some sparkle, or simply use the same components to create a similar look. "I like it when people are open to wild ideas!" says Jason. "Most people who wear glasses don't just have one pair. So if you are getting married you could have different looks for say the ceremony and the reception. Think of what you might spend on a pair of wedding shoes – something that others may only look at once or twice. But when they are talking to you they are looking into your eyes. So it is a really important investment on your wedding day." (And you can definitely wear them again!)

BRIDE ON A BUDGET

Cleverly accessorising a simple wedding gown or evening dress is a fantastic way for the bride on a budget to look a million dollars. "A dress can be very simple. It is the accessories that give it the end look," says Basia Zarzycka. "Sometimes a bride on a very tight budget can create something lovely because it is not about money. You can have a lot of money and look absolutely horrific because taste has nothing to do with how much money you have. It's about flair, imagination and style and how you piece everything together. I've seen the most creative weddings done on a shoestring."

Look through fashion books and magazines for inspiration. Take your dress as the canvas and embellish it with your accessories. "Look for something that is a little more special than you would wear everyday," says Basia. "Maybe a headpiece, a hat, a little hair pin or a feather to make the dress more special and make you feel more special. Add a small buckle detail to a shoe. You can make these things yourself. Pick off beads from old clothes bought at charity shops. Learn how to wire them – it isn't hard. Scour antique markets and fairs and vintage shops for accessories and trimmings. You could add old trimmings to a simple new dress. Add a pair of elegant gloves or a vintage parasol. Mix it in with the new. Instead of a bouquet carry a basket, pom-poms or just a few real or silk flowers held together with a beautiful ribbon. Or something jewelled like a fan." And remember that you can make a simple statement with just one beautiful accessory.

What can you borrow? Who has recently married and could lend you a veil, tiara or jewellery? Guests at the same wedding as the bride you have borrowed from are not going to notice that these items are exactly the same. What have your mother and grandmother got in their jewellery boxes (or even your mother-in-law to be)? The internet is also a wonderful market place for the bargain bride to find items both new and second-hand. Try auction sites too.

TOP TIPS FOR THE BRIDE ON A BUDGET

What can you borrow?

Who has recently married and could lend you a veil and/or accessories?

What goodies lurk in your mother's jewellery box (or your grandmother's or that of your mother-in-law to be)?

Scour antique markets, vintage and charity shops for beads and trimmings and make your own accessories.

Choose one beautiful accessory to make a simple statement.

Shop on the internet for new and used items and check auction sites.

TOP TIPS FOR SHOES & ACCESSORIES

Choose your outfit before shopping for accessories.

Remember you are not dressing the occasion. Don't let your accessories overtake your outfit.

SHOES need to be comfortable and worn–in.

Scuff the soles beforehand so as not to slip on gleaming floors.

Don't be put off wearing heels if you are not used to them – just practise!

Have a pair of slip–on shoe covers for a wet weather dash to the car.

Silicone foot pads will ease tired feet!

Remember to have a pedicure if you'll be wearing open–toed or backless shoes.

GLOVES Know how to elegantly remove them (page 139) and decide when you'll do it.

GLASSES Don't allow your wedding day to be the first occasion you're seen without them – it is all your guests will notice!

GARTER If you must wear one (and most brides do) ensure it can't be detected through the fabric of your dress.

JEWELLERY Start with head and neck.

Make sure gilding on separate items of jewellery matches.

HEADPIECE Does it feel secure?

TIARA Know how to wear one and practise (page 134)

VEIL Decide ahead of time how you will secure your veil and if you will want to remove it for the reception. If you will, can other headpieces stay in place? Do not allow a gap between your veil and head dress.

EXPERTS' TOP TIPS FOR SHOES & ACCESSORIES

shoes & accessories

ideas

UP TO 6 MONTHS BEFORE YOUR WEDDING

Find your dress or outfit FIRST.

Purchase your shoes as soon as you have chosen your outfit, as they will determine the exact length of the skirt.

Know what accessories are available where.

decisions

6 – 4 MONTHS TO GO

Start with your head and neck:

Will you wear a veil or headpiece?

Will you wear other accessories in your hair?

If wearing a necklace choose that before earrings.

Consider gloves.

Will you want a small handbag?

Order accessories to arrive at least a month before the dress.

4-phase timeline

details

UP TO A MONTH BEFORE

Take hair accessories to your hairdresser for the trial run and decide how they will be secured on the day.

If you are wearing a veil and will want to remove it after the ceremony, warn your hairdresser at the trial and decide who will do this for you on the day.

Start 'breaking-in' your shoes (indoors on clean floors!) and scuff the soles.

Source slip-on shoe covers (or ask your local swimming pool for a pair) and buy gel cushion pads.

Take accessories with you to your final dress fitting.

event

AND THE WEEK PRECEDING THE WEDDING

Have your accessories laid-out with your outfit the night before.

When you are dressed, check that all your accessories feel secure – especially headpieces.

Switch your engagement ring to the same finger on the opposite hand.

Ensure someone knows how to assist you to remove your veil without spoiling your hair. Agree together when and where you will do this (don't do it in public).

a bride's guide to gorgeousness

"A wedding is a photo shoot." So states Mahogany founder Richard Thompson, one of the top names in UK hairdressing and a winner of British Hairdresser of the Year. "What you want on your wedding day is to look how Kate Moss wants to look at a photo shoot for the front cover of *Vogue*: Your clothes have got to look great; Your skin has got to look great; Your hair has got to look great."

The good news is that you couldn't be better placed than in the UK to get great hair and marvellous make-up. British hairdressing is widely acknowledged as the finest in the world. If you haven't got a hairdresser, or are unhappy with the one you have, it's easy to find a good one. British make-up artists too work on some of the world's most beautiful and glamorous people. Hair and beauty today go hand in glove. But it wasn't always so.

In Victorian society a fancy hairdo was fine, but make-up was considered such a taboo that a man could divorce his wife for wearing it. As an act of defiance the suffragettes wore red lipstick as they fought not only for the vote, but for the right to look as they pleased. But by the 1920s Selfridges was selling rouge and face powder, women were wearing kohl around the eyes and plucking their eyebrows. Cinema then set the standard with women the world over wanting to look like movie stars. Max Factor,

the Oscar-winning Hollywood make-up artist and former wig-maker to the Russian Imperial Court, seized the moment and initiated the most successful marketing ploy of all time – celebrity endorsement. Then came Elizabeth Arden and Helena Rubinstein; women have not looked the same since! The global beauty industry now generates more money than armaments. In the build up to the bride's big day it wants and takes a large slice of the several billion pounds spent every year on weddings in the UK alone. You have been warned...

Today's glowing bride can radiate a flawless complexion with silken hair having sought as much or as little assistance as she needs. She can fake it on her hair, her face and her body and without anyone even knowing. But the important thing on your wedding day is to still look like you. Don't reinvent yourself. Aspire to look your very best, but not someone your guests will barely recognise.

The experts in this chapter have styled the great and the good and the fabulously rich and famous. They know how to work with what you've got and get the best out of it. This is their "Guide to Gorgeousness". Some of it's obvious, some of it's not. Some advice is painstakingly laborious and/or down-right expensive. Adapt the advice to suit you, your purse and your own sense of style.

what the experts say

FINDING A GOOD HAIRDRESSER

For great wedding hair you need a great hairdresser. If you love the one you've got stick with him or her. If not, and you've friends with great hair, you could ask them where they go. Or the Fellowship for British Hairdressing can help. They represent the top ten percent of hairdressing talent in the UK and all the experts quoted here are members. The Gold Star Salon Scheme is the symbol of Fellowship membership. To find a Gold Star Salon near you go to their website *www.goldstarsalons.com*. It will provide you with the details of a top salon or salons near you. All Gold Star Salons offer a consultation service enabling you to be sure they are right for you before they get the scissors out. Many will be able to assist with make-up too.

"I'd recommend checking-out a couple of salons and then deciding which is right for you," says Richard Thompson, the Fellowship's Chairman. "Like restaurants, hairdressing salons have certain styles depending on the people who own them, and those styles are their trademarks. Go in and have a blow dry and see what you think. The relationship between you and your hairdresser is a very personal one. You need to feel confident in their hands and like them. If you don't, find someone else."

If you are using your usual hairdresser check that he or she regularly styles brides' hair. "I would not want a stylist on my wedding day who does not normally do wedding hair," advises Carol McNeil of the international award-winning Brothers Hair Sculpting Team in Oxford. She has more than a decade of experience dealing with brides from all walks of life. "Check your stylist does wedding hair. If not, do not try and persuade them to do yours. Get them to recommend someone else."

Carol McNeil
Richard Thompson
Zelda Christian

Brothers

MAHOGANY

richard ward

PRELIMINARIES – CUT, COLOUR & CONDITION

Once you're happy with your stylist, have an informal chat about your wedding outfit and hair ideas. Before you can make any decisions about your hair, other details, such as the style of your outfit and overall look, have to be decided. If you've time, then simply ensure you are happy with your hairdresser and work with them to get your hair in good condition.

"Start by using really good salon quality products. They're better," advises Zelda Christian, Bridal Stylist at Richard Ward. Owned by the celebrity hairdresser of the same name, Richard Ward and Zelda style brides whose weddings really are photo-shoots featured in glossy magazines. But salon products are also a lot more expensive because of their base ingredients. "Many of the mass-market brands' products build-up on the hair over time. That can dull your hair and eventually weakens it; it then splits and breaks," warns Zelda. Richard Thompson agrees. "It's like the difference between using a soap on your face or a cleanser. If you look after your scalp you are one stage closer to looking after your hair." Hair's appearance is also partly down to what you eat. Therefore no pre-wedding crash diets that could wreak havoc with your hair and complexion. Enjoy a well-balanced healthy diet and drink plenty of water.

Getting your hair in peak condition also means investing in regular haircuts. Our experts advise about every six weeks. Even if growing your hair the ends need to be trimmed to avoid them splitting. If you already colour your hair you know the drill, but if you don't, be sure you've enough time before the big day to start experimenting. Certainly don't be tempted to try out new colours at home unless that is something you do regularly. "If you have never coloured your hair I would not recommend doing it just before the wedding," advises Carol McNeil. "Try it out at least three months beforehand, to give yourself a chance to get used to it. Then if you don't like it you can go back to your normal colour."

To start with, therefore, the experts advise you to establish a rapport with your hairdresser, ensure they do wedding hair, and start getting your locks into tip-top condition.

IDEAS

Do not buy a veil, tiara or any hair accessories until you have chosen your outfit. Then talk to your hair stylist about your ideas and seek theirs. "Start to build a collection of images that you like," suggests Carol McNeil, "but keep an open mind because we could do many things with your hair that you couldn't actually do yourself. So don't write-off any ideas. Just collect images – almost like creating a mood board." Richard Thompson agrees. "Pictures are a good starting point. A good hairdresser will tell you what is achievable and will help you down the route that is best for you." Bring your ideas, swatches and clippings with you to each appointment. Start looking at what is available to wear in your hair. If you have several months before the wedding you can try-out a few styles in the salon to see what suits you. Certainly if you have never worn your hair up, you at least need to see what it looks like. Then, as soon as you have set the date, secure the wedding day booking.

SECURE THE BOOKING

Before you book you will need to have an idea of the actual hour the marriage will take place. You'll also need to advise how many other people, such as bridesmaids, will require a hair appointment (and possibly make-up too). This is crucial information. The more of you there are, the longer it is going to take for you to get ready. You also need to build-in any travelling time to the salon and allow yourself an extra hour in the day for emergency flexibility. The more there are in the bride's party, the later in the day we advise you get married. You do not want to get up at the crack of dawn on what is going to be a very long day. If it's not possible to avoid an early ceremony, seek help and advice from the professionals assisting you. They'll recommend the quickest and easiest way to timetable your day. Do not underestimate this advice. "In addition to the time needed to do the bride's hair, a stylist will need at least forty-five minutes for each blow dry. If there is a make-up artist, each person will also need forty-five minutes for their make-up to be applied. If anyone is wearing their hair up that could take even longer," advises Zelda Christian.

You also need to decide whether to go to the salon or to ask your hairdresser to come to you. That's likely to be a financial decision. "If your hairdresser is taken out of the salon, then the salon needs to be recompensed. They still need to bring-in what they would have done from that stylist on that day," states Zelda. You will also have to pay travelling time and expenses. "Ask for a quote based upon how many people the hairdresser or hairdressers will have to work on, what sort of hair they have (long or short) and where you are located," advises Carol McNeil. "Things don't flow as fast at home because you do not have the same structure and there are more distractions. The salon will need to allow plenty of time and this will be reflected in the price." And on no account spring an extra hairdo on your stylist on the day. They'll either have to refuse to do it, or compromise somewhere. So do not forget anyone – such as your mother!

Carol also suggests you consider how practical it is to ask your stylist to come to you. Is there enough space? Is it well-lit? How many people will have to work in it? Are there suitable mirrors and enough power points? If you are asking your hairdresser to come to a hotel room check that it is going to be big enough. Reserve a separate room for your bridesmaids to get dressed in because they are likely to be just as concerned about how they look as they are about you, and you need some quiet and a calm space.

If you have the space and can afford the several hundred pounds it could cost you to have your hairdresser come to you, and possibly a make-up artist too, it will take a lot of pressure off you. "It totally takes the stress out of the day," says Zelda. "It means there is someone making sure you are running to time and keeping you calm. Family and well-wishers come in and out, bridesmaids are worrying about their outfits and hair. The bride can't tell these people to go away – but I can! If you can afford it then I'd definitely recommend it."

If such luxury is beyond your means, don't lose any sleep. The salon option can give you more flexibility. Several of you can have your hair, nails and make-up done at the same time allowing you to get in and out of the salon quickly. As well as being a lot cheaper it can be great fun.

Apart from doing your own wedding day hair, which is an option, you could also consider a mobile hairdresser. Check in local press and regional bride's guides. It's pot luck, so try them out first and ask to view photographs of brides they've styled. If you find a good one you'll save big bucks. They might also be able to help you with your make-up.

Whichever service you opt for, ask for a bridal package price. It should include a trial run for the bride, and styling for everyone who is seen on the day. If appropriate the price could also include nails and make-up. Again, ask to see some photographs of their work. Once you have made a booking get the details confirmed in writing. Often a salon will consider an appointment card sufficient, but you can always follow this up with a letter of confirmation.

HAIR DECISIONS & DETAIL

When you have chosen your dress show a picture of it to your hair stylist along with a swatch of the fabric. "I need to know what a bride's aspirations are image-wise," says Richard Thompson. "What will the dress be like? What will the photographs be like? Will they be black and white, colour or both? I want to know the whole vibe of the day."

Things to take into account also include your venue, colour schemes and flowers, the theme (if there is one) and the likely conditions on your wedding day – especially if you will be somewhere unusual or doing something different. If you are tying the knot in a hot air balloon, skiing down a mountain or strapped to the front of a biplane, it's likely to be more about what you are doing than how perfect your appearance while doing it. Make sure you have a style that is suitable and appropriate to the day and location.

There are all kinds of things your hairdresser can do for you in addition to crimping, curling or straightening your hair. They can colour-match hair pieces and extensions, either temporary or permanent (the latter being much more expensive) and match the exact texture of your hair. They can wire-in accessories that will withstand a gale force wind or simply give you a great blow-dry. "Long hair can look really sexy down," says Richard Thompson. "And hair down is much less severe on photographs. Just be who you are and reflect that in your look." Richard also asks his clients who their inner style icons are. "Everyone has an inner icon they want to emulate, and that can be a great place to start."

"Don't look too different on your wedding day. Your groom wants to see the woman he knows coming down the aisle to marry him!" is Carol McNeil's advice. "I would also never create a style before I knew what the hair accessory was. The same with any significant jewellery – we don't want to create a style that obscures it."

As well as veils and tiaras, there are jewelled combs, grips and clips available for your hair. Some have feathers or fur, others can be wired with fresh flowers or herbs. If you decide to put fresh flowers on a hairpiece be sure you've accurately conveyed what it is you want to your florist. Put it in writing. You don't want a comb arriving if you thought you'd ordered a clip or grips. And are you supplying the florist with these items? Also check when and where they will be delivered to on the day.

If you opt to wear a veil seek your hairdresser's advice. The style could dictate what you can do with your hair. "It's no good having a veil that is pinned to the nape of the neck if you want to pull it over your face for the ceremony," advises Carol. "Similarly, if you want to take your veil off for the reception, advise your hairdresser so that it can be taken out without spoiling your hair. And bring your veil or hairpieces to the trial run." A trial run is advisable and it's a good idea not to schedule it too far in advance of the wedding. "I want to have the trial

fresh in my mind," adds Carol. "The length and condition of the hair won't then change too much. Ten days before is ideal."

The trial is the time to take firm decisions. If you are not happy with any aspect at the trial, say so. Don't leave it until your wedding day and worry in the meantime. Also note how long it takes and ensure you have the appropriate amount of time scheduled for the wedding day appointment and with enough time left to get dressed.

THE BUILD-UP AND THE BIG DAY

Have a trim or cut ten days before your wedding day as hair settles nicely in that time. If you colour your hair have that touched-up too as you want the colour to be as close to the root as possible – especially if you plan to wear your hair up. Double-check your wedding day appointments and ask whether they expect you to have already washed your hair – some styles work better if hair settles overnight. If a hairdresser is coming to you, finalise transport arrangements and give written directions. Get a phone number in case they are late.

If you are wearing a veil ask your hairdresser to show someone other than you how to secure it in place. "I always advise against securing the veil at the salon. It could get damaged or dirty, trapped in a car door or someone could tread on it," warns Carol McNeil. Veils are generally easy to secure and remove without disturbing your hair, but someone needs to know how.

If you follow the experts' advice, then on your big day you simply have to get to the salon on time and enjoy it. This might be the only chance you have to sit down and relax. If you work with your stylist, then your hair will remain perfect throughout your celebration – including any unexpected gusts of wind and energetic dance floor activity. Know at all times where you will have access to a mirror, comb and hairspray (as well as lipstick and a compact) and enjoy looking and feeling fabulous!

Marvellous make-up

IDEAS & STARTING POINTS

The experts' advice for wedding day make-up is to look as natural as possible. Less is more. That doesn't mean minimal make-up, however, it means carefully selected colours and shades, expertly applied and blended make-up that will stay fresh for hours. "Make-up is not all about colour. It is about how you use it. It's about enhancing the good and disguising the bad," says top wedding make-up artist Clare Mackinder.

Again we remind you of Richard Thompson's advice at the start of this chapter. "A wedding is a photo shoot." Remember this, because your photographs will be the only record of how you looked on the day. You want those images to be perfect. That means your make-up has got to look good close-up in-the-flesh and under the glare of flash bulbs. "Wedding make-up has got to be flawless. You don't want to look like you are wearing a mask," says Clare Mackinder. "You want to look amazing, but without anyone being able to say what exactly it is that makes you so."

How you will achieve marvellous make-up is largely up to your budget. As always, if you can afford it, call in the professionals. The best in the business, including our experts, Claire Hanson and Clare Mackinder, are mostly independent (or freelance) and many are available through top agencies. But top agencies charge top dollar! Local independent make-up artists will be more affordable and will travel to you on the day. More realistic for most brides will be to have their make-up done in the salon at the same time as their hair. Alternatively, if you are good at it, you could apply your own.

Whatever route you eventually choose to achieve 'facial attraction' on your wedding day, the bridal magazines are a great place to start. You can read-up on the latest trends and products in wedding make-up – including all the new glamour-enhancing wonder lotions and potions, disaster remedies and quick-fixes.

BEAUTY & THE BRIDE

As with your hair, it's never too early to start getting your skin in great condition. If you've got a good complexion, stick to what you do. "Your skin is the basis for looking radiant on the day," says Claire Hanson. She's applied the gloss to a host of high profile people: pop stars and musicians, actors, supermodels, Bond girls and brides. "If you cleanse, tone and moisturise already, that's fine. But don't be seduced into buying loads of expensive stuff you don't usually use unless your skin needs a boost. And don't try any new products in the weeks leading up to your wedding – they could cause a reaction." If you have bad skin, get advice as early as possible. "As soon as you get engaged; choose the companies who have been out there some time and go to more than one counter. Listen to the advice they offer and decide if it makes sense to you. Ask for samples," says Claire Hanson.

Clare Mackinder is an advocate of the cleanse, tone and moisturise regime. "Every night and morning. Without question!" she says. "Use an eye cream, especially if you are a smoker or spend a lot of time at your computer. It's around the eyes you get more lines and wrinkles." If you can afford it, have a few facials, but not within three weeks before the wedding – they can promote a breakout. If you can't afford a facial, Claire Hanson says do your own – under a towel over a bowl of steaming water. Get your eyebrows into shape, but without going tweezer-happy. And don't forget hands, feet, elbows and knees – they like a little extra moisturising too. Most important of all, drink plenty of water to keep you and your skin well-hydrated. Eat a balanced diet with plenty of fresh fruit and vegetables. Go easy on the alcohol and get plenty of sleep. All this will do wonders for your skin – all over!

MAKE-UP ARTISTS

If you decide your budget will stretch to a make-up artist, how much can you spend? This will determine whether you need to look locally or can bring in a name. Most of the top make-up artists are represented by London agents such as Joy Goodman. Such agencies provide for red carpet events, photo-shoots, catwalk shows, film and television. They will do weddings, but expect to pay several hundred pounds in addition to travel time and expenses. Agency fees and charging methods vary, but many make-up artists are London-based and not all will travel beyond the capital. A web search will reveal agencies like Joy's, and most of their artists work can usually be seen on-line. But only investigate this route if you really are prepared to part with a large amount of money.

If you are looking for a local make-up artist where do you start? "Get a recommendation," says Claire Hanson. "Ask your friends, local hairdressers and at make-up counters. Your photographers will also know whose work photographs well." Clare Mackinder agrees. "Your photographer will have been to many, many weddings and know when they have seen a good make-up artist. Word of mouth is your number one way to find a make-up artist." When you think you have found someone, what should you be considering and what questions should you ask? "It must be someone you can establish a rapport with. You must feel you can communicate what you want to them and be able to trust their advice." First ask to see a portfolio and references from other brides. "You want to know that they have done weddings before and that the make-up looked not only good, but good in the photographs," states Claire Hanson. Claire has worked in every kind of medium under every kind of light: for film and television, catwalk events, commercials, pop, rock and classical concerts, fashion photography and in the theatre. Each of these media requires a different style of make-up, and not every make-up artist is good at all of them. Whoever you approach, she advises you ask to see evidence of their work in the form of photographs of real brides. If you like the artist and their work, start negotiating a fee. The cost will depend on how far they have to travel and how many people they'll be making-up on the day. Ask if the fee includes a rehearsal. "You should expect a full make-up trial before the day and that could include a make-up lesson. You can also expect skin-care advice," says Clare Mackinder. "In some respects the trial run is as important as the day itself. It's when you make the decisions."

If you will be made-up in the salon on your wedding day, have a make-up trial when you go for your hair rehearsal. (The salon is likely to advise this.) As with hair, whether at the salon or with an independent make-up artist, a couple of weeks before the wedding is a good time for a rehearsal. Your skin colour and condition won't change too much in this time. Wear clothes similar in colour to your wedding outfit and advise your make-up artist if you will be in the sun before the wedding or are planning a fake-tan. It's at the trial that you will need to make decisions, so ensure that you are happy with the choices you have made and speak up if not.

Go through the timings with the make-up artists at the trial – especially if you are at the salon. Check that your hairdresser and make-up artist have liaised and scheduled those timings to work on the day. Also double-check that you have allowed yourself sufficient time to travel (if necessary) and to get dressed. As we've stated elsewhere, always over-estimate how long things will take.

middle Claire Hanson
far right Clare Mackinder

DECISIONS: CHOOSING YOUR LOOK

Whether doing your own make-up or employing the services of a make-up artist, you will still need to decide what look you are hoping to create. "Don't go for a look you don't normally wear," advises Clare Mackinder. "Most grooms don't like it. Indeed most men like their bride to look natural. So find out what your man likes." Claire Hanson agrees. "Don't go over the top just because it is your wedding day, but at the same time don't under-do it either." Aspire simply to look your best. If you are used to being seen with brightly coloured lipstick and funky eye shadow then you are likely to be reflecting this in your overall look already – so don't let us put you off. Similarly, if you are a person who likes to make a statement, make-up is a great way to pull that off. Whatever your personality, however, think of how you like to be seen and how people are used to seeing you. You can go that extra mile on your wedding day, but be sure it is still a reflection of you and your personality. You might want a subtle or a glamorous look, or perhaps you want your eye shadow or lipstick to pick out a colour from your outfit or flowers? Think too about how you will wear your hair; if it is to be swept back, your face will look very different. You will also need to take into consideration the time of day and the time of year. "How long will you be wearing the make-up?" asks Clare Mackinder. "Are you going from afternoon to dusk and into the evening? Will you be under natural or artificial light, or both?" The harsher and more artificial the light the more danger you could look washed-out in the photographs. You'll need to take account of this when applying your make-up base.

If you have not got a make-up artist to advise you, consider investing in a make-up lesson. Go to a salon or local make-up artists. Ask for a couple of different looks and compare them. Alternatively, the make-up counters can assist. "The risk of seeking advice from commercial make-up counters is that obviously it's their job to sell you make-up, and preferably from their latest colour range. These may not suit you or your colouring," warns Clare Mackinder. Several of the leading make-up companies employ professional make-up artists at their counters. This is a great way to get affordable and often free advice. But test the products before you buy them. Choose your colours according to your skin type and colouring, your eyes and the colours you will be wearing on the day. If you are purchasing new make-up, carry with you a fabric swatch of your dress so that you can seek advice at the counter.

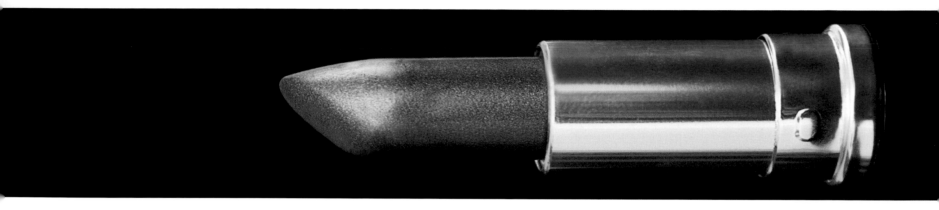

DOING YOUR OWN MAKE-UP

Having selected your colour palette, the purpose of make-up is to enhance your face and features. Think about how long you'll be wearing your make-up and how strong the light is. If it's winter or night time you may need slightly heavier or moodier make-up, or in summer a more matte finish. If you are wearing white or pale colours don't make the mistake of over-compensating with deeper shades than are necessary. Experiment and practise in the right light. Do this at least twice in the two weeks before the wedding when your skin tone and condition will be similar to how it will be on the day. "Do not think that you are going to have to buy lots of fancy new make-up," says Claire Hanson. "Look through your make-up bag to see what colours you can mix together to create new shades – you'll be amazed. You need a good base, a mini compact and a nice lipstick. And a waterproof mascara is an absolute must!"

Follow 'Claire Hanson's Tips for Make-up Application' (page 162), bearing in mind the golden rule: blend, blend, blend! Apply gradually; it's easier to add more make-up than remove it. Use brushes which are affordably priced from most high street chemists. "Don't slam your brushes and applicators into your make-up," says Clare Mackinder. "Apply to the back of your hand first so you can measure what is on the brush. Similarly don't apply straight from the pot to the face." Clare Mackinder then suggests you go back to the mirror twenty minutes after you have applied your make-up to see afresh whether you need more of anything. "Don't be afraid to experiment and mix goods together," reminds Claire Hanson. " Blend well and remember that less is more."

CLAIRE HANSON'S TIPS FOR MAKE-UP APPLICATION

SKIN PREPARATION The key to a gorgeous complexion and perfectly natural make-up is to begin with clean, well-moisturised skin. Your make-up will also last longer.

FOUNDATION For flawless skin that will photograph well, apply a non oil-based foundation (oil-based products can make you appear shiny) in a colour that matches your skin tone. The correct colour will blend well and you will not detect it at the jaw line. If you don't like to wear a base, mix a little with your moisturiser. Warm on the back of your hand before applying. Apply a little at a time blending as you go. If you apply it too thickly foundation can streak.

ALL-OVER GLOW Use a little bronzer on forehead, nose and chin to give you a healthy glow – but use very lightly to avoid a shine.

SHINE To avoid shine and be powder free, try using an all-in-one foundation and powder. Alternatively, with a brush, apply a small sweep of translucent reflective powder over the base. Do not use a shimmer which will make you look shiny, and do not pile the powder on. Sweep in a downward motion over cheeks, nose and chin, and across the forehead. Do not use a powder puff. Take a small powder compact in your bag to blot any shine later in the day, or a sachet of shine control papers.

DARK CIRCLES Be careful not to overdo it with the concealer on dark circles. A light dab starting from the inner corner of the eye is enough. Light-reflecting powder is also an excellent way to reduce darkness. Apply with a sweep of a brush under the eye.

BREAKOUTS Don't panic, don't pop it – just cover it over! Apply a little antiseptic cream to any spots and pat them dry. Or a tiny, tiny amount of toothpaste will instantly dry up a spot. Apply a dab of light concealer or a cover- up stick, blend with foundation and finish with a dash of powder. But do not over-cover blemishes – that's when you draw attention to them.

EYELINER To create different colours line the rim of the eye nearest the lashes with a thin line of black or brown. Then apply your eye shadow.

EYE SHADOW For long-lasting eyes apply a colour-free lid foundation. Dab loose powder around the lashes and on cheek bones so that you can brush away any residue that falls from the lids as you apply your eye make–up. Apply a small amount of light reflecting powder to the eye sockets, nearest the nose, to open your eyes and make them appear brighter. Then blend and apply your colour, beginning with a natural shade on the lid. You can build up–and–out slightly deeper shades, finishing with the darkest shade at the outer edge of the eye socket. The secret is to build gradually and blend as you go.

The eyes are naturally warm and greasy and no matter how fantastic your make–up, so if you are wearing it all day, the eyes will crease and you will need to freshen them up.

LASHES Vaseline on the lashes last thing at night will condition them by morning leaving them soft and perfect for a sweep of mascara. Use an eyelash curler first. To avoid 'clumping' wipe the wand first to remove any excess. Take the mascara brush deep to the root, both above and below the top lashes, and give a little wiggle from side to side.

BLUSHER Apply using a large brush and with a sweep to each cheek, the temples and forehead. Do not apply to your nose or chin.

LIPS Don't forget your lips in your skin care regime – especially if they are dry. Apply Vaseline or a lip balm night and morning. Once a week exfoliate by applying a generous amount of Vaseline with a toothbrush, wipe and soothe with lip balm. There are some great 'lip plump' products available to promote a pout – but be sure to test them well in advance of the big day.

LIP COLOUR Before applying colour, line the lips with a dab of foundation – this fixes the colour. Use a lipstick shade similar to your blusher to avoid a multitude of colours. To keep lipstick long–lasting apply a natural lip liner (not a coloured one, but a shade similar to your lips) and then fill in with your lipstick using a lip brush. Blot with a tissue and apply a second coat. For sensual, luscious, kissable lips finish with a coat of gloss. However, if wearing a nude gloss or sheen do not use a lip liner.

EYEBROWS Don't forget them – they really do frame the face. Reshape a month before the wedding and then keep them in shape. No plucking on the day – it causes redness. Finish with a brow comb after your make–up has been applied.

THE BUILD-UP AND THE BIG DAY

As a precaution, during the week leading-up to your wedding do not try any new products on your face or body. Give yourself a head start in the beauty stakes by eating well, drinking plenty of water, avoiding alcohol and getting as much sleep as possible. This will also keep you tip-top mentally which is the best way to really enjoy your wedding week. If you are well-rested and well-nourished it will be easier to keep nerves under control and you will be less inclined to forget any-thing. If you are employing the services of a make-up artist, give them a call up to ten days before the wedding and confirm the details. Get a mobile phone number in case you need to contact them in an emer-gency. If you are doing your own make-up have at least one practice a couple of days before the wedding and make sure you have everything you need, including clean brushes, make-up remover, cotton wool, cotton buds and plenty of tissues.

If you are getting ready at home or at an hotel and having your hair and make-up done there, set aside the right room for this. It needs to be well-lit with enough power points and a comfortable chair. "Stress al-ways shows in your face," warns Clare Mackinder. "Don't have every-one with you in the room while you are getting ready. When you choose your bridesmaid be sure she or they are going to be good people to have around you on-the-day: people who will not make it about them. If they are not calm, remove them from the room or get them to sit and quietly have their hair and make-up done. Just get them away from you!"

If you are going to the salon for your hair and make-up, as already stated confirm the appointment a couple of weeks before, turn up on time and enjoy it. If you are properly organized, then everything will go like clockwork. If you have followed our experts' advice, then you will be wearing a fabulous outfit, your hair and make-up will be beautiful and you will be a gorgeous bride!

HAIR OR MAKE-UP FIRST?

Should you apply your make-up before having your hair styled or vice-versa? Our experts disagreed on the answer! The majority, however, favoured make-up last. If you are in the salon they will have decided for you. At home, if you have a hairdresser and a make-up artist they'll have to liaise and make it work - but don't get involved if they can't agree, make the decision for them. If you have one and not the other you are probably best to take the advice of the professional who is with you - they'll know how they like to work. If you think you'll get hot and bothered under the heat of the hair dryer, electric rollers or straighten-ing irons then opt for your make-up last, but don't apply any hair-fixing sprays until after your make-up is on.

ON-THE-DAY FRESHEN-UP

Know at all times during the celebration where you have a lipstick, small compact, a brush or comb and tissues. If you are carrying a bag that's obviously a great place for them. If not, ask your bridesmaid or mother to carry them for you, or eventually your groom's pocket is a good place for emergency repair items.

To keep your make-up looking fresh throughout the celebration, "first check for shine," advises Claire Hanson. "A little dab of powder can rectify that. If you are going from day into night you could add a richer lipstick, but be careful - especially if you are not changing. Or apply lip gloss for the evening which adds a spot of glamour. Check for creases on your eye-lids and touch-up with either your finger or a small brush. Also keep your perfume handy, and a mini deodorant stick or spray in case you get warm."

faking it

SELF-TAN

When Coco Chanel fell asleep in the sun in the 1920s she inadvertently established the beauty accessory of the century – the suntan. However, the weeks before your wedding are unlikely to provide you with much spare time to acquire one. It's also not necessary to spend days worshipping the sun. Far safer, and in less than half an hour, you can look like you just stepped off a sun-drenched St. Tropez beach. If you have ever applied a self-tan, the chances are you have experienced orange palms and streaky legs! An all-over glow could be just what you want on your wedding day, but it is not the occasion to experiment with a self-tan that clearly states you have faked it. It is a time in your life we recommend you leave it to the professionals. "Never allow a bride to apply fake-tan herself before her wedding!" states Clare Mackinder. If you want to avoid super-dark ankles, elbows and knees and streaks up the back of your arms, legs and neck, go to a salon.

Self-tanning products and methods of applying them have come a long way in the last decade. Faking it is both effective and affordable. "Consider trying out a self-tan in a salon several weeks before," suggests Clare Mackinder. This is good advice. The different products and methods of applying them produce very different results. No two people will get the same tan from the same product, so you need to experiment.

Beauty salons will apply self-tan by one of three methods. The first technique involves a tanning product being sprayed by hand using an air compressor and airbrush delivery system. This takes about twenty minutes to apply and dries within ten. Based on similar technology are spray tanning booths where the tanning solution is automatically sprayed as you stand in the booth. The downside of this method is that you will be asked to perform a set of contortions within the booth to ensure an even application. If you get it wrong you can end up with a less-than-perfect result. But the process is quick - about fifteen minutes. Finally, there are tanning creams and lotions that are rubbed-in by hand. These take longer to apply, but it is a very relaxing process which usually involves a full body exfoliation first.

Whichever method and product you use, the darker your natural skin tone the darker the result will be. The airbrushing technique has the advantage of the tanning solution containing a bronzer which shows up on the skin immediately to aid an even application. Areas to watch for are the hair line and neck where the tanning solution can collect. Especially watch out for this if you use a tanning booth where your hair will be covered and the solution can collect around the head-cap they'll give you to wear. Tell the salon why you are having the tan and if you are

planning to wear your hair up. Ask them to ensure an even application and to remove any residue in problem areas.

For the best results it is a good idea to start preparing your skin a few days before your tan by exfoliating in the shower daily and moisturising night and morning. Pay particular attention to ankles, knees, elbows and knuckles. Moisturiser can interfere with the absorption of the tanning product so avoid using it immediately before. Have the tan applied two days before your wedding day, not the day before, and keep your skin well-moisturised to prolong the effects.

A WHITE SMILE

Thanks to modern dentistry we can now all have a Hollywood style smile: one that is white, bright and kissable! Tooth whitening gels, strips and toothpastes are available over-the-counter, but more effective and long-lasting results can be achieved by a trip to the dentist. There are two main methods the dental professionals can offer you to achieve whiter teeth. One is an instant, more costly in-chair procedure; the other produces very effective results with an at-home bleaching kit (and you are left with a reusable whitening kit). Top restorative dental specialist, Dr Farid Monibi, has perfected many a bride's smile. "The main difference between over-the-counter and professionally prescribed whitening treatments is the concentration of the whitening product, carbamide peroxide. The stronger the product, the quicker your teeth will whiten. These stronger prescribed versions require custom made whitening trays (that look like gum guards) which ensure the whitening gel does not escape onto the gums causing superficial burns. Most dental practices can offer this treatment or will be able to refer you to a practice that does."

The at-home bleaching kit requires two visits to the surgery. The first to take the imprint of your lower and upper teeth from which the tray is cast, and the second to collect it and be directed how to use the gel at home. The gel is applied to the teeth via the trays which you leave-in for several hours or overnight. "This home whitening typically takes two weeks, advises Farid. "If you are in a hurry there are several treatments we can offer you in the surgery. They typically use a strong solution of hydrogen peroxide and usually in conjunction with a light source that activates the chemicals. This procedure takes about two hours and should be followed by a course of home whitening to maximise the effect. The only advantage in-chair bleaching offers is speed. The same results can be achieved with our home whitening kit and is usually longer-lasting." And the latter is more affordable and offers you the option of purchasing more bleaching gel in the future to maintain that film-star smile!

EYELASH TINTING

Fantastic for the fair-haired is permanent eyelash tinting. "Make-up artists will apply mascara to the top as well as the underneath of the lashes. But most women only apply mascara to the underneath which means you don't get a covering right to the root," says Clare Mackinder. "But eyelash tinting goes right to the root and gives a wonderful finish." It lasts about six weeks. If you are not tinting already, try it a few months before your wedding. If you like it, have your lashes tinted during the week leading up to the wedding.

NAILS

Whether you want lusciously lacquered nails with a dash of colour or a simple clear gloss on your wedding day will depend on your style of outfit. Natural nails are preferable to even the best artificial variety, but few of us are born with great nails. They require cultivation.

According to the New York Times, Jessica Vartoughian is "the first lady of nails". She opened the first ever nails-only salon on Sunset Boulevard over thirty years ago. Her clients include presidents' wives, movie stars and supermodels. Jessica System nail products are now used and sold in upmarket salons throughout the world. "Nails are not all alike," she says. "They differ from person to person – just like hair and skin." To achieve and maintain naturally beautiful nails you need to identify your nail type (see below) and then get into a routine of regular manicures, pedicures and maintenance, including a good hand moisturiser. You can do this at home. You'll start seeing results within days, and within about six weeks you should have strong healthy nails that will look perfect either nude or coloured.

IDENTIFY YOUR NAIL TYPE

Flaking – are the layers separating leaving thin edges?
Soft – do they bend like paper?
Brittle – gently flex the sides of the nail. If they do not move at all, the nail is too hard and brittle and may tend to shatter or break

If you do have problem nails, specialist treatments are available. Some, like Jessica's, are only available from salons, other brands can be purchased from high street chemists. Most nail treatments can be used with or without nail polish. And don't forget your feet: exfoliate hard skin, moisturise and complete with the perfect pedicure. The guidelines are the same as for a manicure.

THE DIY JESSICA MANICURE

FILING Use the correct grit of emery board – soft, normal, hard – depending on your nail type. This will avoid any trauma to the layers of your nail. File in one direction with big stokes – like you are playing a violin. Do not file down the sides of the nail – it needs a 'wall' to support it. The sides are where the stress areas are and where they are most likely to break. The shape of the nail should mirror the shape of the cuticle – a square or oval shape is best. Finally, very gently level with soft downward strokes on the tip of the free edge. This seals the layers of the nail together.

CUTTING Cutting the nail encourages growth and eliminates flaky edges. Cut the nail to reduce its length and file into shape. Use nail clippers – scissors encourage splits and fractures.

CUTICLES Never cut cuticles, it encourages the skin to grow back quicker, thicker and harder. The cuticle is there to protect and prevent bacteria and infection entering the matrix where the new nail is born. (We have eyelashes to prevent dust from getting into our eyes – we don't cut them off!) Soften cuticles morning and night by massaging with a cuticle oil to naturally shrink them and make them look nice. (Jessica make a Phenomen Oil and a Cuticle Formula cream – such products can be combined in a manicure). With a linen towel dipped in water and the corner wrapped around the thumbnail, trace around the cuticle and push the excess back. This will naturally remove any loose, dead skin.

CLEANING Nails must be clean and dry for polish to adhere. When using polish remover, wash it off the nails immediately. Use a nail brush in warm soapy water and brush in downward movements. Dry thoroughly until squeaky clean.

POLISH Keep nails covered and protected at all times. Apply a base coat, two coats of colour and a 'quick dry' top coat. Apply the polish fairly generously, using long sweeping strokes from edge to edge. Always run the brush from side to side, to the centre and across the tip of the free edge. This seals and cushions the nail from everyday breaks.

MAINTENANCE Apply another layer of topcoat every two or three days, sealing the free edge. If the colour wears touch that up too. Only remove nail polish once a week.

JESSICA'S NAIL TIPS

Exercise your fingers by wiggling to increase circulation and activate growth.

Pretend the nail polish is always wet, you'll learn to treat your nails more carefully.

Always wear rubber gloves when doing housework.

Don't use your nails as tools to split open letters or boxes.

Try not to pick things up with your nails and learn to use the pads of your fingers.

Never add nail varnish remover to thin thickened polish. It will damage your nails.

Keep the cap and bottle neck scrupulously clean: after every use wipe off excess polish to ensure an airtight seal and prevent thickening.

Refrigeration reduces thickening – so keep nail polish in the fridge.

EXPERT'S TOP TIPS FOR NAILS

HAIR & BEAUTY DISASTER REMEDIES

The best way to avoid both hair and beauty disasters is not to do or try anything new in the two weeks before your wedding day. If you are used to colouring your hair, waxing your legs, eyelash tinting, eyebrow threading, facial skin peels and electric wave therapy – fine. If not, you can't be certain how your hair or skin will react. Similarly with quick-fix beauty treatments, collagen implants, Botox and anti-wrinkle injections can all be performed in a lunchtime, but it takes far longer for their effects to wear off if you either react badly, or simply don't like the results. When trying anything new for the first time allow months not weeks to see if they suit. If they do, you can return at the appropriate interval before your wedding day.

If you have a hair disaster before the wedding, don't panic! If it's a colour disaster, do not on any account try and fix it yourself, as you could make it worse. Find a salon with a good colour technician. As before, the Fellowship for British Hairdressing's Gold Star Salon website (*www.goldstarsalons.com*) can direct you to a salon near you. Similarly, with a cutting disaster go to the senior stylist at a reputable salon. "Ask for a consultation and make sure that what you are offered makes sense to you. If it doesn't – don't do it," advises Zelda Christian.

Top of the list for on-the-day hair disasters are a hair style you don't like, or discovering you have the wrong hair piece. If you don't like your hair style then it's likely you failed to take our experts' advice and have a trial run. If you don't like a style a hairdresser has done for you, simply say so and ask them to fix it. Try and stay calm; a professional will be able to rectify anything you don't like. When it's a disaster you have created, start again without trying anything complicated. Stick to what you know how to do. If the wrong hair piece has arrived and you are stuck with it, ask your hairdresser how you can still use it. In both events, try not to focus on what has gone wrong. Instead, work with what you have – there will be a solution. Also try and keep things in perspective (which we know is hard on your wedding day!).

Any beauty disasters that cause an adverse reaction are probably best dealt with by your doctor. If you still have visual evidence on the day do not worry – anything can be covered with the right product. If you think you'll need a good concealer go in advance to a reputable make-up counter and seek advice. There are even concealers for disguising surgery marks. For a streaked self-tan disaster there are special disposable wipes specifically designed for the problem. They can be found in high street chemists and in supermarkets. But blemishes are the most likely beauty disaster on the day; follow Claire Hanson's advice on pages 162–163 and they will not be noticeable.

WHAT TO ASK THE HAIR & BEAUTY PROFESSIONALS

Does your regular hairdresser do wedding hair? (If not, don't persuade them to do yours, ask for a recommendation.)

At the salon can they also do your make-up and nails? Can they offer a package price for this?

What does the cost include? Will there be a trial run and how much will they charge for each additional head?

What are the payment terms?

When can you secure the wedding day booking and how long will the appointment last? (Many salons will not take bookings more than six months ahead because of staffing changes and holidays.)

Can you see photographs of real brides? (Does the make-up photograph well? Check especially for shiny faces.)

If your hairdresser and/or make-up artist are coming to you on the day, does the price include travel costs and expenses? How long will they stay? What facilities and make-up do you need to provide?

What do your hairdresser and make-up artists recommend? (You don't have to take this advice, but they may have ideas you have not thought of.)

Who is delivering hair pieces, to where and when?

Ask for everything in writing and receipts for deposits.

HAIR & BEAUTY TIPS FOR THE BRIDE ON A BUDGET

Do your own hair and make-up or consider a simple blow dry at the salon.

Look for mobile hairdressers and make-up artists in local brides' guides and in the phone book.

Ask your bridesmaids if they would be responsible for their own hair and make-up.

Do your own manicures, pedicures and eyebrow shaping.

For a do-it-yourself facial, lean over a bowl of very hot water and cover your head with a towel to trap the steam. Sit for five minutes and then rinse your face in very cold water. Finish by massaging your face and neck with moisturiser.

Don't be seduced into buying expensive beauty products. A moisturiser, body lotion and a minimal amount of make-up is all you need.

Ask for samples, free makeovers and advice from make-up counters.

Use fingers instead of sponges to apply make-up base.

Look through your make-up bag to see what you can mix together to create new colours and shades – you'll be amazed!

Lipstick can double as blusher: dab with a little loose powder if the cheeks are too shiny.

Foundation can double as a concealer: apply an extra dab over problem areas with a cotton bud and blend well.

Vaseline works well brushed through the eyebrows and applied as a lip gloss over lipstick.

GET GORGEOUS! THE EXPERTS' TOP BEAUTY TIPS

Don't reinvent yourself for your wedding day. Stay with a look and style that reflects your personality. Take into account not only what you'll be wearing, but your wedding venue, the time of day and year, the colour scheme and flowers, the lighting and the likely weather conditions. Choose a style that is suitable and appropriate for the day and the location.

Get your hair and skin in tip-top condition. No crash diets: eat a balanced diet with plenty of fresh fruit and vegetables. Reduce the amount of alcohol you drink and increase the amount of water. Get enough rest. Regular exercise will keep you fit physically and mentally.

If your skin needs a boost, begin a beauty regime. If you've a good complexion, don't change anything. If you have bad skin get advice as early as possible. Remember hands, feet, elbows and knees like being moisturised too and get your eyebrows in shape.

Don't do or try anything new, including new products or hair colour, within a month of the wedding. Never apply fake tan yourself. Go to a professional two days before the wedding. Watch-out for the neck and hair line.

No waxing, sugaring, plucking, threading or skin peels within a week of the wedding, and then only if you've done it before.

On your wedding day be on time for all your appointments.

Write a checklist of all the make-up and toiletries you'll need to get ready on the day. A couple of days before, put the make-up in a zip-lock bag. Put everything else into a bag or shoe box.

Do not get married too early in the day, especially if you are having several bridesmaids, or you'll have to get up at the crack of dawn to be ready on time.

If you are wearing a strapless outfit on your wedding day, remember to take off any underwear that will leave strap marks on your skin a couple of hours before you get ready.

Throughout your wedding celebration, know where you have access to your lipstick, a powder compact, a brush or comb and clean tissues. Also have perfume close at hand and consider a mini or travel size deodorant stick or spray if you think you'll overheat.

Just before you leave for the ceremony, apply a tiny amount of cuticle oil around your nails and to the tips of your fingers.

EXPERTS' TOP BEAUTY TIPS

THE EXPERTS' TOP HAIR TIPS

Find a good hairdresser or ensure yours does wedding hair.

If you need to find a hairdresser get recommendations from friends whose hair you like, or visit the Fellowship for British Hairdressing's Gold Star Salon website *www.goldstarsalons.com*.

Regularly trim your hair (about every six weeks) to keep it in good condition and prevent split ends. Use salon quality hair products.

Establish a good rapport with your hairdresser and share your wedding hair ideas with them. Create a 'mood board' of ideas with pictures from magazines of hair (and make-up) styles you like.

Secure the wedding day booking and book a trial run. Check what is included in the price and that you get the trial within a couple of weeks of the wedding.

At the trial run, wear clothes similar in colour to your wedding outfit. Take jewellery and hairpieces with you. If you don't like your hair and make-up at the rehearsal, say so and do not leave until you are happy.

If you are booking a hairdresser (or make-up artist) to come to you on your wedding day, does the price include travel costs and expenses? What will they charge for extra heads?

If asking a hairdresser and make-up professionals to come to you, will you have a suitable room available on the day? It must be well-lit, with a comfortable chair and accessible power points.

Don't purchase hair accessories until you have chosen your outfit and consulted your hairdresser. Be open minded about how professionals can help you, they can do things you can't.

If you will wear a veil, ask your hairdresser to teach someone else how to remove it in case you want to take it off during the reception.

When ordering a hairpiece with fresh flowers in it, get in writing what you have ordered. Know when and where it is being delivered to on the day.

Do not experiment with hair colour within six weeks of your wedding.

Never attempt to rectify hair disasters yourself. Find a good salon and ask for a senior stylist or colourist.

THE EXPERTS' TOP MAKE-UP TIPS

Find a make-up artist. Ask friends, your hair salon, your photographer or look in local brides' guides. If you can afford to, go to an agency.

Don't purchase make-up until you have chosen your outfit .

Get free advice from make-up counters and ask for samples. Beware of being sold products from this season's range rather than what will suit you.

Avoid wearing make-up during the week before your wedding.

When getting ready on your wedding day, wear something that buttons up-the-front so that you don't spoil your hair and make-up when you change.

When applying your own make-up the golden rule is 'blend, blend, blend'. Apply slowly to skin that has been well-moisturised half an hour before. Use clean brushes and never apply directly from the pot to the face.

Use natural coloured lip-liner and consider switching your lipstick to a richer colour later in the day if moving from dusk to evening.

Add lip gloss for a touch of glamour in the evening.

Waterproof mascara is a must!

Once dressed and made-up, don't drink anything coloured that could spill and stain your outfit. Drink through a straw!

Don't over-kiss your groom before the formal photographs – he'll be covered in lipstick!

EXPERTS' TOP HAIR & MAKE-UP TIPS

hair and beauty

ideas

UP TO 6 MONTHS BEFORE YOUR WEDDING

Find a good hairdresser.

Get your hair and skin in tip-top condition.

Regularly trim your hair (about every 6 weeks).

Look through magazines and get ideas. Cut out pictures and gather a 'mood board' of ideas.

Think about who your style icons are.

Start budgeting and assess if you can afford professional help on your wedding day with hair and/or make-up. If so, what can you afford? Know what your options are and have price comparisons for the different services on offer.

decisions

6 – 4 MONTHS TO GO

How many of you will need hair and make-up on the day and who is going to do it?

Find a make-up artist if required.

Secure the wedding day booking(s) and book a rehearsal 2 weeks ahead of the wedding day for yourself.

Begin regular manicures, pedicures and facials and get your eyebrows in shape (DIY treatments are fine).

Only make final decisions about how you will wear your hair and make-up when you have chosen your outfit. Keep your hairdresser informed, show pictures and fabric swatches and ask their advice – they may have ideas you have not thought of.

Try out different styles with your hairdresser when you go for your regular appointments.

Decide if you will wear a veil or hairpiece and whether you need to cut or colour your hair.

If experimenting with colour, do this sooner rather than later.

Get free make-up advice and makeovers at commercial counters and ask for samples. Experiment at home.

Book appointments for the week of your wedding for any other beauty treatments you will require (such as waxing, self tanning, manicures and pedicures).

4-phase timeline

details

UP TO A MONTH TO GO

If wearing a veil, will you want to remove it after the ceremony? If so, tell your hairdresser so that you agree on a style that will work with the veil both in and out.

When wearing fresh flowers in your hair how will they be affixed? If using grips or a comb can your hairdresser help source them and liaise with your florist? Check if you have to collect the finished hair piece on the day, or if it will be delivered. If the florist will deliver it, agree to where and at what time (does this work with your salon appointments?).

Have a last trim/cut and colour about ten days before the wedding.

At the make-up trial wear a colour similar to what you'll be wearing on your wedding day. Take a swatch of your dress fabric.

At the hair trial take any hair accessories and jewellery with you. If you don't like something say so. Don't leave until you are happy.

Double-check the wedding day booking(s) and that the timings will work. When professionals are travelling to you, ensure they have directions and a telephone number.

event

AND THE WEEK PRECEDING THE WEDDING

Double-check appointments and transport arrangements.

Ensure everyone having their hair and make-up done knows when, where and how they are getting there.

Write a checklist for hair accessories and make-up you'll need on the day. A couple of days before gather it all together.

Avoid wearing make-up during the week before the wedding.

Do not try new products on your hair, face or body this week.

If doing your own hair or make-up, practise in the correct light.

Lay-out everything you'll need in a suitable room the night before. Ensure it is well-lit, with a comfortable chair and accessible power points.

Do nails the eve of the wedding. Don't forget toes!

Be on time for all appointments.

Keep beauty products clear of your outfit. Only dress when you have applied everything. If your outfit needs to go over your head cover your face.

If you are wearing a veil and intend to take it off at the reception, get your hairdresser to teach someone how to remove it.

Ensure lipstick, compact and tissues are accessible.

Check make-up before the photographs – you are especially looking to avoid a shiny face.

Once dressed and ready have a long look at yourself in a full length mirror. Enjoy looking and feeling fabulous and do not worry about your appearance – you will radiate gorgeousness!

wedding flowers

Flowers have formed a symbolic part of the marriage ceremony since the beginning of recorded time. They are steeped in tradition and symbolism and are an essential part of any wedding – civil or religious. Brides in Ancient Greece carried herbs to repel evil spirits. At Roman weddings, the couple wore floral garlands signifying new life. Anglo–Saxon couples also wore garlands, which by the Middle Ages were adorned with ears of wheat to symbolize fertility. The Victorians devised meanings for flowers and Queen Victoria wore orange blossoms on her wedding day to represent purity and faithfulness.

The western tradition of tossing the bouquet dates to medieval England when it was believed a bride could pass on her good fortune to others. In an attempt to avoid her clothing being torn by those wanting a piece of her good luck, a bride would toss her shoe or flowers into the crowd as she got away. As shoes were more valuable it was the tossing of the bouquet that became the norm. Hence tradition now dictates that the girl who catches the bouquet will receive the bride's good fortune and be the next to secure a husband.

In modern Britain wedding flowers reflect the cross–cultural, multi–faith society we live in. Blooms from the world over are airfreighted–in and sold at flower markets up and down the country. They can be used to wonderful effect to clearly express and signify who we are as individuals, couples, families and communities. If trying to create a specific style, mood or theme there's a flower or flowers to match. They can transform a venue, bringing it to life, creating a beautiful environment and a stunning sense of occasion.

You can arrange your own flowers, use a local florist, or employ one with a national or international reputation, like our first expert, Jane Packer. Jane is widely recognized as one of the world's most influential florists. From humble beginnings at a small West End flower store two decades ago, she championed the vision that flowers are as exciting as fashion and interior design. Her passion for flowers led the then Lady Diana Spencer to select Jane to arrange her wedding day flowers. Alternatively, you can secure the services of a floral designer specialising in parties and events, such as our second expert, Mathew Dickinson. Like Jane, Mathew is a trend–setter. He trained as a horticulturist and runs international flower workshops. His designs are among those regularly featured by bridal magazine editors.

You might already have a vision of how your wedding will look, or you could be in need of some advice. Either way, be informed before making final floral decisions. What flowers do you already like? Do you prefer traditional floral arrangements or a few wild flowers presented in a simple vase? What flowers do you buy for your home? How do these preferences fit with the style of wedding you are hoping to have, what you'll wear, your choice of venue(s) and the time of day and year you are marrying? Are flowers a priority? Do you want a few simple blooms or huge, elaborate arrangements. Are they the starting point to creating your day?

"Wedding days are dream days and every bride has a different dream," says Jane. "It is our role to understand the dream, interpret it with colour and a wonderful selection of flowers that will bring it to life." What is your dream and how can you create it?

what the experts say

FINDING A FLORIST

Securing the services of a professional florist on your wedding day is an essential luxury. Even if you are planning a small celebration, think very carefully before committing to doing your own flowers. "It's a big risk because it is all last minute," says Mathew Dickinson. "When are you going to do it? What if something goes wrong? How do you know the best place to source your flowers? How do you know what to look for? Do you have the expertise to assess a flower's quality?" Florists are professionally trained; it is their job to know these things and it is their expertise, experience and a guarantee you are buying as well as the blooms. If you do your own flowers, or if anyone close to you does them, you'll be involved and there is an immovable deadline to work to. You need to shop for flowers, transport them, store them, sort and arrange them and this all takes time. Time is at a premium on your wedding day and the days leading up to it. "I would never suggest doing your own. The day is stressful enough without having to worry about wilting flowers," adds Jane Packer.

Also think carefully before encouraging a member of the wedding party to take charge of the flowers because in all likelihood they won't have time either. "If you have a mother or close family member who likes flower arranging and wants to be involved then let them help us," suggests Mathew. "Indeed sometimes that works well as helpers are pleased to be working with a professional florist and pick-up some tips."

If you are holding your wedding locally, you may already know a fabulous florist. If not, a recommendation is your best way to find one. Alternatively, local brides' guides and the internet are useful tools. If you are marrying at a local hotel or other venue, they may offer recommendations too.

Most florists will offer a free consultation. "Look at the quality of the flowers in the shop," suggests Jane. "Also the personality of the people who work there. Did they meet you and greet you? It then comes down to meeting the florist and striking a chord with them – that is the most important thing. Whoever you have selected to do your flowers needs to understand what you want and have empathy for it." And that is an immediate thing Jane says, "Either you get on, or you don't. The florist understands you, or they don't." If you have any doubts then find someone else.

When meeting a florist for the first time allow at least an hour and take as much information with you as you have: the wedding date, photos of the venue(s), a picture of your dress together with a swatch of the fabric (if you have an idea at this stage that is enough), the approximate number of guests, and a selection of clippings from magazines of flowers and arrangements you are drawn to. This information will assist the florist to assess your style and your aspirations for the wedding. You will also need an idea of your budget.

Jane Packer

Mathew Dickinson

BUDGETING FOR FLOWERS

"When first meeting a bride the conversation always begins with a little about her. Budget then comes in fairly close behind. There is no point in getting into long, drawn-out conversations with lots of detail if someone can't afford it. It is a good idea to know roughly how much money you can spend on flowers before you come in and see us," says Jane Packer.

If you are fortunate enough to be a bride whose parents are footing the bill for your wedding the 'traditional' way, then the groom is responsible for your bouquet, the bridesmaids' flowers and the buttonholes.

Allocating around ten percent of your overall budget to flowers is a good starting point when assessing how much you can spend. Flowers are expensive and can only be purchased and arranged within hours of the wedding. The labour costs are high because it is time-consuming. "Brides can usually work out how much the wedding meal is likely to cost, they can see how much wedding gowns are in magazines, but they have never usually bought this many flowers in one go and had them professionally arranged," says Mathew Dickinson. Many brides are shocked at what they see as the cost of the flowers. "But they are paying for the labour as well as the flowers. We go to market, we select the flowers, we put them in the van, then unload them. We wash them, we sort them, we store them. We put them back on the

van and take them to the venue, unload and arrange them, make and secure buttonholes, tie or wire bouquets and so it goes on. Every single flower could be handled up to ten times. And it's all mostly in the two days leading up to the wedding and the wedding day itself. If it is a big wedding we have to throw people at it and they all have to be paid." So ten percent of an average budget is now beginning to feel like good value! "On your wedding day you want fantastic flowers, not second rate. If it is a really hot summer day or a freezing cold winter afternoon we know what to do with the flowers and how to protect them from adverse weather conditions," adds Mathew.

Within your budget you will need to purchase the bride's bouquet, bouquets or corsages (which will be cheaper) for your bridesmaids, and buttonholes and corsages for the wedding party. The rest can be spent on the ceremony and reception flowers. "As a rule I advise you spend your money on your bouquet and reception flowers. Keep the ceremony flowers to a minimum as it rarely lasts more than an hour. The reception on the other hand goes on for several hours so spend your money there," advises Mathew.

If your wedding day is more than six or nine months away you do not need to make any detailed decisions right away, you simply need to select a florist and have an idea of how much you have to spend and where it is to be spent. You and your florist can work out the detail together nearer the time (about six to four months before). If you have a year or more to go simply secure the booking and arrange to meet again at a later date when you have the other specific details in place.

The exact flowers you want are then the biggest factor in determining costs. "Flowers in season will be the best quality, the toughest and the best value for money," says Mathew. "Even in winter there is a huge choice." If you have a year or more to go then look at what is in the florists, flower markets and gardens twelve months before your wedding and seek your florist's ideas so that you can go and look at the flowers when they are in season. "It's then to do with the type of flowers and arrangements you want," advises Jane. "You could throw a handful of petals on a table with a few candles, or you could have a huge and elaborate table centre with say orchids and roses. It comes down to the type of flowers you are using, the quantity and the season. The florist needs to establish whether it is an elaborate affair or is something simpler and understated." The more complicated and time-consuming the arrangements, the more expensive they will be.

Establish with your venue(s) as early as possible what restrictions, if any, there are with regard to flowers. At certain times of the year churches and religious venues do not allow flowers, some Oxbridge colleges and large churches and cathedrals restrict or do not allow flowers at all, and register offices have several weddings every day of the week and cannot accommodate access for the delivery of flowers because of this. Licensed venues may also have considerations that will affect your budget, so seek their advice. Your ceremony venue may have more than one wedding on your wedding day and you may be able to liaise with another bride and share flowers. Church flower volunteers may also be delighted to assist you and that too could affect your budget.

"If money is no object leave it to your florist," says Mathew. "We'll come up with the ideas for you and interpret what you have in mind. Trust us – we'll liaise with you throughout the process." Wholesalers can provide flowers from across the world, so if money is not an issue you can have almost anything you want. But expect to pay, and allow your florist sufficient time to place the order. "The sky's the limit with a large budget!" says Jane. "It is amazing because you can be wildly creative. There is nothing like having a huge quantity of flowers and hearing people gasp as they walk in."

SECURE THE BOOKING

When you have found a florist, secure the booking and get a written estimate of costs. If you have some time before your wedding day you may not know exactly what you want, but you can establish the budget and that your florist will be able to work within it. Most florists can create a customised package for you. Agree in writing the minimum you are expecting in terms of bouquets, buttonholes and corsages, pedestal and table arrangements. Check that the price includes delivery and on–the–day labour costs and gives details of vases and containers and the style of bouquets and buttonholes. But understand that if you have not decided on the flowers themselves, that could eventually alter the price. Try and secure a quote that stipulates flowers in season and an idea of quantity. Similarly, if you have agreed exact details and have been quoted for specific flowers and plants but then change your mind, that could cost you more money.

A good florist will want to visit the venue(s) with you about three or four months before the wedding (if they do not already know venues),

Establish that it will be the florist you are dealing with who will be arranging the flowers on the day. If not, ensure you've met and are happy with whoever will be overseeing them. Check with the venue(s) whether the flowers have to be removed after the wedding. If they do, ask your florist to quote for their collection (if you do not want to keep them). It is likely the florist will need to return to the venue to collect pedestals and containers anyway.

When you have decided on the exact details (advice on which follows) of your bouquet(s), buttonholes and flowers, ask for a written quotation. "Be wary of an all–inclusive package that does not break down the costs for you – you want to know what you are getting," warns Mathew. Ensure all the details outlined on our checklist opposite have been included and that there are no hidden extras. To secure the booking you will be required to pay a deposit.

FLOWER QUOTATION CHECKLIST

Bride's bouquet

Bridesmaids' bouquets, posies or corsages (specify quantity)

Buttonholes & corsages (specify quantity)

Floral headpieces (if required)

Ceremony flower arrangements (specify quantity, style and size)

Reception flower arrangements (specify quantity, style and size)

Dining table centrepieces (specify quantity, style and size)

Cake table decorations

Buffet table arrangements

Additional flowers e.g. for fireplaces in summer, bathrooms, window sills, entry tables, thank you bouquets for mothers

Hire of vases/planters/pedestals/containers

Candles (if part of arrangements), storm lanterns, candelabras

Delivery and collection charges

Does the price include VAT?

Is this an estimate of costs or a fixed quotation?

BRIDE ON A BUDGET

Much of the experts' advice for the bride on a budget is useful also to couples who want their flower budget (however generous) to go further. "Use flowers that are in season – that is the number one way to stretch your budget," says Jane Packer. "In terms of the ceremony and reception, always go for size rather than quantity – have one big arrangement. If you break the budget up into six smaller arrangements dotted around the room no-one sees them." Think about where flowers and plants will have most impact. At the ceremony for example, every-one faces forward – guide their eyes to a wonderful floral arrangement there. Mathew Dickinson agrees. "Get the 'wow' factor. The same with your reception if you are strapped for cash." And spend your money on the reception flowers rather than the ceremony flowers as you and your guests will be at the reception longer.

You could also consider moving arrangements from the ceremony venue to the reception, but you need to think about who will do this and when. "I do not often suggest doing that," says Jane. "Who is going to do it? I have done it, but it looks like the florist is late with the delivery and it does not look professional." If it is your florist who will move the flowers, then there is also likely to be a labour cost, so you could ask someone else to take charge. If your ceremony and reception are in different rooms at the same location then obviously this is going to be easier than transporting flowers to another venue. "Our one proviso is that you do not see us doing it. You need to ensure that it can be done discreetly otherwise it looks awful," adds Mathew.

As with all aspects of your wedding details, simplicity is the key. "You do not need a vast quantity of flowers. You can do something that is simple and stunning. Use nice containers and no clutter on the tables," says Mathew. You could also consider using plants in pots rather than more expensive fresh cut flowers as table arrangements. They can then be given as gifts to people who have helped you plan the day. And you could investigate hiring topiary and box or bay trees if appropriate to your venue. "Explain to your florist that money is a consideration. They may have to be a little more creative, but it is still possible to create something wonderful," advises Jane. "But spend your money on your bouquet – that is crucial."

If marrying at a ceremony venue where volunteer flower arrangers usually provide the flowers, such as at a church, ask if they might be available to assist you. Also find out if there are other weddings taking place at your venue(s) the same day, or within a day, and explore the possibility of sharing flowers with another couple. "Loose, mixed-col-oured foliage is another way to decorate a venue for a reasonable price. It can look divine," states Mathew.

If you decide to do your own flowers, or friends and family help you, keep it simple. Put someone other than you in charge of every aspect. Remember to organize somewhere cool to store and arrange the flow-ers and ask for a few extra flowers to be bought to cover any damaged stems. Ensure that the person in charge is reliable and competent and has some experience as flowers require delicate handling. On the day, do not get side-tracked and involved with the flowers; you won't have time.

FLOWER TIPS FOR THE BRIDE ON A BUDGET

Only use flowers in season.

Use lots of mixed–coloured foliage – it's reasonably priced.

Consider pot plants which are cheaper than fresh cut flowers.

Hire topiary, box and bay trees.

Spend your budget on one large arrangement where everyone will see it, not several that no–one will notice.

Keep the decorations simple: use nice containers and avoid 'table clutter'.

Explore sharing flowers with another couple using the venue(s) the same day or within a day of your wedding.

Check your venue does not already have flowers available.
(Many remove them so as not to clash with wedding flowers they assume you'll provide.)

Ask your venue(s) if they have volunteer flower arrangers who might assist you for a small donation.

If a friend or family member is doing your flowers, do not get side–tracked and involved on the day; you won't have time. Choose someone competent, reliable and with some experience.

If not purchasing bouquets from a florist, ensure thorns and pollen stems will be removed.

Borrow bridesmaids' flowers for decorating areas at the reception.

Corsages and flowers worn on the wrist are cheaper than posies and bouquets for bridesmaids.

DETAILS

Having chosen your florist and established a budget, decided who and where will have flowers, and start thinking about the variety of flowers you want. Your starting points are the time of year, your wedding gown and the venue(s). "I first sit down with the bride and establish the look that she wants. It is about assessing the mood and the personality of the person," says Jane Packer. "One of the first questions I ask a bride is what is her dream? How does she want to look on this day? If she says she wants to look like she has floated in on a cloud, or she wants to look like a Hollywood vamp, then I immediately get a picture in my mind of the direction we are going in."

But do not worry if you initially have no idea what you want advises Mathew Dickinson. "Some brides know exactly what they want and how they would like their bouquet tied, others don't and it does not matter. We love it when brides have no idea and are open to our suggestions. A colour scheme is helpful, but not essential." A colour scheme can unify the various elements of your wedding: the flowers, bridesmaids, the venues (if there is more than one) and the groom, best man and ushers' accessories (waistcoats, cravats and ties, buttonholes and handkerchiefs). Select colours appropriate to the time of year and the venue and that suit your skin tones and your outfit. Flowers are a good place to start when thinking of a unifying colour scheme, and specifically colours of flowers in season (e.g. autumnal russets, winter reds and whites, spring yellows and purples, summer pinks and berry colours). You do not have to select one colour, but a colour palette. Within that you can choose shades of one colour, colours that blend, or complementary colours. "What you can do is endless," states Jane. "It doesn't end with the flower shop and vase. You could have paper lanterns with flowers coming out of them. You could use jam jars. It is about you leading your florist where you are thinking with ideas pictures and drawings."

Cut out pictures from magazines and think whether they will go with the style of event you are trying to create. If they don't, is it the way they are arranged or is it the flowers themselves? If you have admired flowers as a guest at a wedding think about why you liked them and what it was that caught your eye. Would something similar be appropriate for your wedding? Our advice, as always, is to work with and seek the

advice of the professionals you have employed. Be open to their advice and ideas. Study your venues and get a feel for them and what will be appropriate within them. By the time you sit down with your florist to specify exact details you should have a swatch sample of your gown and bridesmaids dresses, pictures of the designs, know your maximum budget and your florist should have visited the venue(s). Your first decision is then the bridal bouquet.

THE BRIDE'S BOUQUET

A bride's bouquet is her most important accessory. "One thing you should never skimp on is the bridal bouquet – it's in all the photographs," states Mathew Dickinson. Your bouquet should complete and complement your look without overpowering it. Avoid extremes of colour and size (which will also make it more difficult to carry). It should also reflect the season and the time and the setting of your wedding. If you are opting for a casual look, a single stem or hand–tied bouquet or posy might be appropriate. For a more formal ensemble opt for something more structured, like a wired bouquet. Or you could choose to have one large bloom constructed from many blossoms or petals.

"Usually the dress starts things off," says Jane Packer. "There are lots of different things to take into account: the shape and height of the bride, what is fashionable and what is not. Flowers are hugely influenced by fashion. We started using beads for example in our bouquets when we saw that happening on the catwalk." As well as beads you can incorporate ribbons, feathers, jewels, tassels, organza, shells or fruit into your bouquet. "Things come in and out of fashion," says Mathew. "Generally speaking the trend is for smaller bouquets because dresses are simpler. The huge bouquet is out – no bride wants to be seen carrying a garden down the aisle! It does not complement the look. But we need to match the flowers to the dress and the aspirations of the day." Avoid styles and blooms that are overwhelming and seek your florist's advice. Ask him or her to take you through the various styles of bouquet and seek a shape and size appropriate to your overall look. If you do not want to carry a traditional bouquet you have other options: in winter you could wear a fur or faux–fur stole or a muff and pin a corsage onto it, you could have a bag created from flowers, carry

a parasol wired with fresh flowers in summer, or have a pomander hanging from your wrist. "But never use anything dyed," warns Mathew. "There is a danger the dye could come off onto your outfit. Also avoid having too strong a colour contrast within your bouquet as it can then look as though it has holes in it. Be especially careful of this if you are having black and white photographs."

Having decided on a style and a size of bouquet (which could be dictated by your choice of blooms) explore how the bouquet becomes the basis for the rest of your wedding flowers, especially the flowers carried and worn by the rest of the bridal party. If you have chosen well, the bouquet will easily form the basis of the other flowers and arrangements you use throughout the rest of the day.

If you have chosen to wear flowers in your hair, remember that your florist is not a hairdresser! The advice of our expert hairdressers is to ensure you have liaised with your hairdresser and your florist and specified in advance how you would like the flowers delivered (for example, fastened to a comb, wired onto grips or a tiara).

Your bouquet may be delivered several hours or more before the wedding ceremony. If so, ask your florist for advice on how and where to store it. Generally speaking it should be dampened, covered with moist tissue or muslin and kept as cool as possible.

If you are doing your own flowers, or a friend or family member has volunteered to do them, be sure your bouquet is free from thorns and that pollen stems (many of which can easily stain) have been removed. If you have opted to do your own flowers, seriously consider purchasing just your bouquet from a professional. They are time-consuming to construct and require a high level of expertise. If this is not an option, choose something very simple.

After the wedding you may want your bouquet professionally preserved. Not all florists recommend this "They never look as good," advises Mathew Dickinson. If you do want to preserve yours (either as it is, or as a smaller version) there are specialist companies who offer various preservation methods. But you must arrange this in advance as your bouquet will need to be delivered to them straight away. If you want to still toss your bouquet, order a less expensive version of it for the purpose.

HOW TO CARRY A BOUQUET

Correctly carrying your bouquet will ensure you look elegant and sophisticated. It will also make you appear taller and slimmer. "Hold the bouquet with both hands and tilt it forward at the hip. Keep your shoulders back. Your father then leads you by slipping his right arm through your left," states Mathew Dickinson.

Practice using a rolled-up newspaper or magazine as it is not as natural as it might at first appear. Having put so much effort into your look do not spoil it by inelegantly carrying your bouquet. And on no account point with it (which we've all seen)!

BRIDESMAIDS' BLOOMS

The bridesmaids' bouquets do not have to match the bride's. Indeed they do not have to carry a bouquet at all. "Some don't want the traditional fussy look, they might want a single flower worn on the wrist *Sex and the City* style," says Jane Packer. Younger bridesmaids could carry baskets of flowers, hoops or pomanders. All could simply wear a corsage. "But bridesmaids have one or the other – never a corsage and a bouquet," advises Mathew Dickinson. If bridesmaids are carrying bouquets, the shape and colour should complement the bride's bouquet, but without overpowering it. They should be smaller. If you have several bridesmaids, the chief bridesmaid could carry a slightly larger or more elaborate version than the others. Bridesmaids wearing different colours could have the same flowers but the bouquets could be tied with ribbons to match their outfits. Their flowers could match yours, or be made with just one of the blooms in your bouquet (or the other way around). Your flowers could match the bridesmaid's dresses or their flowers match yours. The possibilities are numerous. Pageboys should wear buttonholes.

Pass-on the advice to your bridesmaids on how to carry a bouquet. And all of you should remember how to correctly hold your bouquets during the photographs (you could ask your photographer to remind you). During the reception you could ask bridesmaids to place their flowers in bathrooms (or other specified places) for decoration until the end of the celebration.

CORSAGES

As with buttonholes, giving a corsage to mothers, grandmothers and other special ladies at your celebration is a thoughtful way to acknowledge them without breaking the bank. Many of our *Wedding Bible* experts don't like wedding favours cluttering the tables; you could consider giving away corsages and buttonholes instead. As with buttonholes, corsages should reflect the rest of the flowers, but they also need to be appropriate to the outfits they'll be pinned on. You could find out what the recipients will be wearing, or suggest they contact your florist direct to ensure they receive something they want. Alternatively, you could choose fairly neutral blooms. Seek your florist's advice. Again, you don't need to stick with flowers – especially as these are for the ladies.

A corsage is pinned to the left shoulder, or to the left lapel of a suit, or you could order single blooms that can be tied at the wrist. Sometimes women secure their corsages to handbags, scarves or wraps.

Have the corsages delivered with the buttonholes. If you need some to be delivered with your bouquet, specify which ones to your florist and have him or her label them all – especially if they are not all the same.

BUTTONHOLES

Thankfully, buttonholes have come a long way since the carnation with the tin foil covered stem! Although not a requirement for anyone other than the groom, his best man and the bride's father, they are a relatively inexpensive way of singling-out the wedding party and other close family members. They also look really smart. Buttonholes should really be provided for the ushers and groom's father too, and for readers, brothers and close male family members if the budget allows.

Buttonholes can be created from a cluster of blooms or a single flower. Or they need not be flowers at all but could be made from herbs, leaves or berries and with beads, feathers, ribbons and other fancy trimmings. Buttonholes can be simple or elaborate, casual or formal. A starting point will be the bride's flowers. "I would always suggest that the flowers in the bouquet should be part of the general theme," advises Jane Packer. You could single-out one bloom or one colour. It will need to complement the detail in the groom's outfit and, as with the rest of the flowers, ensure the buttonholes reflect the style of the event and the venue.

The groom's buttonhole may be the same as the those worn by the rest of the wedding party, or completely different. It could be a more elaborate or larger version. It could match the main flower in the bride's bouquet whilst the others match a bloom the bridesmaids are carrying. If all the buttonholes are different try and link one detail, such as style or colour. Also ensure that they are suitable to withstand several hours without water, and lots of hugging and kissing!

Agree in writing with your florist where and when the buttonholes (and corsages) are being delivered, especially if it is not to the same address as your bouquet, and know who will be there to receive them. "Have a list of names of who the buttonholes are for so that they are not taken by people who should not have them," advises Mathew. "If not your florist, then give the job to a reliable usher. You could have a removable name label on each one." Also ask your florist to provide extra pins.

Buttonholes should be securely fastened with a pin to the left lapel. And Mathew Dickinson's top-tip for the groom: "I have a 'no hugging' policy after he has secured his buttonhole until after the photographs – you don't want it crushed!"

VENUE FLOWERS

You may be holding your ceremony and reception at one venue or they might be at different locations. Consult with your venue(s) and establish what restrictions, if any, there are with regard to flowers. Check when your florist may have access on the wedding day and possibly the day before, and whether the flowers need to be removed after the celebration. Your venue(s) may also have flowers of their own displayed, so liaise as appropriate.

If your florist is already familiar with your venue(s), they will be able to offer advice on what works well there. If not, arrange a visit together at least four to six months before the wedding. Once again the style, size, mood and formality of the event needs to be reflected in the flowers. If your ceremony and reception are in different rooms at the same location, they will need to be similar. If at separate venues,

however, you have more options. "The bridal flowers should match or complement the bride and bridesmaids. The reception flowers should complement the venue. But you do not need to match the ceremony and reception flowers if they are being held in different venues," states Mathew Dickinson. "Everyone thinks the flowers have to be the same throughout the day – they don't! It depends on the style, the venue and the budget." Take your cue from the venue(s). Study the interior and gardens, the lighting and assess the mood.

Remember the experts' advice earlier in the chapter and opt for one large display rather than several smaller ones. If money is a consideration spend it where you'll be most of the time – at the reception. And as already advised, only move flowers from room-to-room or venue-to-venue if it can be done discreetly.

...quet of muscari, guelder roses, lisianthus and ...rangeas.

Yellow is a powerful, vibrant colour, so consider a mix of ranunculus shooting out between bright yellow 'Illusion' roses and green foliage, hand-tied with Indian-style gold sequin fabric.

CEREMONY FLOWERS

Because of the number of weddings performed in them every day, it is not usually feasible to decorate a register office. Therefore, go to town with the bouquets, buttonholes and corsages, using the bridal bouquet as the inspiration and centrepiece.

For locations where you can decorate with flowers, think about where you'll place them: at entrances and doors, gates and porches, pew or row ends, window sills, and at the alter, pulpit, huppah or equivalent. "Put flower arrangements where everyone is looking at them," reminds Jane Packer.

What you can create with flowers is endless. Your starting point for your ceremony flowers is your bouquet. If you have an idea of how you want that to be, the choice of the rest of the flowers can develop from there.

Work with your florist and venue(s) and do your homework: seek inspiration from magazines, websites and flower markets. If you've time, visit a flower show. Study the venue, what you like about it and what you don't, how it looks and feels and the mood you are trying to create. Take into account the time of year and the time of day and remember what is in season. Think of weddings you have been to at similar venues and what did and didn't work, what you liked and what you didn't like. "It is about you leading your florist where you are thinking with ideas, with pictures and drawings," advises Jane.

RECEPTION FLOWERS

For many couples the wedding reception is the area they want to concentrate on in terms of decoration and setting the scene. You may be holding your reception at a tried–and–tested venue where hundreds of couples have already celebrated their union, or at a village hall or at home. Wherever you are holding the celebration, and whatever your budget, you can create a unique and personal event that reflects you, your personality, your style, your values and what you represent as a couple. Flowers are a valuable source of inspiration to help you achieve this. You could reverse the advice previously given in this chapter and start with an overview of the event, concentrating on the venue and the style and mood you are trying to create at the reception and work backwards from there. You may discover that you have been drawn to hold your reception at a particular venue precisely because it reflects and suits the occasion you are trying to create. Should you find the process is not flowing or ideas are not gelling, ensure you have selected the appropriate venues and professionals to assist you. If something does not feel right, that might be the one thing you need to change to make everything else fall into place.

When decorating your reception, again think of entrances, window sills, as well as fireplaces (in summer), bathrooms, alcoves and hallways. If there are large expanses of space seek your florist's advice on how to fill them. Ask the venue how others have decorated them before and ask if they have photographs.

In a marquee, you can really go to town as you have a blank canvas. Think of entrances and poles (if not a frame marquee) and consider hanging arrangements (we've hung an upside down Christmas tree as a chandelier at a New Year's Eve wedding – see pages 44 and 45). In summer you can bring the garden into the marquee in the form of pots, containers and steel watering cans. Your marquee may be constructed within a garden and that could therefore be your inspiration. If it is your garden, or belongs to your parents, the longer you have to plan and plant, the better. It may be that you need to do little more than think what is in bloom in the garden at the time you are holding the wedding. If you are having a marquee, whether at home or another venue, give your florist a floor plan showing the exits and with a layout of the table and dance–floor.

"Candles are also wonderful and create a fantastic and intimate mood," says Mathew. They can be incorporated within table centrepieces as well as other floral arrangements. They can also be placed in storm/hurricane lanterns or night lights can be placed in pretty holders to stand alone or in groups on tables, staircases, on window ledges and up garden paths. However, check with your venue as fire regulations sometimes prohibit the use of candles.

Don't go overboard with other decorations at your reception. "Balloons are an absolute no, no!" states Mathew. "No streamers, no horseshoes, no hearts. People also get carried away with too much clutter on the tables. Get rid of the favours (an American import). Simplicity is the key. Also beware of looking too contemporary which can make it feel like a corporate event. Go for something that is elegant and timeless." But Jane adds that everything dates. "Be it from the food that you eat to the dress. Choose what you want. If you worry about every aspect you'll end up with something boring designed by default."

TABLE CENTREPIECES

Many brides spend hours deciding on their table decorations. Flowers are the obvious choice. These are the arrangements guests will have the most opportunity to study. Budget is a serious consideration, especially if you have a large number of guests and therefore tables: if you overspend on each one the total amount could well exceed your flower budget. Remember the more complicated the arrangement, the more it will cost. Think of favourite flowers, your bouquet, the style and colour scheme of the room, the lighting, the time of day and year and how formal or informal the event will be. Again, look through magazines and on websites. "If someone comes in with a picture of a huge table centre then you know they want lots of flowers on the tables. Or it might be three little bud vases reflecting they've a simpler style in mind," says Jane Packer. So assess what styles you are drawn to and how appropriate and/or affordable they will be.

Each table could be the same, the top or main table could be more elaborate, or each table could have a different arrangement. Keep the centrepieces similar in style and size and have them either low or high for cross-table conversation. Vegetables, fresh or sugared fruits, pebbles, feathers, beads, coloured gel, candles can all be incorporated within table arrangements. Simple pot plants are also an option. Tables can also be edged with flowers or foliage, garlands can be woven through chairbacks, and blooms can be placed on napkins.

"If you want to give the flower arrangements away at the end of the evening but you have to return the containers ask your florist to use plastic containers within the decorative ones," is Mathew's tip. If you are planning to give guests the table flowers or other arrangements make a list of recipients and perhaps leave them a note on their chair. Other ideas could include giving them to the youngest or oldest seated at each table, to the person with the nearest birthday or to the couple with the nearest wedding anniversary. You could also consider giving them to a local hospice or home for the elderly.

WHAT TO ASK THE FLOWER PROFESSIONALS

When choosing a florist, ask to see a portfolio of their wedding work and testimonials from other couples.

Assess the quality of the flowers in the shop and the greeting you received upon arrival.

Will yours be the only wedding on the day? If not, who will be overseeing your flowers – is it the person you are liaising with?

Does the florist know the venue(s) you have chosen, and if so what ideas do they have?

Can they visit the venue(s) with you?

Can they make up a table centrepiece for you to see in advance free-of-charge?

Ask for an estimate that specifies exact quantities, sizes and blooms.

Does the final quote include delivery (and to more than one location if required), collection and VAT?

What are the florist's terms and how much is the deposit?

When do they need you to make final floral decisions?

THE EVENT

Delivery and storage at your venue needs to be agreed in advance. Your florist should liaise with the venue manager without you needing to be involved. A week or so before the wedding, give your florist a list of where all the flowers are to be delivered to on the day. If there is more than one delivery point specify exactly which flowers are to go where, as well as who will be there to accept them. Remember that churches and other venues are often locked, so know who to contact to arrange delivery, and set up delivery times in advance (you may need to make such arrangements). Put someone in charge at each location (such as the best man for the buttonholes and your mother for the bouquets). Give your florist a copy of your 'Wedding Day Contact List' (page 248). That list should include the florist's

mobile number, in case of any unforeseen last minute changes in delivery arrangements.

If bouquets, buttonholes and corsages are delivered with several hours or more to spare, store them somewhere cool and seek your florist's advice. Remember to send the buttonholes ahead of time to the ceremony venue, but keep your father's with your bouquet (a common mishap is for his buttonhole to be sent along with the others to the ceremony, but the ushers think it is spare and give it away!).

When you are dressed and ready to leave, pick up your bouquet – you are now a bride!

THE WEDDING FLOWERS TOP TIPS

Flowers in season will be the best value and quality.

Allocate around 10% of your wedding budget to flowers.

Take as much information as you have to the first consultation (venue(s), date and time of wedding, number of guests, style of gown, number of bridesmaids and a swatch of your dress fabric).

Seek inspiration from the venue(s), your wedding gown, the time of day and year and what flowers are in season.

Be open to your florist's advice.

Do not skimp on the bride's bouquet – it will be in all the photographs.

Spend less on your ceremony flowers than the ones for the reception as the latter lasts far longer.

Place flower arrangements where they will attract the most attention.

Go for the 'wow factor' with a couple of large floral arrangements, as opposed to several smaller ones.

The flowers in the bride's bouquet should be part of the general theme.

The bridal flowers should match or complement the bride and bridesmaids. The reception flowers should complement the venue. You do not need to match the ceremony and reception flowers if they are being held at different venues.

Remember flowers for entrances, window sills, alcoves, fireplaces (in summer), row ends, alter, pulpit, huppah (or equivalent), hallways, cake table, buffet tables and bathrooms.

Avoid 'table clutter' – keep your floral centrepieces the focal point.

Keep dining table centrepieces low for cross–table talk.

The more complicated or elaborate arrangements and centrepieces are, the more they will cost.

If hiring pots or vases, ask your florist for plastic containers within the decorative ones, so you can give arrangements away as gifts.

Practise carrying your bouquet correctly. Never point with it.

In addition to the bridal party, if the budget allows, provide buttonholes and corsages for important family members and special guests.

Avoid paper confetti – it can stain clothes if dampened in a downpour. Therefore use fresh rose petals.

Do not be tempted to do your own flowers, you will not have time and wedding flowers are mostly a last minute job.

If a member of your family or a friend has volunteered to do your flowers, invest in the services of a florist for the bride's bouquet, or keep it very simple.

If money is no object, go to town with the flowers!

EXPERTS' TOP TIPS FOR WEDDING FLOWERS

wedding flowers

ideas

UP TO 12 MONTHS BEFORE THE WEDDING

Select a florist, establish a budget, ask for an estimate and secure the booking.

If you've a year or more to go, study flowers in season at the appropriate time of year. Visit gardens, parks, flower markets and flower shows for inspiration.

Study magazines, websites and begin creating a 'mood board' of ideas to show your florist.

decisions

6 MONTHS TO GO

Decide who and where will have flowers.

Establish what restrictions exist at your venues (also ask if candles are allowed).

Start narrowing–down your ideas: do they fit the style of your wedding, your dress, the venue(s), the time of day and year and the mood you are trying to create?

4-phase timeline

details

6 – 4 MONTHS TO GO

Take fabric swatches of your dress and bridesmaids' dresses to your florist, along with pictures of the designs.

Visit the venue(s) with your florist.

Discuss your ideas and concerns and make your choices together. Be guided by your florist.

Start by deciding on the bride's bouquet.

Establish quantities (arrangements, bouquets, buttonholes, corsages and table centrepieces).

Discuss style and size of arrangements.

Get a detailed quotation – not an estimate of costs. If you are over-budget discuss this with your florist now.

Establish on-the-day contact and delivery details.

event

AND THE WEEK PRECEDING THE WEDDING

A few days before the wedding, double-check delivery details and timings – particularly if there is more than one delivery address.

Check access and contact names and numbers with your venue(s).

Give your florist the 'Wedding Day Contact List'. Include your florists mobile number in case of last minute changes in delivery requirements.

Ask your florist to label buttonholes and corsages (even if they are the same) and bridesmaids' bouquets. Request they include a few extra pins.

Have your father's buttonhole delivered with the bride's bouquet and keep them together.

If bouquets and buttonholes arrive early, store them somewhere cool.

wedding cake

When Pierce and Keely Brosnan were planning their wedding, she said, "If I have a great man, a great dress and a great cake, nothing else matters!" She chose Mich Turner, founder of the Little Venice Cake Company in London, to bake her fairytale wedding cake. Mich boasts an enviable client list and her cakes have taken centre stage, not just at weddings and parties, but in films, on television and at glittering awards ceremonies. "Have a spectacular cake!" she states. "Cutting it is the first official duty the wife has to perform, is a natural and wonderful photo opportunity and a fantastic memory of the day."

The modern wedding cake is the result of an evolution. In Ancient Rome small wheat cakes were broken over the bride's head, symbolizing fertility. Guests caught the crumbs and kept them for good luck. In medieval Britain guests brought small cakes to the wedding feast and piled them on the centre of a table. The newly married couple then kissed over them. Then a French baker began icing small cakes together to form one large cake. The now traditional three-tiered wedding cake was conceived by a Victorian, Fleet Street baker who created a cake for his daughter's wedding based upon the spire of St Bride's Church. The cutting of the cake represents the sharing of the first meal as husband and wife. One superstition states that a bridesmaid who places a slice of wedding cake under her pillow will dream of her future husband!

Mercifully, long gone are the days when wedding guests risked breaking a tooth on icing that resembled cement, only to find a piece of dry, stale fruit cake inside! Now your wedding cake options are endless: chocolate truffle torte, sponge cake layered with ganache and buttercream, rum-soaked sultana and carrot cake with coconut, luscious lemon cake with lime curd buttercream filling, meringue pavlova decorated with fresh flowers, crispy cream doughnuts, chestnut, hazelnut or orange cake, coffee and walnut cake, profiterole croquembouche... the list goes on. If you can't decide, you can have a different filling for every tier of your cake and as many tiers as you like! "Certainly A-list Hollywood couples having big showbiz weddings that are featured in magazines have had an impact on the quality and design a modern couple expect," says Mich. She should know having baked cakes for, among others, Sir Paul McCartney, Emma Thompson, Dame Kiri Te Kanawa and the Beckhams. You too can ask a patissier to create almost any mouth-watering cake for whatever style of celebration you are planning and for any number of guests.

what the expert says

STARTING POINT – CHOOSING THE STYLE OF YOUR CAKE

Your wedding cake could be provided by your venue or an outside caterer, a patissier, a supermarket (many do bake some smashing cakes), an ambitious novice, or specialist cake designers such as the Little Venice Cake Company. As always, a recommendation is the best place to start when sourcing a supplier. Your venue or caterer may try and insist they provide your cake, or they may recommend a preferred supplier. Before agreeing to this, or to anyone supplying your wedding cake, ensure you see and taste examples and use the following advice to assess their suitability and expertise. Cake baking and decorating is a specialist craft. What kind of specialist you go to will depend upon your budget, the style of cake you want and how complicated it is. A simple cake, especially if you have limited funds, could be provided by someone with less expertise and experience. But for a formal spectacular cake you'll need to call-in the experts.

"A good time to come and talk about your cake is when you have chosen your dress and flowers and have an idea of the style of your day. Ideally, allow at least three months," advises Mich. Take with you any ideas you already have. Books, magazines and the internet can offer inspiration. Think first about the style of your celebration: is it a simple contemporary wedding or a more formal and/or lavish occasion? Do you need a formal, tiered, iced cake or a sculptural creation? Should the cake form a dramatic centrepiece or can it be something more informal, funky or fun? Think too of the venue; scale is important, particularly if the cake is to be a focal point. How many people has it got to feed? When will you serve it and what will you have eaten already? Do you want to serve the cake as dessert (if you do, you could opt for a cheese course instead of a pudding from your venue or caterer)? Do you want tiers of several flavours? Consider your flowers, colours, themes you may have chosen, the time of year, the time of day and how long the cake has to stand before it is cut and served. These are your starting points. But visit suppliers with an open mind. Trained cake designers may think of things and have ideas that you have not thought of. "As with the rest of your wedding day, the cake should reflect your personalities. Think how the wedding cake is going to be part of your day," suggests Mich.

"It's a good plan to have an idea of the menu for your wedding breakfast so you can see how the cake is going to fit-in. The first question to ask is: how many people will the cake need to serve? That gives an indi-

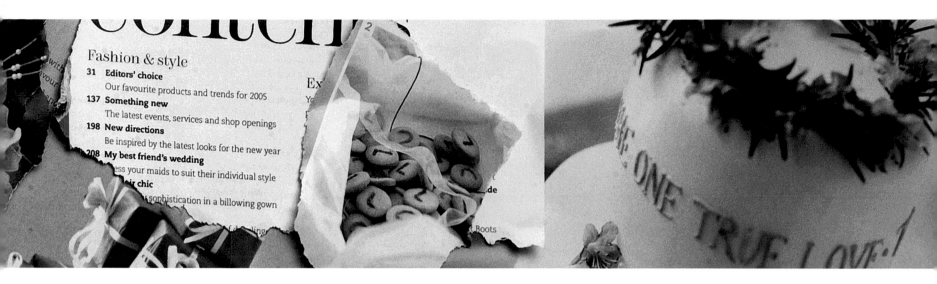

cation of how big your cake should be. For a more intimate wedding, or perhaps a second marriage celebration, a beautifully decorated, two-tiered, stacked cake could be appropriate. Or for smaller celebrations you could have individual cakes set-up on a stand; because the number of tiers builds-up very quickly the result is quite dramatic and beautiful. For a very large gathering we'd suggest working with fake tiers: you have a base tier for the bride and groom to cut, but the rest of the tiers are made up with polystyrene inside – but iced and decorated in the normal way. We bake an additional cake to the cutting cake that can be plated-up in the kitchen. This greatly assists the caterer as all they have to do is pre-slice the cake, then plate and serve it as soon as you have cut the other cake."

If serving the cake as your dessert, you can add other accompaniments; perhaps brandy sauce with a fruit cake, raspberry coulis with chocolate cake and garnish with fresh fruit and berries, edible flowers or nuts. Because it can take time to plate and serve the cake, you may decide to cut it either before the wedding breakfast (perhaps with a blast of confetti from a confetti gun as you enter the room?) or following the first course.

If you want a cake in addition to dessert, think about what you are serving for pudding. "If you are having a chocolate pudding, consider an alternative flavour or flavours for the cake. The cake is usually served following speeches and toasts. Bear in mind when you are sampling the cake, that by the time you eat it on your wedding day, you may well have consumed canapés, champagne, a substantial meal and wine, so you will need a cake that will satisfy the palate without having a huge slice. It needs to have a gusty flavour that stands up to a champagne toast and 'packs a punch'." You could also consider serving your cake later in the celebration, maybe towards the end of the evening when dancing guests might feel peckish.

It has become increasingly popular for couples to opt for different flavours in different tiers of their wedding cake: "A lot of couples do still have the traditional rich fruit cake somewhere in their wedding cake, either as a base tier to support the weight of the other tiers, or as the top tier to keep for their first child's christening." Or you could freeze and keep a tier to enjoy on your first wedding anniversary. Alternatively, ask your supplier if at the same time as baking your wedding cake, they could make you a smaller cake for freezing.

CAKE QUESTIONS

Wedding cakes are costly because creating them is time-consuming and most of the decoration is done by hand. A large, formal, tiered wedding cake will make a large dent in your budget. Therefore you have a right to expect a high level of service and the opportunity to both see and sample the cakes of potential suppliers. Don't be bamboozled. If you can't sample a cake, how do you know what you will get on the day? The cost of your wedding cake is likely to be calculated upon the number of servings. Check whether the price includes delivery and assembly. Cakes are rarely sent-out ready assembled; they need to be set-up on the day. If they are decorated with fresh fruit or flowers they can only usually be delivered within a couple of hours of the start of the reception. If the supplier is unable to deliver and set-up the cake, who will? How are they going to suitably transport the cake and when? If it is a complicated tiered cake or a large sculptural design, does the person have experience of setting-up and dressing celebration cakes? If not, it's risky and it's therefore worth paying extra for the cake supplier to do it for you. Alternatively, your caterer or venue may be willing to assist if they have experience, but check first.

Also ask about the ingredients. For example, will they use butter rather than vegetable shortening? If they won't, does the quality of the cake match the price? The use of organic ingredients may also be a consideration; if so, are you willing to pay extra?

You will also need to liaise with your reception venue. Ask when the cake can be delivered and set-up on the day and whether they can provide a cake stand, knife and cake table – preferably with wheels if a large tiered cake has to be removed to the kitchen for plating. The cake table is likely to be one of the focal points of the room. Check with your cake supplier that the table on offer is a suitable size and stable. A huge round table can make even a large cake look tiny and make it very difficult to reach the base tier for cutting. If it isn't the right size consider hiring one. Ensure you have discussed with the venue exactly where the cake table will be placed and that it will be provided with a clean cloth. It needs to be positioned in an area that will be well-lit and with no distractions near or around it to spoil the photographs. If you are adding special lighting to the room, add a spotlight for the cake table too. If you want the table decorated with flowers, ask your florist to liaise with the cake supplier to ensure they are both happy and that each understands what the other is providing.

If you would like to send cake to family and friends who are unable to attend your wedding, bear in mind that many cakes will not stay fresh enough once sliced. Seek the advice of your supplier who may be able to bake small individual cakes, or a different suitable layer of the wedding cake specifically for sending-out. Some bakers will offer to do this for you. "We have individual cake boxes made exclusively for us," says Mich. "We photograph all our cakes and print a personalised small label with a picture of it saying 'From the wedding of ...' so those who couldn't make it see how the cake looked when it was set-up at the reception.

SPECIAL CONSIDERATIONS

Cakes are made from fresh ingredients, therefore they can spoil if left out for several hours. "A mousse or cheesecake, or a cake containing fresh cream will not last more than four hours if left out of a refrigerator. Your reception is likely to last longer than that," warns Mich. So avoid fillings and decorations that will not keep if you are having an outdoor summer wedding or a reception in a summer marquee.

Receptions in marquees or aboard boats and barges also bring some special considerations. "If you are in a moving venue stacked cakes are advisable rather than tiered," states Mich. The layers of a stacked cake are placed directly upon one another and supported by cake boards. This makes them more stable than the traditional wedding cake with tiers separated by pillars. "Likewise, marquee floors tend to be uneven, so it is worth having a spirit level and some cardboard handy to prop-up the table legs and ensure a stable level base. If the table is level from the start you have a hope of getting the cake level by the time you get to the top!"

If you have not ordered your cake from your venue they may try and charge you 'cakeage' (really!). This is usually a per plate charge to cover the cost of cutting, plating and washing-up. Try to remember to ask if there is a charge for supplying your own cake before you sign the contract when you are in a stronger position to negotiate. If you have strong feelings about how appropriate a charge is, attempt to expunge the clause from your contract early on.

MAKING OR DECORATING YOUR OWN CAKE

Don't be tempted to make your own wedding cake unless you are confident! Even if you are an enthusiastic amateur baker, during the week leading up to your wedding you are unlikely to be wanting to be icing and decorating a cake in the wee small hours. If you do, delegate the task of setting-it-up on the day to someone trustworthy.

"If a friend or relative offers to make you a cake I would suggest checking they have some experience of baking, decorating and setting- up a wedding cake," advises Mich. "The internal construction is as important as the outside of the cake. You can't simply pile one tier on top of another; with each layer more support is needed as the cake gets heavier and heavier. The tiers have to be on separate boards and you have to dowel the cake all the way through. The icing must be allowed to set overnight before you attempt stacking the cake. And if you are working with a very tall cake of several flavours, position the heavier fruit cake at the base with the softer, lighter tiers near the top."

If you are buying an off-the-shelf cake – and there are some beautiful ones to choose from at leading supermarkets and small local suppliers – you might want to consider decorating or dressing it yourself. Consider how much time this will take and don't be overly ambitious. Is there someone else who could do this for you? Perhaps your mother, your mother-in-law-to-be, an aunt or a friend with an eye for detail? "There are some lovely ways in which you can decorate off-the-shelf cakes. Put them in your own style with lots of fresh flowers." A word of caution if you want to decorate a cake with fruit: "Do not use fresh fruit, especially berries, on iced cakes. The moisture from the fruit will soak straight into the icing. Because icing is water based it absorbs the moisture like blotting paper," warns Mich. "We tend to work with fresh flowers on an iced cake and fresh fruit on our chocolate covered cakes. You can use fruit on a cake decorated with chocolate because the cocoa butter in the chocolate is oil based, that means the moisture from the fruit is held on the surface of the chocolate."

If you are using flowers, think about their colour and texture and remember that they do not have to be edible (but should be removed before serving). Other embellishments could include sugared or crystallised fruits, nuts, ribbons and sweets. For more inspiration on baking and decorating your own cake, see Mich Turner's beautifully illustrated book, *Spectacular Cakes*.

Mich Turner

HOW TO CUT AND EAT CAKE

The cutting of the cake is the perfect photo opportunity! At the agreed time, ask the Master of Ceremonies or the best man to announce your intention to cut the cake. Your photographer should be in place. The bride stands to the left of the groom and takes the cake knife in her right hand. The groom places his right hand upon hers. Together you slice through the bottom layer of the cake. The room will be filled with the flash of photography, you'll feel like a movie star and then you have to eat cake whilst being photographed! Traditionally, you serve one another from that first slice – this is a great photograph; the groom, using a cake fork, feeds the bride first. If you can, remember not to overload the fork. If your cake is so delicious that you must continue making your way through a large slice of it, make sure you take tiny mouthfuls so that you continue to look demure in the inevitable snaps your friends and family will be taking. Having cut the cake, move away from it and have it taken to the kitchen for slicing and plating. No–one, especially you, wants to see the messy destruction of this expensive but marvellous creation!

MICH TURNER'S WEDDING CAKE TIPS

Ask your venue staff who their recommended cake suppliers are.

Only bake your own wedding cake if you are confident and have done it before.

Ask to see, and more importantly sample, cakes from potential suppliers.

How do they charge and does the price include delivery and assembly?

Will your venue charge a fee for a cake they have not provided?

When choosing your cake, consider the style of your celebration, the scale of your reception venue, how many people the cake has to serve and the wedding breakfast menu.

Do you want tiers of several flavours and will you want to preserve one layer for a later occasion?

Will you want to send cake to absent friends and family?

Will you serve the cake as dessert? If not, choose an alternative flavour to the pudding.

If you are having a large wedding cake, or are serving the cake as pudding, consider a cake with a real base tier to cut and additional fake tiers, with extra serving cake that can be pre-plated in the kitchen.

For summer weddings, avoid ingredients that will spoil in warm weather.

Avoid tiered cakes on boats and other moving venues. Opt instead for stacked designs.

If an enthusiastic amateur is baking your cake, ensure they have made a similar one before.

When decorating an off-the-shelf cake, never use fresh fruit on icing – it will absorb the moisture like blotting paper.

Check your venue has a suitable cake table, stand and a knife. Agree timings for access on the day.

Agree the position of the cake table in advance. Ensure it is well-lit with no distractions to spoil the photographs. Give your cake supplier set-up details as you are unlikely to be available on the day.

Provide a spirit level and cardboard to set the cake up on the day – especially in a marquee.

For great cake photos, gaze longingly and lovingly into the eyes of your new spouse as you feed one another. Add a blast of confetti for a romantic, showbiz, glamorous effect!

EXPERT'S TOP TIPS FOR THE WEDDING CAKE

picture perfect
photography & videography

The photographer is probably the most important professional you will hire on your wedding day. Top of the list when you've set the date is finding a good wedding photographer. Poor wedding photography is one of the biggest let-downs for a couple after their wedding. If you try and save money here you are likely to be disappointed. Your photographs, and the video if you have one, are the only visual memento of your day.

Formal, stylized photography grew from the tradition of portrait painting. Early photography was a slow, uncomfortable and strange process. The subjects were required to sit still, sometimes in neck splints, for long periods. Rarely before the 1930s do you see anyone smiling in a photograph! Early film stars glamourized photography and by the end of World War II brides were opting not just for a couple of formal portraits, but for albums recording the events of the entire wedding day. Hollywood glamour met wedding photography when Grace Kelly married Prince Rainier of Monaco in 1956. Her wedding day images were published in magazines across the globe and the trend was set for glamorous, stylish wedding photography. We've never looked back.

Whilst photography captures a moment in time, videography records time in motion. Digital camera and editing technology means you, your family and friends can relive moments of your wedding day on DVD or even the web. Paying good and experienced professionals to capture those moments creatively and present them in an imaginative and beautifully edited wedding film is expensive. But if you can afford it, don't hesitate to part with your cash; you'll never regret it. If your budget can't stretch, we've the very man on-hand to avoid a home made video nasty! Michael Metcalf has nearly three decades experience in real television. He's worked on hundreds of multi-camera 'live' programmes and outside broadcasts. His credits include *Razzmatazz*, *The Roxy*,

The Big Breakfast and he is currently the Senior Director at *GMTV*. Michael also makes wedding DVDs! He's the man those in the know call-upon to make theirs. Here in the *Wedding Bible* he tells you what to expect from the professionals, how to hire the right one and offers his top tips to the amateur videographer.

Our *Wedding Bible* photography experts are among those who have raised the standard of wedding photography in the UK over the past decade. They are the photographers of choice for some of our most glamorous, sophisticated society and celebrity brides. Pascal Plessis founded London based Contrejour in 1998. The company's much imitated style is true-life reportage: 'beauty, simplicity and honesty' they state on the their website. The photography of Susie Barker and Harley Evans, of Oxford based Barker Evans, speaks for itself. It is their images that are exclusively presented here in the *Wedding Bible*, mostly of real brides from real weddings. Susie and Harley have worked together for over ten years and are in demand by brides at home and abroad for their stylish, fresh, glamorous approach to wedding photography. All our experts come from a background of press and fashion. Knowing how to react to events as they unfold, and quickly, is the key to good wedding photography.

The options for the 21st century couple seeking a photographer are numerous. Many completely reject the formal stylized photography of the past and opt for a more relaxed reportage (or documentary) style. But bad reportage – random pictures, badly framed and poorly reproduced – can be worse. A mixture of good quality, elegant portraiture and spontaneous reportage will result in a beautiful wedding album that will stand the test of time. Couple that with a beautifully shot and selectively edited wedding film, and you will have the complete story of your day forever captured for you and future generations to enjoy.

what the experts say

WHY HIRE A PROFESSIONAL PHOTOGRAPHER?

"If you ask a friend to take your wedding photographs you will get holiday snap quality. They may be good on one section of your wedding, with the people they know, but they will not capture the full story. We will give you the full story of your day," says Pascal Plessis. "I am constantly surprised at how little money couples want to spend on a photographer compared with the cost of the wedding. Especially when you consider the one thing you can keep from your day is the photographs. The reality is that good quality photography and good quality reprints cost money."

"A lot of people like the style of shots a friend can get for them. They therefore think they do not need a professional photographer," says Harley Evans. "They say they do not want the formal shots and therefore will save money and ask a friend to take their photographs for them. With a friend you will get one or two nice shots – you'll always get that – but you should not leave it to chance." For the modern bride who is likely to want a more informal reportage or documentary style of photography, the fact that it looks easy is a trap that it's all too tempting to fall into. "Bad documentary photography is awful!" says Harley. "It's just backs of heads and closed eyes because that it how it was. But in the right hands it can be glorious! Documentary does not mean failing to think about the images. A good photographer is thinking, creating and looking all the time, but no-one is aware of this creative process bubbling-away inside the photographer's head. It's about knowing when to dip-in and tease the best out of people and knowing instinctively when to draw back. That

is a skill you acquire with experience. A good wedding photographer knows how to read people so that they feel comfortable. You are often photographing them without them even being aware of it. But you are also doing this quickly and spontaneously. When you hire a professional photographer you are buying their professional expertise. That also includes expertise in processing standards, film quality and the quality of the camera. Everyone now has a digital camera, but a professional's will be head-and-shoulders above a conventional one. With a professional photographer you have a guarantee of wonderful wedding photographs."

" We think outside the box and see the event as a whole," says Susie Barker. "It's our job to get wonderful, stylish pictures. We seek-out those perfect shots. It is about knowing when to hold back and when to jump in. It is about reacting to the atmosphere of the event and reading when you can get right in there with the camera and how intimate you can be with the bride and groom. Some couples are private and don't want to share those moments with the camera, others want you to capture everything. A good and experienced wedding photographer will know how to read a couple and react accordingly. Your guests will take some great photographs, but they won't be consistently good. It's not their job to be."

So there you have it! Resist the amateur's offer. There are no short-cuts or cost-saving devices to great wedding photography. You must immediately seek-out a professional photographer!

FINDING A PHOTOGRAPHER

If you know a fabulous wedding photographer, book them straight away – even if you have yet to fix upon other details of the day. Indeed it is even worth setting the date around the availability of your chosen photographer. Personal recommendation, wedding fairs, bridal magazines, the internet and phone books, local brides' guides and professional photographic organizations are all avenues you can explore to find the right photographer for you. You do not need to get bogged-down in the detail of the technology – which is ever-changing. It doesn't matter what the format is, what matters is that you choose a photographer who produces results you like. So see several, compare styles and prices. What style of photography you are seeking will obviously determine the photographers you will be drawn to. Are you looking for reportage, formal or a mixture? Black and white, colour or both? Choose someone who specialises in what you want. If you don't know what you want, simply go for those whose style and images attract you. "Most couples have never had to think about hiring a photographer before. It can be bewildering," states Susie Barker. "You might not know whether you want formal or more natural photographs. We would always opt for both: some natural reportage and a few traditional shots of the bride and groom, their families and close friends. Those traditional family photographs that are passed down the generations are important, but you also want pictures that capture the mood and feel of the people and the day."

"Word-of-mouth is the best way to find a photographer," states Pascal Plessis. "If you know someone who has great wedding pictures, ask who took them. It's good for us too as we immediately know a bit more about you. And don't be frightened to look far afield for your photographer. One who does the same venues over and over again might well be taking the same pictures over and over again."

If you can't get a recommendation, do some research. "Select three or so photographers whose images in their ads you like," suggests Susie. "Phone them up. You'll immediately know if you like the sound of them and whether you are establishing a rapport. I can usually tell straight away whether we'll get on. Think about whether you like the way they deal with you on the phone. If you do like the sound of them, arrange to meet to see more of their work." Meeting your photographer is important. If you phone a large company and they can't tell you who will take your photographs on the day, look elsewhere.

"The first chat is really important. When a couple point-out shots from our portfolio that they like we can see where they are coming from, what they are hoping to achieve, how they see themselves on their wedding day," says Harley Evans. "Some people are extrovert and love being photographed and will flirt with the camera. Others are more reserved and our approach will therefore be different. It is about finding a way to work where the camera is not an obstacle between you and them. The couple need to feel that they are spending part of their day with me, not the camera. They need to know they can relax and feel comfortable with me. It is in those early stages when we find out about a couple and what approach we might take."

When you meet you want to see images and albums, and lots of them. They should be consistently good – remember that what you see is what you get. "It is important you are shown albums of whole weddings. Every wedding is different and you need to see that it is not the same pictures and poses over and over again," advises Susie. "Be suspicious of albums of 'best shots'. You must see pictures of at least three complete weddings."

"Check that these albums capture the atmosphere of the whole day," adds Harley. "As well as glamorous shots of the bride and groom, you are looking for great shots of the guests and family, fragments and details (flowers, dress, shoes, bouquets). Find a style that suits you and your day. But you must see consistency through a number of weddings." Pascal agrees. "Every album of every wedding should be different. You should be able to see what kind of people they are by their wedding photographs. If you see three albums with the same shots, it means the photographer is always going for the same format. If the pictures are different you can see he is committed."

A good photographer will also be quizzing you. He or she is looking to learn how the style of photography you are interested in complements the style of your wedding. They'll want information about your chosen venues, the approximate number of guests, dates and timings. This is also an opportunity for you to decide whether you like them. "Feeling relaxed and at ease with the photographer is as important as liking the work," emphasizes Susie. "Photography is a passion, but you also need a passion for people to be a good wedding photographer." Are they confident enough to direct guests in an appropriate manner, without bullying or annoying them? Will you enjoy being with them all day?

WHAT TO ASK THE PROFESSIONAL PHOTOGRAPHER

When you see what you like, you need to ask what you'll get. Photographer's wedding packages vary and it can be difficult to compare like with like. "There are many forms a package could take," advises Harley Evans. "Generally it will include the on–the–day costs for the photographer, the proofs and a certain number of reprints. You need to ask if you will get all the proofs, or just the photographer's selection? How many prints will you get in addition to the proofs, will they come in an album and what will the charge be for additional prints? You need to know the reprint price because if you want lots of them, you do not want the cost to be prohibitive."

"Some photographers, including ourselves, make their money up-front on the wedding day," says Susie Barker. "Others are cheaper on the day and make their money on the reprints. So you need to know exactly what you are getting."

The photographer owns the copyright to your wedding photographs. This is standard across the profession. "People want the negatives (or the digital file) to save money. But I want to ensure that the quality of every reprint of my images is professional. Do you know where to get photographs professionally printed to our standard? Do you know how to store the negatives or disc properly?" asks Pascal. It is unusual, but for a large fee a few photographers will sell you the negatives or the digital file. "Now that people use scanners to make their own extra prints, some photographers would rather offer the originals than have people make poor quality copies at home on their PCs to save a few pounds. But it is not something every photographer offers, neither should they feel obliged to." Remember that scanning and reproducing photographs when you do not own the copyright is against the law. Having forked–out for really good photographs surely you want top quality reprints and on paper that will not fade? "Has your printer been professionally calibrated?" asks Harley. (Do you even know what that means?) "There may come a day when you can get the best quality images at home on your computer and printer. But that day is not here yet. For now, leave it to the professionals."

The photographer's package price should include a meeting the week of the wedding. On your wedding day it should include some pictures of the bride getting ready, arrivals, the ceremony and the reception. It might not include the photographer staying to the very end of the day. So check if it will include the speeches and the first dance. If not, and you want those photographed, will they charge extra to stay? "When will you get your photographs?" asks Pascal. You should expect to receive them within two to four weeks of the wedding. "When you return from your honeymoon it can be a bit of a anticlimax, so it is nice to have the photographs to look forward to." And how will you receive them? "A good photographer is going to feel comfortable meeting-up with you to go through everything," says Harley. "But make sure you know exactly what you are going to get in your hand on that day and what your options are." Many photographers can also post your photographs on their website for friends and family to view and order directly.

Other factors that affect cost include whether you will get an engagement portrait, whether you will be presented with an album and what type of album that will be. If the photographer has to travel a long distance there may be additional expenses such as overnight accommodation. Many photographers now also offer a 'Wedding Book' – a hard–backed coffee table style story book of your day. You can create your own layout, write your own text and include details such as invitations, place cards, menus and add your honeymoon pictures. Smaller paperbacked versions can also be produced to give to family and friends. However, these are expensive!

A good photographer will be covered by professional indemnity insurance in the event of something going wrong. But it is photographs, not a cash refund you want because their car broke down or the camera jammed. "Do you want money, or do you want good photographs?" asks Pascal. "Instead of asking whether they have indemnity insurance, ask what their back–up plan is if something goes wrong."

If you are happy with both what you see and what you'll get, secure the booking without delay. But only pay a deposit when you have all the details you have agreed in writing. Also arrange a date to meet within two weeks of the wedding.

PHOTOGRAPHY PACKAGE CHECKLIST

Does the package price include expenses and VAT?

How long will the photographer be with you on the day?

Approximately how many pictures will they take?

Will you see and keep all the proofs?

Will they have PROOF stamped across them?

Will they be presented in an album?

Will they be available to view and order on–line?

What is the cost of reprints?

PHOTOGRAPHY DETAILS

On your wedding day you want to be able to leave the photographer to it. Therefore some details need to be worked-out in advance. As soon as possible your photographer will need information about timings, venues and any restrictions. Some venues, particularly religious buildings and historic houses, do not allow photography everywhere and may restrict flash photography – especially during the wedding ceremony. "If you are hiring a grand venue do not assume you have free and easy access within or around it. So if you have a location for a photograph in mind, ensure you ask if you will have access to it on the day," warns Harley Evans.

The time of year will also have some bearing on what is and is not possible. "People really love the idea of the romance of a winter wedding. You can get some fantastically atmospheric shots. But if the service is late in the afternoon just know that you are not going to have any daylight shots at all," warns Harley. If you are planning a winter wedding, lack of natural light will be your photographer's main challenge and they will need to be well-versed in low-level lighting. Therefore ensure you have seen winter weddings represented in his or her portfolio. "The conditions can be quite harsh to work around for the natural stylish shots of the couple. So discuss this with your photographer in case you decide you want some daylight time – even if it is just enough to get the guests arriving. But you could also consider having some fun with guests by setting-up a photo corner with some studio lights."

Bright sunshine also brings problems. It can bleach-out a white wedding gown, you and guests could be perspiring, eyes can be squinting and wide-brimmed hats will cast a shadow on their wearers' faces. Softer light is far more flattering than full sunshine. So if your photographer seems happier to wait for a cloud to come overhead, he knows what he is doing! "If you are marrying abroad in a hot climate the light can be too strong early in the day," warns Pascal Plessis. "Also the guests get hot and sweaty, so don't marry in the heat of the midday sun."

Have a wet weather contingency plan if you are hoping to have some formal photography outside, and discuss this in advance with your photographer. They will want to see the locations when visiting the venue (which a good photographer will want to do if they do not already know it). "Each season brings considerations of its own," adds Harley. "Don't worry about it. A good photographer will get the best out of the conditions whatever they are."

When you have a schedule for the big day's events, let your photographer have it. Discuss when and where you'd like to set aside some time for formal and family shots. "Usually after the ceremony is a good time, or at the drinks reception," advises Susie Barker. "Also look for the best backdrop for that symbolic shot, that will be passed-down through the generations, of you and your new husband on your wedding day." For your formal family portraits, your photographer will be able to offer an opinion as to the best location. "The only time we take control of the wedding is for the formal photographs," says Pascal. "You don't need to spend a long time on these pictures; everyone has come to enjoy the celebration, not to wait and watch you having your photograph taken. Just twenty minutes or so."

"That's plenty of time," agrees Susie. "You can still get the groups without the formal poses. I spend a lot of time photographing groups of guests. I follow the bride and groom around and take some shots.

Sometimes I'll ask people to put their heads together and take a very informal shot with them all looking into the camera."

Also build into your day some informal time with your photographer. "Documentary style photography, whilst it will produce lots of natural shots, might not produce the volume of romantic images that you are looking for. So set—aside five or ten minutes to wander hand—in—hand around the venue and let the photographer document it. That is a really good way to get some great shots of you together," is Harley's tip.

For your formal photos avoid giving your photographer a long shot list. A list of faceless names will mean nothing to them. "I just ask to be told in advance who is important so that I know I have got them. I want to tune into the day rather than dictate how it will be photographed." says Susie. Harley agrees. "You don't want a long shot list as that makes the wedding uncreative. But you do need to satisfy family, parents and grandparents. It is the one opportunity where you have family members together. It doesn't have to be outside the church either. Indeed it is

better to find a good backdrop at the reception when everyone has had a chance to say hello and relax with a drink. Just draw the family together in a group, look directly into the camera, and get something that is glamorous and stylish."

Also tell your photographer if there are any family dynamics that might affect how people behave on the day. "I need to know if anything has happened recently, like a death in the family, or if a parent is not there for some reason, whether there are divorced parents who have remarried, children and stepchildren. The formal photographs can be a bit of an ordeal for some family members. I don't want anyone to be uncomfortable. So just set aside the right amount of time and decide who, where and when, together with your photographer," says Harley. Also tell your photographer anything you think he needs to know about you. "I want to know everything!" says Pascal. "Even the sad stories that are part of your life and that have brought you here. It is really important to understand the people you are photographing. That is why meetings are so crucial."

PHOTOGRAPHY AT THE EVENT

Arrange to meet your photographer a week to ten days before the wedding. If that is not possible, set aside half an hour to speak to one another over the telephone. Run through the detailed schedule for the day and discuss timings. Ensure your groom knows to arrive at the ceremony at least forty-five minutes before it starts. This will give your photographer time to get some nice shots of him, his best man and the ushers. A phone call from you to the best man to advise him to tell the ushers to arrive in good time is probably not a bad idea!

On the day just trust your photographer and leave him or her to it. "The best tip for great photographs is to just be yourself. Anything contrived shows," warns Harley Evans. "So many people adopt a camera pose. They think they will look better if they raise their chins or hold themselves in. They don't! Adopting an unnatural pose produces an unnatural style."

"Pictures are about movement. Keep moving, keep talking and looking into the lens." says Pascal Plessis.

"Keep make-up natural with a matte finish," advises Susie Barker. "But we do not have any input into how you look on the day. It's not our job or area of expertise. It is up to us to photograph you well, not for you to make it happen. That is why you have hired a professional photographer. We know all the tricks of the trade and will make you look gorgeous." Pascal warns not to apply make-up with a shimmer which will make you appear shiny on the photographs. And watch-out when kissing your groom in bright red lipstick. "The couple spend all day kissing and the groom ends up looking like a strawberry!"

Be careful not to drink too much before or during the wedding celebrations. "The groom can usually get away with it, but never the bride," states Pascal. "A drunk bride does not look nice and looks terrible in the photographs." When you have cut the cake a lovely shot is you feeding it to one another. If the budget will stretch, a confetti gun (which you can hire from a party shop) fired over you during the first dance or as you enter or leave the wedding breakfast also looks great. But the biggest secret to wonderful wedding photography: "A bride and groom in love!" says Pascal. "If there is real love showing, you will have happy guests and great photographs!"

VIDEOGRAPHY

"Everyone has seen bad wedding videos, even bad professionally-made ones," says *GMTV's* Michael Metcalf. And he's right! Happily, out-of-focus, wobbly, sloppily edited wedding videos with terrible soundtracks are easily avoidable. For a slick, polished wedding day film that captures the key moments of your day in an enjoyable and imaginative way, hire a professional. If your budget won't stretch, have a couple of enthusiastic amateurs read this chapter and make a simple video. It won't be worthy of a BAFTA, but with Michael Metcalf's advice it won't be embarrassing and will be watchable.

HIRING A PROFESSIONAL VIDEOGRAPHER

Memories are priceless. However, capturing them on film is expensive. That's because, in addition to the labour costs, the equipment used to shoot and edit your wedding film is expensive. Be suspicious of anyone able to offer you what they describe as a professional wedding film on-the-cheap. A good and experienced video company may provide two camera operators on the day. They will shoot up to ten hours of footage. Not all videographers are good editors, so a third professional may be employed to sort, select and edit the material and turn it into your fabulous wedding day film. That could take him or her several days. Do not underestimate the importance of good editing. It is not just what you film that counts but how it is put together. Where many wedding videos disappoint is in the editing; it's the extra time the skilled professionals give to this process that transforms a mediocre film into a masterpiece.

The individuals you entrust with this once-in-a-lifetime purchase must demonstrate expertise in both filming and editing. It might be that one person possesses both skills, but they must be able to demonstrate this to you. If you can't secure the services of a good professional locally, cast your net far and wide because many will travel. As always, a recommendation from someone you trust is the best place to start your search. Professional bodies, such as the Association of Professional Videomakers *(www.apv.org.uk)* can assist.

As with photography, what you see is what you get. Therefore, before hiring professionals, ask to view at least three complete wedding videos or DVDs – not edited highlights, compilations or montages from several weddings – but entire events. View them from start to finish. If you are bored so will the viewers of your wedding film be! Ensure you have seen the key moments of the day captured on film (the guests arriving, the groom waiting for his bride, her procession down the aisle, a selection of shots from the marriage service, the cake cutting, the first dance etc.). You will notice any bad camera work; camera movements should be slick and smooth, everything should be in focus with no fast zooms in and out. Watch for good colour balance and clarity, good lighting (you'll notice if it is bad) with no sudden cuts or distorted sound. The film should not just capture the bride and groom, but the atmosphere and flavour of the entire day. "In my view the video should not run longer than an hour," states Michael. "All too often people shoot a wedding video which runs longer than the *'Lord of the Rings'* trilogy. Your friends and family do not want to sit through the entire day again. They want to be reminded of the best and most enjoyable moments. A really good wedding video is a record and celebration of the day, not a documentary. Some of the best I've made are where the service is simply set to beautiful and evocative music chosen by the couple which runs all the way through. The film starts with the guests arriving, the groom waiting anxiously, wonderful shots of the bride's arrival, the exchanging of glances. It's a celebration and the music drives it through."

Ensure that the person or people who will shoot and edit your video worked on the ones you have viewed. When you are happy with what and who you have found discuss details. What will they charge and what is included? How many cameras were used in the videos you viewed and how many will they provide on the day? (It's well worth paying the additional cost for an extra camera operator if you can afford to, as it offers more flexibility. One camera can shadow the bride and groom whilst the other captures everything else.) How many copies will you be given and what is the cost of additional DVDs? Will they keep the original material (as is normal) or can you purchase it? When will they arrive on the day and how long will they stay? What is their back-up plan in the event of camera failure? How long will the final version of your film run, will the cover be personalised and can you choose the text? Will the film include any sequences set to music, can you choose that music and will it cost extra? Will they include short sound bites of guests comments or greetings? Can you add a message or thank you on the credits? Will you be able to view the film before the final edit and be able to ask for any changes (a common complaint is the accidental omission of important family members)? How long after the wedding will you receive the finished product?

You should also expect the professionals to ask you questions. In addition to seeking the obvious information about where and when the wedding will take place, are they finding out about you? To make a truly watchable video they need to get as much information about you and your families as possible. Are they asking you about the style of the event, who will be important on the day and how you are going to identify these people to them? It is often a good idea to assign a bridesmaid or usher to liaise with the videographer and point-out the significant people. "The pretty young things in the gorgeous outfits are not necessarily those the bride and groom want to be reminded of in years to come. It's the shots of Granny and family that are important. I've been caught-out before by camera operators at celebrity weddings who only film the celebs. The couple don't just want shots of them, they want to see shots of all the people they love!"

Do not part with cash or sign a contract until you have satisfied yourselves that you will receive a well-shot, high-quality production along the lines you are satisfied with.

VIDEOGRAPHY AT THE EVENT

Whether hiring a professional or using an enthusiastic amateur videographer, it is essential you properly brief them. They need to have a detailed schedule of the day's timings, exactly when and where everything is happening and who is in charge. "If the wedding includes a religious service, check what is and isn't allowed and tell the videographer. Don't assume he knows," states Michael. Request permission for the presence of a videographer from the person officiating at the ceremony: some religious venues will not allow filming and most impose some restrictions. Seek advance confirmation, don't be disappointed on your wedding day because you failed to check.

If the videographer is unfamiliar with the form of your marriage service, inform him. Tell him about the key elements and what he must capture on film. Also advise him of any customs or practices he needs to know about, including dress code. If he has to take his shoes off or cover his head don't let it be a surprise on the day. The videographer needs to feel comfortable and confident to work at his best.

Ensure you have introduced your photographer and videographer beforehand, or brief your groom to do this on the day. They need to work together at certain points and be sensitive to one another's presence. As with your photographer, trust the videographer on the day to do their job. Be yourself in front of the camera and don't try any trickery in an attempt to make yourself look better – that's their job.

VIDEOGRAPHY PACKAGE CHECKLIST

Does the package price include expenses and VAT?

How many cameras will be present on the day?

Approximately how long will the edited video/DVD run?

Will there be an additional charge for music?

How many copies are provided within the package price and how much will extra copies cost?

How will the film be packaged and do you have any input?

AVOIDING A VIDEO NASTY:
TIPS FOR THE AMATEUR VIDEOGRAPHER

According to our expert, Michael Metcalf, the top-tip for the amateur videographer is to keep it simple. "You are not Steven Spielberg! The ultimate aim is to make something watchable. The mistake so many amateurs make is that they try and be too clever. They take too many risks with the camera and end-up with a lot of unusable material. When I make a wedding video I constantly ask myself, 'Would I watch this as a TV viewer at home? Would it be of interest to me if I did not know the couple?' The trick is to make it look like a professional programme and not a home video."

Researching their subject is a priority for any film maker. Michael advises the amateur to ascertain from the couple what they are expecting from their wedding video. "Remember it is not a documentary. It should be a series of images capturing the key moments and highlights of the day and offering the viewer a flavour of the atmosphere." Do you really need a long record of the day, including every aspect of the service and unedited speeches. "Would you not prefer edited highlights, set to music, interspersed with what we in the trade call "voxpops" (sound bites from guests)? A film that simply captures the day is a record of it and presented in a watchable and enjoyable format of a reasonable length. No-one wants to watch more than an hour."

If you can find two enthusiastic amateurs all the better! One can follow the bride and groom and the other can film everything else. But what are the tricks-of-the-trade that these amateurs can employ? "We have in TV a term called 'cutaways'. These are the shots that form a bridge between sequences," says Michael. For example, you can't edit a shot of the bride getting out of a car straight to a shot of her at the alter. The film will look as though it has 'jumped'. You need to insert a relevant short shot of something else in-between – perhaps a close-up of some flowers or a shot of the venue's exterior. "At weddings there are literally hundreds of cutaways you can film: flowers, architectural details, candles, bouquets, table settings, guests! Film lots of them, keep them simple and slow and be careful of zooms in and out. Try and make every shot a useable one. A wedding is not a race, there is a lot of waiting around, so you have plenty of time to get some good shots and there is plenty of detail you can film."

New digital cameras will solve many of the problems previously associated with lighting. A word of warning, however, if you are filming people in front of windows. "Expose the camera for their faces because it will automatically expose for the strongest light level. If you don't have the correct exposure the faces will be a silhouette.

"Audio is a big problem with wedding videos and it's importance is often overlooked. It is crucial to get a microphone as close to the action as possible. You can't switch the camera off during the service or you'll lose the sound and won't be able to edit it together. If the couple wear microphones, it looks awful, so how are you going to hear them? You could rig-up a microphone beforehand, but where are you going to position it to pick up everything you need? How are you going to hear the readings, for example? It's really difficult. I'd advise simply setting the service to music, then you can get lots of beautiful shots and edit together the highlights and most moving images. It will be more watchable too."

If you have got two cameras available have one of them positioned at a good vantage point to capture the bride and groom during the ceremony. Use a tripod to keep the camera steady. The other camera operator can film the guests, and if he is allowed to move around a little (he'll need permission from the person officiating at the ceremony) he can film a variety of different shots and images. Both cameras can film the procession and recession from agreed camera positions which will offer greater flexibility at the editing stage.

"If the videographer is going to record any of the music, he needs to keep recording during the whole of it. If he doesn't, when it comes to editing the music, some of it will be missing! Although obvious, it is an easy mistake to make," warns Michael. Remember this during the speeches and with the first dance too.

"For a really professional production get lots of shots of people – as many as you can. If possible, get them when they arrive and whilst seated waiting for the bride to arrive. Start the film with some beautiful music and wonderful shots of the guests arriving. Also, film the groom; brides love to see the groom waiting for her. I had one bride who was so surprised to see her groom pacing up and down and rubbing his brow. She said she had no idea he had been so nervous because he's normally very composed.

"After the ceremony, the pre-wedding breakfast drinks usually last around an hour. You don't need to film an hour of material, just about fifteen minutes which can be edited down to about two minutes. Use the rest of the time to get guests to say a few words to camera and to film the details in the room where the wedding breakfast will be. Film the flowers, the table centres, the favours, the cake. These are the details the bride will not have time to take-in, but they are the very things she has spent many months planning. These shots are also great cutaways to take you from one sequence to another when editing the film together. When the guests come in, film them taking their seats, but don't film them eating; just get a close-up or two of the plated food and switch the camera off until the speeches start."

With the speeches, again consider if you really do need them in their entirety. You can always ask for a written copy as a record. If you do want them on film, the videographer will need to rig a microphone and film the speaker not the guests. If you have two cameras, however, one can concentrate on the guests' reactions. The speeches can then be cut down to edited highlights.

"The videographer must remember that it is the bride and groom's day," warns Michael. "He should be in the background observing the event. The guests are there to see the bride and groom and enjoy the wedding. They can't do that if the videographer is constantly in the way. If you are not experienced with camera work, just keep it simple. No crash zooms in or out or attempting to be clever. Keep all the shots slow and make them useable. It's worth using a tripod, especially for the ceremony and speeches, as the shots will be steadier. Try not to over-or under-shoot and get lots of cutaways. Remember to hold each shot for a few seconds before cutting."

MICHAEL METCALF'S AMATEUR VIDEOGRAPHY TIPS

Keep it simple – you are not Steven Spielberg!

Two cameras offer more flexibility than one.

Research your subject – learn as much as you can about the key players and venues in advance.

Check on filming restrictions with venues and officiants.

You do not have to make a documentary – produce an entertaining, watchable wedding film of the highlights of the day.

Make every shot useable. Keep shots simple and slow with no fast zooms in and out. Hold each shot for several seconds before cutting.

Do not attempt to reproduce the service and speeches in their entirety.

Consider using music sequences.

If recording music, record the whole of it to avoid problems when editing.

Get lots of shots of guests – especially their arrival.

Ask someone to be assigned to you who knows close family and friends.

Shoot plenty of cutaways and film all the details.

Use a tripod to steady the camera when filming the service and speeches.

Introduce yourself to the photographer and work with them so as not to get in their way.

Remember to stay in the background observing the event.

VIDEOGRAPHER'S KEY SHOTS LIST

Guests' arrival
Groom, best man and ushers seating guests
Bride's arrival and procession
Ceremony highlights
First kiss
Bride and groom's recession
Key family members
Receiving line
Drinks reception highlights
Sound bites from guests
Details (flowers, table centrepieces etc.)
Plated food (a few simple shots)
Toasts
Cake cutting
First dance
Bride and groom's departure

PHOTOGRAPHY AND VIDEOGRAPHY TIPS

Hire a professional photographer – amateurs' images will not be consistently good.

Opt for a mixture of relaxed reportage photography with a few traditional formal portraits and groups.

Meet photographers and videographers before booking them. If you cannot be told who will be photographing or filming your wedding day, look elsewhere.

Ask photographers to show you albums of whole weddings, not best shots. Look for consistency and whether they have captured the atmosphere of the day. What you see is what you'll get.

Ask videographers to show you videos or DVDs of complete weddings, not edited highlights or montages of the best shots from several events. Look for expertise in both filming and editing. Is the style of the film similar to that which you are looking for?

Preferably have two video cameras filming your wedding.

Consider an edited version of the marriage service, capturing the highlights and set to music.

If having a winter wedding or marrying abroad, check similar weddings are included amongst your photographer and videographer's portfolios.

Ensure you like and are at ease with the professionals – they'll be with you all day.

Ask for a detailed breakdown of costs including the cost of reprints with your photographer and extra copies of the film with your videographer.

Ask what the back-up plan is in the event of something going wrong.

Check photography and videography restrictions with your venue(s) and those conducting the marriage ceremony. Is flash photography allowed and can photographers and videographers move around?

Ensure you have informed professionals of the form of your marriage ceremony if they are not familiar with it. Advise of customs or practices, including dress code.

Have a wet weather contingency plan for the formal photographs if outside.

Set-aside some informal time with your photographer on your wedding day for some informal shots of you and your groom.

Don't have your photography or videography requirements dictate the day. Avoid long shot lists.

No camera poses – stay natural.

Don't drink too much – it looks terrible in the photographs and worse on film!

On the day, trust the professionals to do their job.

photography and videography

ideas

AS SOON AS YOU'VE SET THE DATE

Select a style of photography you like and find a photographer who matches it.

Find a really good videographer or ask a couple of keen amateurs to film your wedding. Ensure you are clear about the style of wedding film you require.

decisions

6 – 4 MONTHS TO GO

Check on photography or videography restrictions with your venue(s) and pass on details to your photographer and videographer.

Arrange to visit the venue(s) with them if they are unfamiliar with it.

Give your photographer and videographer provisional on–the–day timings as soon as you have them.

4-phase timeline

details

UP TO A MONTH TO GO

Decide with your photographer where your formal photographs will be taken.

Have a wet weather contingency plan if outside.

Agree what time your photographer and videographer will arrive on the day.

event

AND THE WEEK PRECEDING THE WEDDING

Confirm details and timings with your photographer and videographer and when and where they will be arriving.

Give the photographer and videographer your 'Wedding Day Schedule' and 'Wedding Day Contact List' (page 248). Tell them who to liaise with in the event of a problem.

Assign an usher or bridesmaid to direct the photographer and videographer to important friends and family. Ensure this is someone who can recognise the key people.

Advise the groom and best man what time the photographer and videographer will meet them before the ceremony. Ensure they've told the ushers.

Remember to feed your photographer and videographer – they are with you all day!

all the rest

In this chapter we cover everything we've not mentioned so far. To keep you organized, we share with you how we store and keep track of guest information when arranging weddings. You'll then know at a glance who has replied, who needs special food, who has small children, where you will seat guests and what gifts you've received. Our Wedding Bible Company designer has some tips about wedding stationery and we offer suggestions on how to draw-up a successful seating plan. To assist with your gift list, we've sought advice from professionals working in the retail side of the wedding business. Finally, you may take your husband's name as soon as you are married, but who will need to know and under what name will you book your honeymoon, and does it matter?

Happy guests make happy weddings! But weddings can be expensive events to attend. There are travel costs, often accommodation to pay for, a gift to buy, sometimes a new outfit or hat is required and drinks might need to be purchased at the bar during the reception. From the moment your invitation falls on their door mat, indicate to your guests that they'll be well-looked-after and that you appreciate the effort they are making on your behalf. Your invitation is the first hint at the style and formality of your wedding day or week-end. Enclose with it as much additional information about the celebration as possible. As well as being witnesses to your union, it is important your guests feel included. If friends or family are likely to be unfamiliar with aspects of your celebration (perhaps because yours will be a multi cultural one, or because your religious service will be new to them) give advance warning about what to expect, especially if they will be required to observe or participate in perhaps unfamiliar customs or practices.

what the experts say

GUEST SPREADSHEET

The easiest way to keep track of your guest information is to create a 'Guest Spreadsheet' on your computer. In addition to names and addresses and responses to invitations, include columns across the top of the spreadsheet for everything relevant to your celebration. For example, dietary considerations, accommodation details, table number, gift received and thank-you note posted. Enter guests' last names in the first column and forenames in the second. Type adults' names in capital letters and children's names in lower case. If people in a couple invited do not share the same last name, leave the partner's first column entry blank, and enter their full name in the second column. This will ensure your guest numbers are accurate, that you can see at a glance who is accompanying whom and who has children.

Work to one spreadsheet – this is crucial to avoid losing information. Decide who is in charge of it. Only they should add and remove details. Always keep a back-up and print a hard copy when amendments are made. When you have received all guests' replies, you can save a second copy with the names of those not attending deleted. Thus you will have a master list to work from for your table plan. You can see an example of a' Guest Spreadsheet' on our website and can find one in the *Wedding Bible Planner* (see *www.weddingbible.co.uk*)

STATIONERY & INVITATIONS

There is more to wedding stationery than simply invitations. In addition, you might want to send engagement announcements, 'Save the Day' cards and thank-you notes as your gifts arrive. For your wedding day you may choose to print Order of Service sheets, menu and place cards and a table plan. Your stationery can set or reflect your wedding day style or theme. It's also the first indication your guests have about the formality and style of your celebration. Wedding Bible Company designer, Yvonne Macken, has designed stationery for numerous weddings. "The style of your stationery will often be an expression of your personalities. That doesn't mean you have to hand-make it or have it custom designed. You can order beautiful, high quality predesigned stationery on the high street and in department stores. The cost benefit is that you are not paying a set-up charge for a one-off job. Generally you choose from a set of designs and your personal details are added, often with a choice of typeface. Features such as embossing, gold and silver foiling or intricate and ornate cut-outs will cost less than bespoke stationery from a printer. There is so much choice you are bound to find a style that is 'you'. Matching stationery will look really smart and many of your guests will keep the printed items from the wedding as a memento of the day, so give them something to treasure!"

If you want to produce your own design, have a chat with a local printer. He or she will be able to assist you with both layout and design if required. "Your stationery is a great opportunity for you to stamp your mark on the day," advises Yvonne. "When the Wedding Bible Company arranged the wedding of television presenter, Kate Garraway, I was inspired both by the couple and the venue they chose when designing their stationery. Kate and her husband, Derek Draper, have a great sense of humour – slightly mischievous – so I thought I'd design a little caricature of them and use it as the thematic image on all their printed stationery. However, it also needed to be stylish and glamorous to match the style and formality of their celebration. So I used the Art Deco venue as my starting point. I took photographs of the mirrors, carpet patterns and decorative detail and colour-matched them with the materials used in the ballroom where the wedding breakfast took place. On-line I searched for images from the twenties and thirties and period posters to further inspire me. I found the perfect image of a twenties couple which formed the basis of my drawing of Kate and Derek. If you decide to go down the quirky and individual route, there are things you need to consider, such as the appropriateness of the design and how it suits the style of your celebration. In the case of Kate and Derek, I printed the caricature very small on the reverse of the Order of Service sheets. Thus it provided a reference point, indicated that it was part of the stationery set, but was at the same time respectful to the solemnity of the religious marriage ceremony. I was then able to exaggerate it on the menu cards, place names, table plans and the gift and luggage tags we also made for them. It was a fun way to give potentially ordinary items a little pizzazz."

You may have a photograph or a picture you would like to use and a printer can scan this professionally and incorporate it in your design. Before securing a printer's services, ask to see examples of their work and get cost estimates in writing. Confirm deadlines and allow time for delays with proofing and any changes required. The cost does not have to be significantly more than predesigned stationery, but bear in mind any additional touches will add to the price. "If you select an ornate typeface, make sure it is legible, especially the numbers. If you are hand-writing stationery, that too needs to be easy to read, however neat your writing. In addition to a traditional fountain pen, you can also try calligraphy pens and rollerballs which give a lovely finish."

A traditional wedding invitation is a folded 8 x 6 inch white card. The text is engraved on the front, states who is hosting the event and includes the words 'request the pleasure of your company'. The names of the guests are hand written on the top left hand corner in black ink (some couples employ a calligrapher to do this). Traditional or otherwise, the wording on your invitations should include the following information:

> Full name(s) of the host(s).
> Bride's first name and her relationship to the host(s)
> Bridegroom's title and full name.
> Ceremony Address.
> Date and time of the ceremony.
> Reception address (if different).
> *RSVP* address.

When sending your invitations, give your guests as much information as possible. Include as appropriate: an accommodation list, maps and directions, details of other wedding-related gatherings, information about public transport and local taxi numbers. Order your invitations at least three months before the wedding. Post them ten to eight weeks in advance. Two-weeks before, chase up anyone who has failed to respond.

Providing a reply card with pre-addressed envelopes will speed-up the response process. You can also ask for dietary preferences to be indicated on the card as well as details of where out-of-town guests will be staying (that information may be useful to you if you are providing transport, or if additional events are being planned before and after the wedding). If you know where guests are staying you could leave a note welcoming them. At Wedding Bible weddings we often arrange a welcome pack which includes a bottle of wine, nibbles and a hangover cure!

WEDDING STATIONERY CHECKLIST

Engagement Announcements

'Save the Day' cards

Invitations

Reply cards & addressed envelopes

Invitation enclosures :	Maps & directions
	Accommodation list
	Public transport information
	Taxi telephone numbers
	Additional information as appropriate
Wedding Day Stationery:	Orders of Service
	Menu cards
	Seating cards
	Place cards
	Table plan
	Thank-you cards

GIFT LIST

Traditionally, a gift list existed to help couples set-up-home together. Typically it included china, glass, linens and kitchenware. The bride's mother managed the list, sending-out relevant information on request. Nowadays most newlyweds will already have homes of their own (not necessarily together) and will have accumulated the household basics. Thus today's gift lists are more 'wish lists' ensuring you receive at least some of the items you want or need.

The first wedding-list service was developed by London's General Trading Company nearly a century ago. The store was founded to provide newly married couples with everything they'd require for their new home. Today, most large high street stores have gift registry services where guests can browse and shop on-line. Specialist wedding list shops also exist around the country. A gift list avoids duplication of presents and most companies will allow you to change your mind and exchange items before they are delivered.

Gift list services usually take only a limited number of clients and work on a 'first-come-first-served basis'. Therefore, register at least six months before your big day. "Before registering with a company or store, check you are being offered an expert opinion as you shop," advises Giles Rees, head of the Wedding List at the General Trading Company. "Do they offer a personal, face to face service? Are sales staff on hand to advise both you and your guests? Can you see products on-line?" Three or four months before the wedding, allow at least half a day to draw up the list in-store so that it is up-and-running before you send your invitations. Once opened, you'll be updated weekly about the progress of the list, know who has given you what, and be able to alter and add items if necessary. Guests will be able to buy in-store, over the phone and on-line. Most registry services deliver free of charge either as gifts are purchased or all at once when the list has been closed. Guests who prefer to give your present in person will be able to take delivery themselves upon purchase.

Giles says the most successful lists – those where everything is purchased – include a variety of items to suit all budgets. But with the larger department stores offering a choice of around half a million products, where do you start? "Have a really good look at what you've already got between you and come with an idea of what you think you need," advises Kerry McCulloch, head of the John Lewis Gift List. "Start with the basics: crockery, kitchenware, linens and household items. Include some hobby gifts, perhaps a BBQ and garden furniture. You might also want a second dinner service or something special."

It was traditionally frowned-upon to mention gifts in an invitation, but most couples now consider it acceptable to mail gift list details with their invitations. If you decide to do this, include details discreetly – perhaps at the bottom of an accommodation list or with directions. Record all the gifts on your 'Guest Spreadsheet' as they arrive. Don't expect all your guests to purchase from your list, and accept all gifts graciously, writing a thank-you note as you receive them. Alternatively, wait and send a card with a photograph from the wedding when you return from honeymoon. Arrange a secure area at the reception for gifts brought on the day, and assign someone (usually the best man) to deliver them to your home.

SEATING PLAN

A good seating plan is crucial to the success of any wedding reception where you will be sharing a meal. Even if you are planning a buffet-style lunch or dinner, a seating plan is a good idea. It avoids a chaotic, unseemly rush for places and couples being separated, ensures important guests are seated where they can see and hear everything, and allows you to place people together who you believe will enjoy each other's company. It can be a difficult and time-consuming task, so set aside at least an afternoon, about ten days before the wedding, to properly complete it.

There are no hard and fast rules to table planning, but generally it is best to seat people of a similar age together and to look for things that guests have in common. By the time you are ready to work on the seating plan you should have a table plan indicating how tables will be arranged in the room, how many people will be seated at each one and where you will place your top table (see 'Tables & Place Settings' page 79). Attempt an even balance between men and women, with couples seated on the same table, but not necessarily together. Your immediate family and close friends should be seated at tables near to, or surrounding, the top table.

Do not print the plan until you are certain there will be no changes made to it. If having it professionally printed, discuss the deadline with your printer. Display the seating plan at the reception on an easel or easels where they can be easily seen. If there will be more than eighty guests consider individual seating cards with guests' names and table numbers, either set out on a table alphabetically, or distributed by older children or a bridesmaid during the drinks reception. Give a copy of the table and seating plans to your caterers, highlighting those guests with specific dietary requirements. Remember to order high chairs for infants.

TIPS FOR CREATING THE PERFECT SEATING PLAN

Place each person next to at least one other they already know.

Seat speech makers where they will not have their backs to anyone, if possible.

Place young children next to, or between, their parents.

Consider a children's table for those aged over seven. Place this in the least favourable position!

Avoid mixing age groups, unless family.

Ensure a balance between men and women at each table and alternate wherever possible.

Sit families together and place work colleagues on their own table.

Look for things guests have in common and for a balance between extroverts and those of a more reserved disposition.

Do not seat all the single guests together. Work them into the seating plan early to avoid using them to fill places.

If you know people do not get on, seat them apart from each other.

Be considerate to the needs of the elderly and any disabled guests.

TOP TIPS FOR THE PERFECT SEATING PLAN

THE HONEYMOON

Don't leave arranging your honeymoon too late. As soon as you have set the date and secured a venue, start planning. You will be glad later that you took the time to get it right and allocated funds when budgeting for the rest of the wedding. Traditionally it is the groom's responsibility. If he is happy to take the lead, it's another task delegated so let him! If he wants the destination to be a surprise, ask for an indication of what to pack.

Co-ordinate your schedules to determine the dates to book. The tradition of dashing-off to catch a train, boat or plane before the reception is over has long passed. Consider allowing a couple of days before departing on honeymoon to climb down from your wedding day high, and enjoy a lazy day or two at your first night venue.

Officials are under no obligation to accept your marriage certificate as proof of identity if your tickets do not match the name in your passport. If you want to travel in your married name, apply to the Passport Office for a new passport not earlier than three months before the wedding day, and not less than a month before. Your registrar will need to sign the application form to confirm the wedding date, and your passport will not be valid until then. Check visa and inoculation requirements in good time, order foreign currency and take-out travel insurance (if you already have a policy which includes free cover for a spouse, advise the insurers of your impending change in marital status to ensure you are both covered). Always stress to tour operators, travel agents, airlines and hotels when booking that you will be on honeymoon as they may offer upgrades or special packages. Take your marriage certificate with you in case you need to prove you are honeymooners.

NAME CHANGE

There is no legal requirement for you to change your surname when you marry. But if, like most women, you decide to do so, your marriage certificate is the only documentary evidence you will require to prove your change of name. However, if you want to add your husband's name without surrendering your maiden name, you can only do this by deed poll. Legally you are adding your maiden name as a middle name. If you wish to do this for signing on your wedding day you should apply to the UK Deed Poll Service at least two weeks before (you can do this on-line at *www.ukdps.co.uk*). Because your name change is officially by deed poll, you will only need this document as proof. Remember to also indicate the change in your marital status when advising of your name change.

Even when retaining your maiden name, some institutions insist it is a requirement to advise of the change in your marital status – particularly insurance and mortgage companies. To do this, and to advise of a name change, you will need to provide your marriage certificate or deed poll (not copies) as proof. You might also want to consider seeking advice about drawing-up wills.

HONEYMOON CHECKLIST

Ensure the name on your tickets matches the name in your passport.

Check visa and inoculation requirements in good time.

Confirm travel details and flight times the week of the wedding.

Gather together passports, tickets, driving licences, insurance certificate and currency. Agree who is responsible for them and where they will be stored before and during the wedding.

Travel with your marriage certificate in case you need to prove you are honeymooners.

NAME CHANGE CHECKLIST

Bank

Building society

Mortgage company

Credit & store cards

Insurance companies

DVLA (driving licence)

Inland Revenue (quoting your National Insurance number)

Utility companies

Subscription services

Doctor & dentist

Passport

wedding week

It's your wedding week and everything is arranged! The key now is to delegate what tasks remain, get plenty of rest and enjoy what is essentially double–checking what you have already put in place. If you have been organized and have chosen reliable suppliers (which you will have done by asking them the right questions!) your wedding week and day will run like clockwork. Have confidence in those to whom you have entrusted your day – if something unexpected occurs, they will have a contingency plan. If the wedding party know what is required of them, everything will run smoothly, so go through their duties with them. Pay particular attention to the ushers. It is their responsibility to guide guests and help them to their seats, but also to make sure all the guests are where they should be and have everything they need. Make a special effort to be on time for all appointments this week – and especially on your wedding day.

In the last few days complete the tasks in the final checklists on the following pages (not everything applies to everyone – so do not feel overwhelmed when glancing through them). Delegate what you can to a trustworthy friend or relative. When working on your 'Wedding Day Schedule' (page 249), if you have not already done so, decide who is in charge on the day – it should not be either of you. If the best man is not naturally a good decision maker or reliable enough, appoint someone who is. They should liaise with the celebrant at the ceremony and banqueting manager (or wedding co-ordinator) at the reception. If your wedding is being hosted from home, ensure your mother (or you, if at your home) has appointed someone to be in charge who knows where everything is. Create the 'Wedding Day Schedule' mainly so everyone involved knows what is happening and when.

Check what should be in your 'Ceremony Box' and 'Reception Box' (page 249). If you can't fit everything in, write on the lid with a thick marker pen the extras to be included. Appoint someone as their keeper and ensure they are delivered and securely stored, if necessary.

Place all the make–up you'll require in a shoe box or bag. Also have tweezers, nail scissors, a nail file, safety pins, a needle and thread (or hotel sewing kit), spare tights, cotton wool and cleansing wipes handy. Prepare your 'Bride's SOS Kit' (page 249) and place it in the 'Reception Box' (if you are staying at the reception venue, have it handy in your room instead). Lay your clothes and accessories out the night before.

You are likely to have people with you on the day (such as bridesmaids) who bring bags and belongings which will need to be returned to them at the end of the evening. Purchase some cheap luggage tags and use them on the day to label bags with names and destinations. Delegate the task of transporting them – bridesmaids should not arrive at the ceremony with plastic bags in tow! If you are getting ready at an hotel, ask others to remove their belongings before you depart for the ceremony – you don't want bridesmaids knocking on your door on your wedding night!

Sleep, or at least rest, as much as you can during the last few days. Avoid alcohol and drink plenty of water. On your wedding morning, eat breakfast. Limit those around you – willing hands can become clumsy feet! Have only those you really want or need near you. Get dressed somewhere quiet with good lighting and enough power points. To remove stains use soda water. If you get pollen on your clothes do not brush, rub or wet the stain – tack it off with sticky tape. And no hugging bridesmaids or mothers when their corsages are affixed – you will squash the flowers! Read page 250 a couple of days before your wedding day.

You've done it – now let's get this show on the road!

WEDDING WEEK CHECKLIST

Confirm final guest numbers with venue/caterer.

Arrange with your venue for food, and an area to sit down and eat, for suppliers and professionals (eg. photographer, videographer, entertainers) who will be at the reception.

Complete seating plan and take to printers.

Check honeymoon details and gather together passports and travel documents (agree who will store them until the day of departure).

Confirm access times for suppliers with venue(s).

Confirm on-the-day contact details, delivery times and addresses with all suppliers.

Inform florist of final buttonhole and corsage requirements and agree delivery details.

Confirm first dance with band/DJ.

Compile and distribute 'Wedding Day Schedule' and 'Wedding Day Contact List'.

Collect hired outfits (delegate their return).

Collect wedding gown and accessories.

Arrange manicures and beauty treatments as required.

Confirm rehearsal times with those attending.

Collect Orders of Service and reception stationery.

Arrange for a 'wedding announcement' in local or national newspaper if required.

Prepare fees due on the day, place in envelopes in 'Ceremony Box' or 'Reception Box' as appropriate.

Double-check that the wedding party know and understand their roles and arrival times.

If doing your own make-up have a trial run.

Pack for honeymoon.

Wrap gifts for wedding party.

Deliver or delegate delivery of the 'Ceremony Box' and the 'Reception Box'.

WEDDING DAY CONTACT LIST

Create an on-the-day contact list of telephone and mobile numbers of everyone playing a key role in the wedding, including suppliers and venues. Distribute it to everyone on the list. Do not include yourselves. If something goes wrong, or is delayed, allow others to solve the problem.

Adapt the list below as appropriate.

WEDDING PARTY

Best man
Chief bridesmaid
Mother of the bride
Father of the Bride
Ushers
Groom's home/hotel
Bride's home/hotel
Groom's parents
Readers
Additional helpers

SUPPLIERS AND PROFESSIONALS

Hairdresser
Make-up artist
Florist
Photographer
Venue(s)
Registrar/officiant
Cake company
Caterer
Transport/drivers
Videographer
Band/DJ/Musicians/Entertainers
Toastmaster/Master of Ceremonies
Local taxi firm

CEREMONY BOX

'Wedding Day Schedule'
'Wedding Day Contact List'
Instructions for ushers
Orders of Service
Buttonhole/corsage List
Mini sewing kit (including a shirt button)
Fees for officiant and venue
Wipes to remove lipstick marks from groom's face!

RECEPTION BOX

'Wedding Day Schedule'
'Wedding Day Contact List'
Seating and Table plans
Menu & place Cards
Favours
Gifts
Fees due
Scissors, post–it notes, pen, sticky tape
Spirit level and cardboard (for levelling cake table)
Speeches
'Bride's SOS Kit'

BRIDE'S SOS KIT

(Know where you can store and have access to this kit at the reception.)

Lipstick/gloss
Small compact
Brush/comb
Hairspray
Tissues & cleansing wipes
Cotton wool & tips
Nail file
Soda water (to remove spills/stains)
Deodorant wipes
Perfume

'WEDDING DAY SCHEDULE

When working on the time–tabling of the schedule below, allow for most things to take longer than you think. In the preparation stage, work backwards from the ceremony start time. Attach your 'Wedding Day Contact List' and distribute to your best man, chief bridesmaid, photographer, videographer, venue co–ordinator or caterer, and Toastmaster or MC. Include the names of those mentioned in it for identification purposes. Place a copy in the 'Ceremony' and 'Reception' boxes.

PREPARATION

Cake delivery to venue
Flowers to venue(s)

BRIDE

Hair/Make–up appointments
Bouquet & buttonhole delivery
Photographer arrives
Bridesmaids/bride's mother depart for ceremony
Bride departs for ceremony

GROOM

Meet best man
Buttonhole/corsage delivery
Depart for ceremony
Groom & attendants' photographs
Guests arrive

CEREMONY

Arrival of the bride
Official photographs
Depart for reception

RECEPTION

Drinks reception
Wedding Breakfast
Speeches & toasts
(Father of the bride, groom, best man)
Cake cutting
First dance (title)
Dancing
Tossing of bouquet
Bride & groom depart
Carriages

WEDDING DAY

Today is going to be an amazing day. That's guaranteed! You will probably feel a variety of emotions, which is perfectly normal. In all likelihood, declaring your love publicly is not something you are used to doing. But on your wedding day you are relating to someone publicly in a way you usually only do privately. Saying it out loud only adds to the sense that it is real and it can be overwhelming. Reread voice coach, Andrew Wade's advice on page 60 so it is fresh in your mind.

There is a perceived pressure on a couple, especially the bride, to look and be perfect and for everything everywhere to look as it does in glossy magazines. This only increases the tension. Wedding days are dream days, filled with the hopes and expectations of you and your loved ones. As Dr Kristina Downing-Orr told us in the first chapter, "The biggest day isn't called that for nothing." If you are essentially a shy person or couple, you will need to embrace the idea that you will be the focus of attention. Everyone wants to see you, coo over you, admire your dress and take your photograph. This is your moment under the spotlight, the one time in your life when it is all about you. Enjoy it – it's like being Madonna for the day!

Your mood and behaviour today will be contagious! How you carry yourself as you enter before the assembled congregation for your marriage ceremony will help set the atmosphere and mood of the day.

A radiant, relaxed and happy bride ensures an inclusive and joyous celebration. Therefore, try to keep control of your nerves. As you enter with your father (or whoever is giving you away) pause together and survey the scene before you. This is a room filled with family and friends, those who have loved and guided you to this point in your lives. They want your marriage to succeed and are here to offer you their support. Acknowledge this. Walk slowly, smile and make eye contact with as many guests as you can. Smile for your groom and remember the same (or a squeeze) for your father. This is a subtle but simple way to win–over the entire congregation at the very start of your celebration.

When the ceremony is over the celebrating begins. Relax and enjoy yourselves. Stay close together as once you are separated, it might be difficult to break away from guests to find one another again. Make the effort to speak to as many of your family and friends as possible during the drinks reception. And remember not to be the last to leave at the end of the evening. End your day on a high and give your guests a wonderful last image of you.

Finally, and most important of all, have a wonderful day! It has been a pleasure planning it with you. May we be among the first to wish you a long, healthy and happy life together. Congratulations!

Congratulations!

wedding bible experts

My heartfelt thanks to the following individuals, companies and organizations for agreeing to be interviewed for this book. I am lucky enough to regularly work alongside many of you featured here both in words and pictures. You continue to be my inspiration in every aspect of my work.

GETTING STARTED
Inspirations: Carole Hamilton of *You & Your Wedding*, Christine Weaver of the National Wedding Show, Sue Maddix of the Designer Wedding Show. **Dealing with Stress:** Dr Kristina Downing–Orr. **Bride on a Budget:** Laura Bloom, author *The Wedding Diaries* **'The Seven Week Wedding'** and **'Bride with a Bump':** Zelda Suite–Pedler of *Cosmo Bride* and *Your & Your Wedding*.

WEDDING DAY VENUES
Hotels: James Partridge of Claridge's, Corina Tibbetts of Hotel Portmeirion, Roger Hayward of Lucknam Park. **Country Houses:** Nigel Baring at Ardington House, Norman Hudson of *Hudson's Historic Houses & Gardens*. **Marquee Weddings:** Stephen Keyes of The Made Up Textiles Asscn.

WEDDING CEREMONY
Legal Preliminaries: General Register Offices of England & Wales, Scotland and Northern Ireland. **Voice Coach:** Andrew Wade.

WEDDING RECEPTION
James Partridge at Claridge's, Corina Tibbetts of Hotel Portmeirion.

WEDDING GOWN
Gown: Amanda Wakeley, Basia Zarzycka, Caroline Parkes, Catherine Walker, Christina Marty of Christiana Couture, Neil Cunningham, Phillipa Lepley. **Vintage Clothing:** Virginia Bates of Virginia. **Underwear:** Jill Kenton at Rigby & Peller. **Bridesmaids & Mothers:** Sharon Cunningham.

STEPPING OUT – SHOES & ACCESSORIES
Shoes: Basia Zarzycka, Elizabeth Rickard of Rickard Shah, Olivia Morris. **Veil:** Amanda Wakeley, Caroline Parkes, Christina Marty of Christiana Couture, Neil Cunningham. **Tiaras, Headpieces, Jewellery & Handbags:** Basia Zarzycka, Maria Merola of Merola. **Gloves:** Genevieve James of Cornelia James. **Spectacles:** Jason Kirk of Kirk Originals.

BRIDE'S GUIDE TO GORGEOUSNESS
Hair: Carol McNeil from Brother's Hair Sculpting Team, Richard Thompson of the Fellowship for British Hairdressing and Mahogany, Zelda Christian the 'Image Doctor' at Richard Ward Hair & Metro Spa. **Make–up artists:** Claire Hanson, Clare Mackinder. **Nails:** Jessica Vartoughian of Jessica Cosmetics. **Restorative Dental Specialist:** (tooth whitening) Farid Monibi of 33 Beaumont Street, Oxford.

WEDDING FLOWERS
Jane Packer, Mathew Dickinson.

WEDDING CAKE
Mich Turner of the Little Venice Cake Company.

PICTURE PERFECT – PHOTOGRAPHY & VIDEOGRAPHY
Photography: Susie Barker and Harley Evans of Barker Evans and the Wedding Bible Company, Pascal Plessis of Contrejour. **Videography:** Michael Metcalf of *GMTV*.

ALL THE REST
Gift List: Giles Rees at the General Trading Company, Kerry McCulloch for John Lewis. **Stationery:** Yvonne Macken of the Wedding Bible Company.

The '*Wedding Bible* Experts' have not advertised with us, neither have we paid them for their interviews.
For more information with contact details and links to their websites, please visit www.weddingbible.co.uk.

acknowledgments

It's taken nearly three years to complete this project. We launched the business off the back of the wedding work we were already doing. Then, having identified the need for a book such as this, we saw others fight over it, but ultimately didn't like their plans for our idea. How hard could it be to launch our own publishing company we wondered? Now we know! This is the first of our *Wedding Bible* titles which we're producing alongside a range of greetings cards. The events side of our company continues to flourish; that keeps us focused. Weddings are our business: planning them, photographing them, writing and being interviewed about them. We simply love them! Working alongside so many dedicated and talented people is a privilege and inspiring. Many of them are our '*Wedding Bible* Experts' opposite. So our first thank-you goes to you. Next we must thank our *Wedding Bible* brides and grooms who have allowed us to reproduce images from their weddings: Karen and David Allen, Sara and Jonny Allison, Hannah and Ray Baker, Emma and Marcus Bateson, Theresa and Alan Booker, Emma and Daryn Buckley, Rachel and David Clarke, Selena and Henry Coleman, Lauren and Stuart Dennis, Molly Russell and Stuart Ford, Shahin and Alminaz Gulamali, Carolyn and Danny Hanwell, Eunice Tan and Owen Hawkes, Angela and Brian Henderson, Kate and Nick James, Hannah and Nick Lake, Annabell and Antony Licata, Karen and Nathaniel Liddy, Jacqui Lewis and Paul Lyon, Meabh and Dave McInerney, Torie and John Newby, Antonietta and Lee Shepstone, Alex and Greg Suthern, Charlotte & Thomas Weedon, Lesley and Trevor White, Katie and Alex Woodeson and our cover couple, Charlotte and Gary Worden. Thank you too to Kate Garraway and Derek Draper for allowing us to discuss your wedding and for being so nice about us (we loved the challenge that was 'The 5-week-Wedding'!).

There are then those who have advised, helped and encouraged us in many and different ways: Howard Arnes, Roger Bonnett, Douglas Bowen, Ruth Bowen, Ruggero Franich, Ed Glover, John Gould and Amanda Weller. A special thank-you to Anna, Natasha, Aaron and the team at Butler and Tanner. Kenny, Mark, Steve and Kafui at Presstoprint for last-minute, late-hour mock-ups. Natalie Belcher of Colorbase. Phil Green and Chris Darling of Meridian.

A special thank-you to our proof readers, David Pitcher, Catherine Barker and especially Fiona Edwards. Any errors are now mine. Thank you to Robin Llywelyn and Hotel Portmeirion for the use of your stunning backdrop for our photo shoot. Also Deborah Wong and Anton Dean for looking gorgeous, Jacqui Lewis at Flowerworks for your fabulous flowers, Claire Hanson for hair and make-up, and Deborah and Gwynfor at the Gwrach Ynys B&B.

Richard Craze and Roni Jay at White Ladder Press, we are overwhelmed by your generosity of spirit, wise counsel, and will be eternally grateful to you (*White Ladder Diaries* is our 'bible'). The lovely Carole Hamilton at *You & Your Wedding* – you have no idea how much your support continues to mean to us. Hazel Cushion at Áccent Press, when you came into our lives a short time ago it was as though someone had switched the light on. In addition to the hard work you have put in our behalf, thank-you for your enthusiasm, advice, encouragement and straight-talking. We must also thank Signature Book Services – keep up the good work team! And our heartfelt gratitude to our families who have had to live and breathe the *Wedding Bible* with us all this time.

Finally, my personal thank-yous. First the men in my life; my brother Andrew Pitcher, and his company Avatarweb.net – thank-you for so generously lending us your talents and for giving up so much time to our website – we love it! Next my father; walking on your arm on my wedding day is a memory I'll treasure until my dying day (I watch the video over and over). To my husband, Tim, thank you for making me a bride; saying 'yes' is the best decision I have ever made. And last, but by no means least, the women in my life; my business partners, Harley, Susie and Yvonne. Without you there would be no business, no books, no cards and I'd not be having half as much fun...

Thank you!

index